American Compact

American Political Thought
edited by
Wilson Carey McWilliams and Lance Banning

American Compact
James Madison and
the Problem of Founding

Gary Rosen

University Press of Kansas

Published by the University Press of Kansas (Lawrence, Kansas 66049),
which was organized by the Kansas Board of Regents and is operated and
funded by Emporia State University, Fort Hays State University, Kansas
State University, Pittsburg State University, the University of Kansas, and
Wichita State University.

Library of Congress Cataloging-in-Publication Data

Rosen, Gary, 1966–
    American compact : James Madison and the problem of founding /
Gary Rosen.
        p.   cm. — (American political thought)
    Includes bibliographical references.
    ISBN 0–7006–0960–1 (alk. paper)
    1. Madison, James, 1751–1836—Contributions in political science.
    2. Social contract. I. Title. II. Series.
    JC211.M35R67   1999
    973.5′1′092—dc21   98-55508

British Library Cataloguing in Publication Data is available.

Printed in the United States of America
10 9 8 7 6 5 4 3 2 1

For Leslie

The first question that offers itself is, whether the general form and aspect of the government be strictly republican? It is evident that no other form would be reconcileable with the genius of the people of America; with the fundamental principles of the revolution; or with that honorable determination, which animates every votary of freedom, to rest all our political experiments on the capacity of mankind for self-government.

James Madison, *Federalist* 39, 16 January 1788

Whatever respect may be due to the rights of private judgment, and no man feels more of it than I do, there can be no doubt that there are subjects to which the capacities of the bulk of mankind are unequal, and on which they must and will be governed by those with whom they happen to have acquaintance and confidence. The proposed Constitution is of this description.

James Madison to Edmund Randolph, 10 January 1788

Contents

Acknowledgments

This book began as a dissertation in the Department of Government at Harvard. There I was privileged to study with two matchless teachers, Harvey C. Mansfield and Judith N. Shklar, who for all their philosophical differences were of a single mind in recommending a serious acquaintance with American political thought. I am grateful as well to the other members of my dissertation committee—Stephen Macedo, for his close reading and constant encouragement, and Michael J. Sandel, for graciously taking on my project after the cruel loss of Mrs. Shklar.

Others, outside the department, also read and commented on parts of the present work. My thanks go to Walter Berns, Charles R. Kesler, and Gerald Mara, as well as to the editors and anonymous reviewers of the *Review of Politics*, where a version of chapter 4 appeared as "James Madison and the Problem of Founding" (vol. 58 [1996]: 561–95).

My years as a graduate student were made far more productive, and certainly more agreeable, by financial support from a number of institutions. I would like to express my appreciation to the National Science Foundation, the Jacob K. Javits Fellowship Program, the Mellon Foundation, the Harry S. Truman Scholarship Foundation, and the Intercollegiate Studies Institute.

At the University Press of Kansas, Lance Banning and Wilson Carey McWilliams, the editors of this series, offered many helpful suggestions that markedly improved the book. And on the production side, Fred M. Woodward and his staff were a model of professional competence and courtesy.

Finally, I have two primary and ongoing debts to acknowledge: one to my parents, whose support of my work, like their love, never wavers; and the other to my wife, Leslie, for all the reasons she knows so well.

Introduction

Many Madisons

For students of the early American republic, James Madison has long been something of a riddle, the member of the founding generation whose actions and thought most stubbornly resist easy summary. No one disputes, of course, his vital contributions to the establishment of the Constitution. A leading critic of the Articles of Confederation—the feckless league under which the newly independent states were governed for much of the 1780s—Madison was among the first American statesmen to contemplate a more far-reaching union, one that would attend more energetically to national needs while offering a measure of security to those who had suffered at the hands of local majorities. He would go on to become the most influential member of the Federal Convention of 1787; co-author of *The Federalist*, the classic defense of that gathering's handiwork; and the primary sponsor of the Bill of Rights, which he viewed as a harmless palliative for such foes of the new regime as still remained. Here, then, we have the familiar Madison: nationalist, centralizer, wary observer of the states.

But what of the less familiar Madison, the one who emerged shortly thereafter? As most historians would have it, the Virginian underwent a radical transformation in the early 1790s, renouncing his expansive nationalism and embracing a doctrine of states' rights and strict constitutional construction. The watershed event of the period was his opposition in 1791 to the chartering of the first Bank of the United States, an act made more emphatic by his stand against the other financial measures of Alexander Hamilton, his chief collaborator on *The Federalist*. Madison's eventual authorship of the Virginia Resolutions in response to the Alien and Sedition Acts of 1798 and his subsequent defense of them in his Report on the Virginia Resolutions are taken to be the climax of his metamorphosis from a nationalist centralizer to a paladin of Jeffersonian Anti-Federalism.

To compound this riddle still more, it would appear that Madison changed his constitutional views yet again during the closing days of his presidency. The grounds for this charge are two seemingly contradictory acts: his signing into law in 1816 the charter of the second Bank of the United States—the very institution he had previously condemned as a constitutional abomination—and his veto less than a year later of the bonus bill, a plan for internal improvements that he supported as a matter of policy but declared outside the constitutional authority of the national government. Critics argued that he had reverted to Hamiltonianism with respect to the bank while remaining an orthodox Republican on the question of roads and canals.

Unable to explain Madison's shifting political and ideological allegiances, most historians and biographers, from Henry Adams to Irving Brant and Ralph Ketcham, have concluded that he was hopelessly inconsistent. They suggest that Madison's career, taken as a whole, lacks principled justification, making him at best a pragmatist and at worst a trimmer or a hypocrite.[1] Moreover, according to this narrative, the "Father of the Constitution," the brilliant theorist of the extended republic, eventually became a derivative thinker, a man defined less by his own views than by those of Hamilton and Thomas Jefferson, the period's great political antagonists. A discerning and disinterested politician early in his public life, Madison thus emerges as a mere partisan in his mature years.

The aim of this study is to rehabilitate Madison as a constitutional thinker and a statesman. At a superficial level, this means demonstrating the consistency of his most controversial public acts. For students of Madison, the decisive test in this regard has generally been his devotion to the cause of nationalism. But Madison never equated the regime established in 1789 with a simple elevation of the whole over its parts. For him, the *form* that this division took was the heart of the matter. As he declared toward the end of his career, "there were few, if any, of my contemporaries, through the long period and varied scenes of my political life, to whom a mutability of opinion was less applicable, on the great *constitutional* questions which have agitated the public mind."[2] Madison asked to be judged not by his fealty to one side or the other in the early disputes between the nation and the states but rather by his allegiance to the Constitution itself, the instrument designed to regulate this conflict.

More fundamentally, rehabilitating Madison requires a far deeper appreciation of his originality as a political theorist. This is not to say that his writings are best understood as exercises in speculative reason; every one of his significant works arose in response to some practical need. But Madison was a self-consciously philosophical statesman and freely related the issues of his day to a wider theory of politics. By his own lights, his public activity was neither anti- nor sub-theoretical, as some have argued in an attempt to distance him (and the founding generation more generally) from the taint of modern political thought.[3] To the contrary, Madison was a profoundly original thinker with respect to the problems and possibilities inherent in the root idea of his political thought: the social compact. His critique of received notions about the social compact, I will argue, provides the necessary philosophical backdrop against which to see the consistency of his constitutional claims. Madison the theorist vindicates Madison the practitioner.

To say that Madison's first principles arose from the social compact is to say, of course, that he was a liberal. In itself this is uncontroversial. No serious student of Madison denies the primacy of property and civil liberty, consent and tolerance in his political thought. Various influences have been adduced to account for these priorities—Thomas Hobbes and John Locke have their scholarly advocates, as do David Hume and Montesquieu[4]—and each lineage produces a slightly different interpretation of Madison's views. But the basic fact of his liberalism remains. Even Madison's severest academic critics have taken it as their starting point, charging him with infidelity to his own principles for selfishly favoring only certain sorts of property (Charles Beard) or for needlessly throwing up institutional obstacles to the will of the majority (Robert Dahl and James MacGregor Burns).[5]

What complicates this profile is that Madison had very definite ideas about how his liberal ends were to be achieved. Monarchy and aristocracy were out of the question for the United States, however effectively they might protect the rights of person and property. The American regime was to be republican—based, that is, on the political participation of the great body of the people. Furthermore, it was to operate entirely through the mechanism of representation. So complete a reliance on representation was a novelty in Madison's day and has generated heated disputes about the character of his republicanism in our own. *Federalist* 10, Madison's single best-known writing, has become the chief exegetical battleground. Commentators argue endlessly about his emphasis there on the problem of faction and on the need to select "fit characters" to represent and "refine" the views of the people.[6] The essay has been variously presented as a repudiation of selfish interest-group liberalism (Garry Wills), as an aristocratic critique of classical republicanism (Gordon S. Wood and J. G. A. Pocock), and as evidence of Madison's stubborn attachment to popular government—warts and all—because of its profound contribution to human dignity (David F. Epstein).[7] Disagreements aside, all these writers point to Madison's belief that politics was not merely a source of contention and danger—the orthodox liberal view—but an activity with the potential to elevate and ennoble those who took part in it. Today only a scholar like Richard K. Matthews, in search of a foil for the Jeffersonian democracy he so admires, refuses to acknowledge this crucial dimension of Madison's thought.[8]

Attempting to pull together the liberal and republican strands in Madison's thought is not an entirely novel undertaking, nor is applying such a synthesis to the problem of his consistency. The historian Lance Banning has recently offered a compelling analysis of Madison's break with Hamilton, showing the divisions that existed among Federalists even as they came together in the movement for a new constitution. For Banning, the Madison who helped Jefferson establish the Republican Party was the same one, by and large, who fought for the Virginia Plan at the Federal Convention and co-authored *The Federalist*. Never a nationalist of the Hamiltonian stripe and always a stickler for written constitutions, Madison opposed Hamilton's ambitious plans on entirely predictable grounds.[9]

Banning's account falls short, however, in two crucial respects. In the first place, it concludes with the formative years of the

Republican Party in the 1790s and thus fails to answer the troubling questions raised by Madison's constitutional thinking as president. More seriously, it presents Madison's first principles as an amalgam of "modern" and "neoclassical" elements, combining liberalism and a tradition of civic humanism that extends back, by way of such eighteenth-century Whig Opposition writers as "Cato" (John Trenchard and Thomas Gordon), to ancient Greece and Rome. This argument is a hallmark of the "ideological" school of early American historiography, of which Banning is a prominent (if sometimes dissenting) member. Like Wood, Pocock, Drew R. McCoy, and the other writers who have developed this influential interpretation,[10] Banning conceives of liberalism as a stark world of possessive individuals, utterly indifferent to public things. In this view, Madison ceased to be a liberal when he spoke of republican virtue, his thoughts supposedly turning from rights and interests to the modern equivalents of Spartan gruel and Roman censorship. It is, alas, a thoroughly mistaken premise. Though liberalism does not take the cultivation of virtue to be its end—this being its chief departure from premodern political thought—it cannot dispense with it altogether.[11] As Madison so amply demonstrated, even liberalism, with its unblinking realism about the selfish tendencies of humankind and its narrow focus on mundane goods like security, prosperity, and peace, must look to certain human excellences if it is to create political regimes that can endure.

The account of Madison's thought offered here adds to a growing literature that seeks to restore natural-rights liberalism to the preeminence it once enjoyed in interpretations of the American founding.[12] In recent years, a number of scholars—Thomas L. Pangle, Paul A. Rahe, Michael P. Zuckert, and Jerome Huyler, among others—have responded in convincing fashion to the claims of the ideological school. While acknowledging the rich historical pedigree of republican thinking among the revolutionary generation, they have insisted at the same time on the more fundamental, and ultimately determinative, influence of Locke. The statesmen who presided over the creation of the United States, they have shown, were perfectly capable of integrating the seemingly incompatible domains of civic virtue and natural rights. As a practical matter, the former furnished a potent vocabulary for politics, while the latter supplied first principles and primary aims.[13]

Madison's contribution to this synthesis arose in response to the chastening experience of American nation-building and was expressed most forcefully in his idiosyncratic account of the social compact. The basic features of his version are familiar; they derive in a fairly obvious way from the writings of Hobbes and Locke. But Madison brought something new to this venerable liberal idea: a keen appreciation of the political virtues that his great philosophical predecessors failed to describe or quietly suppressed for fear of undermining their wider project. Madison charged Hobbes and Locke with a certain practical naiveté. Their accounts of government's origin say nothing about the process by which a regime might actually be formed and maintained, as if the simple fact of popular sovereignty over constitution making would lead spontaneously to lasting constitutions. Madison's remedy was to appropriate the characteristic virtues of classical political philosophy—architechtonic prudence for founding a regime and patriotic reverence for securing it—but at the same time to tame and refine them, turning them into liberal virtues. He found classical possibilities within the liberal tradition.

An attentive reader of Madison's writings cannot help noticing his constant resort to the social compact. Its distinctive terms flow through virtually every one of his discussions of political fundamentals, from his earliest days in the Continental Congress to his years of retirement at Montpelier. Property, civil liberty, and public order—the concepts that typically organize analyses of Madison's political thought—make their appearance as well. But Madison did not just assert their importance; rather he deduced it from the social compact, the underlying idea that tied these other concepts together and showed their relation to one another. To see as much demands not only that we look with fresh eyes at well-known Madisonian texts—*The Federalist,* the "Memorial and Remonstrance," the Report on the Virginia Resolutions—but that we consider the whole of his voluminous writings, rich as they are with reflection on first principles.

In the opening chapter of the present study, I show that the social compact was indeed the fundamental idea of Madison's political thought. Its influence is evident both in his general political goals (popularly established government, fidelity to written constitutions, security and prosperity) and in the philosophical idiom (the state of nature, natural rights, the original compact and its stages, necessity versus liberty) that he used to discuss them. Madison had serious doubts, however, about what I will call the *political* right of nature. This notion, implicit in the social compact as it had come down to the founding generation, held that a sovereign people, having resolved to escape the state of nature, was capable on its own of forming a government adequate to that end. The political right of nature suggested, in other words, that the people possessed certain rather exalted political capacities. For Madison, this assumption was difficult to square with the social compact's emphasis on necessity—on the single-minded pursuit of self-preservation—as the impetus for establishing particular political forms. So singularly powerful a psychological force ruled out the sort of deliberation needed to overcome the indeterminacy of the state of nature.

In chapter 2, we see how Madison developed this critique still further in light of the concrete historical situation of the United States under the Articles of Confederation. It was not just the urgency of self-preservation that interfered with the establishment of adequate political forms for the new nation, he concluded. Pride and interest—the less insistent motives of the social compact and the sources of the social diversity that he celebrated in *Federalist* 10—proved to be no less of a problem. Madison regarded them as the prime obstacles to popular acceptance of the extended sphere that might begin to neutralize them. Appreciating the durability of these attachments, he again called into question the practicality of the political right of nature and, with it, the possibility of a true founding by the people.

Chapter 3 points to Madison's solution: the distinctively American political institution of the constitutional convention. As his writings from around the time of the Federal Convention show, Madison came to view such a gathering as a counterpoint to the people, as an opportunity for those of outstanding prudence—understood in both its moral and intellectual sense—to transcend popular opinion and to do for the people what they could not do for themselves. Reviewing Hobbes's critique of Aristotle on the question of prudence, I suggest that Madison's sympathy for the ancient understanding of this faculty created a serious predicament for his liberal, egalitarian principles—one of which he was fully aware.

In chapter 4, I turn to a close reading of *Federalist* 37 through 40, Madison's extended defense of the Federal Convention. These essays contain his remarkably nuanced account of the relationship between architechtonic prudence and both the vaunted modern science of politics and the requirements of the social compact. Here too—and not coincidentally—Madison gives his most forceful plea for republicanism, justifying the prerogative assumed by the Federal Convention (most notably in casting aside the binding forms of the Articles of Confederation) as a necessary but exceptional means for establishing popular rule. For Madison, republicanism was not just useful or politic; it was a plain implication of the proud equality described by the social compact. This series from *The Federalist* introduces the tension, decisive for Madison's constitutionalism, between the claims of the people and those of the prudent few.

Chapter 5 takes us beyond the framing of the Constitution to the constitutional politics of the early republic. Here I lay out the philosophical disagreements that separated Madison not only from Hamilton but from Jefferson as well (despite the two Virginians' obvious affinities). For Madison, the positions taken by both men on the ultimate significance of the Constitution represented a dangerous reversion to original principles. Jefferson, with his insistence on perpetual change in political forms, failed to appreciate the fragility of founding and the people's inadequacies as founders. Hamilton, with his aristocratic disdain for constitutional limits, took the example of the Federal Convention to an antirepublican extreme, entrusting the welfare of the many to the few. Madison's response was to elevate the Constitution itself, to encourage a sort of constitutional veneration—a liberal counterpart to Aristotle's notion of "true opinion"—that would firmly anchor the regime while respecting the people's ultimate right to judge it. This, he suggested, was the surest avenue to the security and dignity promised by America's republican experiment.

I conclude by considering the practical side of Madison's constitutionalism. In the interpretation of fundamental law, Madison promoted a variety of what we have come to call original understanding (though his position departs in important ways from that of today's advocates of an originalist jurisprudence). Madison distinguished sharply between the making of the Constitution at the Federal Convention and its subsequent ratification by the American people, seeing the latter as the legitimate source of its meaning. He hoped that such principled respect for the popular sovereign would constrain the overreaching of both the people and their aristocratic foes. Similar considerations entered into his stringent requirements for a binding constitutional precedent. Thus, by giving a narrow constitutional sanction to the second Bank of the United States because of its long and widespread acceptance, he meant to discourage its use as a license for further usurpation; the forms of the Constitution would be honored even as they were being breached.

Such practical compromises, Madison knew, were inevitable under the social compact, an idea seemingly at war with itself in its simultaneous elevation and demotion of constitutional forms. On the one hand, forms were all-important, for they alone could win a release from the disorder and danger of the state of nature; on the other hand, they were mere instruments, interchangeable means for achieving certain unchanging ends. Madison certainly could not resolve this tension. But he negotiated it with unrivaled subtlety, providing an account of the social compact that is both psychologically persuasive and more consonant than its predecessors with the actual demands of political life.

Chapter One

The Social Compact Reconsidered

To say that the social compact was central to James Madison's political thought is nothing extraordinary. As various commentators have noted, it is not difficult to detect the social compact in the Virginian's contributions to *The Federalist*.[1] Elsewhere, too, his general political priorities and the concepts that he uses to discuss them suggest long acquaintance with the thought of Hobbes, Locke, and their followers.[2] But Madison was no mere acolyte. His writings constitute a profound meditation on the social compact and establish him as both a sophisticated student and a critic of the idea. In this chapter, I will show the extent of Madison's reliance on the social compact and some of the difficulties and tensions that he found in it. The next chapter will explore the implications of his social compact for the problem of American nationhood. As Madison appreciated, the diverse people of a newly independent America were hardly denizens of the state of nature and were held apart by differences more serious in many respects than the common concerns that brought them together.

Here we shall begin with *The Federalist* and then turn to three other statements by Madison: the "Memorial and Remonstrance against Religious Assessments," his famed petition against government interference in spiritual matters; a speech on citizenship, given to the First Congress, in which he describes "principles of a general nature" regarding political obligation; and, finally, an outline of remarks that he delivered before the Virginia General Assembly challenging the legitimacy of the state's Revolution-era constitution and recommending its revision.

These last three writings are a necessary supplement to Madison's *Federalist* essays, which, by their nature, draw attention to the details of the Constitution itself rather than to the principles that vindicate constitution making. In the pages of *The Federalist,* the social compact is assumed, not developed. Though these other works were also written for decidedly practical ends, they are more concerned with the grounds of political life than with particular institutional forms. At the risk of speaking of them too schematically, one might say that the "Memorial and Remonstrance" presents human beings as they appear before any social or political association; that Madison's speech on citizenship shows them in civil society, the initial stage of the social compact; and that his notes on revising the Virginia constitution describe how, in the second stage of the social compact, they move on to establish government. Taken together with *The Federalist,* these writings introduce a problem that preoccupied Madison and that shall occupy us as well—whether the political and psychological premises usually associated with the social compact can begin to explain the act of founding at its heart.

Natural Law and Its Problematic Political Right

In *The Federalist,* as in his other writings, Madison employs the Lockean expression "compact"—rather than the "covenant" and "contract" favored, respectively, by Hobbes and Jean-Jacques Rousseau—to describe the agreement by which human beings escape the state of nature.[3] For Madison (as for his co-authors, Alexander Hamilton and John Jay), "contract" was a commercial term, "compact" a political one.[4] Though this was doubtless a reflection of contemporary American usage, Madison's unvarying choice of "compact" over "contract" may also show a certain resistance to the ideas of Rousseau, whose *Social Contract* appeared in 1762 in its definitive form and was surely known to him.

The distinctive vocabulary of the social compact appears briefly in several of Madison's *Federalist* essays. The most substantial exposition of the concept comes at the end of *Federalist* 51, in which he restates his argument from Number 10 about the salutary effects of extending the sphere of national government. Madison compares the situation of factions of different strengths to that of individuals in the state of nature.

> In a society under the forms of which the stronger faction can readily unite and oppress the weaker, anarchy may as truly be said to reign, as in a state of nature where the weaker individual is not secured against the violence of the stronger: And as in the latter state even the stronger individuals are prompted by the uncertainty of their condition, to submit to a government which may protect the weak as well as themselves: So in the former state, will the more powerful factions or parties be gradually induced by a like motive, to wish for a government which will protect all parties, the weaker as well as the more powerful.[5]

Madison's state of nature, like that of his philosophical predecessors, is based on the presumed vulnerability of human beings outside political society. In the absence of government, natural inequalities are allowed their fullest expression. The threat of violence from a stronger individual deprives a weaker one of security, both physical and psychological. Madison does not specify the motivation for such violence, but the usual suspects—avarice, lust, the sheer pleasure of prevailing—suggest themselves. Although security may not be an immediate aim for such a strongman, Madison does suppose that it is as much a fundamental good for him as it is for a weaker individual, a fact that leads the prepolitical brute to reconsider the advantages of his unequal strength. Calculation, foresight, or some like faculty allows him to appreciate the uncertainty of his own situation and its ultimate similarity to that of his weaker neighbor. In light of this discovery, the stronger individual submits to a government that will extend its protection to all.

Elsewhere in *The Federalist*, Madison describes the relation between the state of nature and particular forms of government as being regulated by a law of nature, a law that in turn implies certain natural rights. His two references to this "transcendent" standard—the adjective he uses in both instances—clearly allude to Jefferson's Declaration of Independence, which makes a similar distinction between the law of nature and the rights that arise from it. In neither case does Madison provide much detail about the meaning or philosophical foundation of these ideas, but his use of them suggests something of their relationship to one another. For Madison, the *law* of nature pertains to the urgency of the prepolitical situation; the *rights* of nature, to the means for escaping it. The great difficulty lay in reconciling the two, namely, in explaining how harried, frightened men could possibly establish effective political forms under such distressing circumstances.

As Publius, Madison appeals to the law of nature itself only once, in the course of justifying the authority assumed by the Federal Convention. He describes it in a peculiar series of appositives. To understand why the delegates in Philadelphia discarded the Articles of Confederation, one must recur, he says, "to the absolute necessity of the case; to the great principle of self-preservation; to the transcendent law of nature and of nature's God, which declares that the safety and happiness of society are the objects at which all political institutions aim, and to which all such institutions must be sacrificed."[6] The three successive formulations seem to derive from one another, as if the law of nature were, as its name implies, the appearance in human affairs of some more general natural force. "Absolute necessity," a term seemingly indebted to the mechanistic physical science of the day, presented itself to the Federal Convention in the form of a "case," in this instance, the conclusion that political disorder had come to pose an intolerable threat to the community. Necessity, thus understood, led irresistibly to "the great principle of self-preservation," a principle that, in its emphasis on the irreducible need for survival, presumably applies to all living things. The distinctively human side of this principle found expression, in turn, in the law of nature proper, the last of Madison's triad. Consulting this law, the delegates transformed it into a political maxim, a rule of action dictating that inadequate political forms must give way.

Madison seems to assign compulsive force to the law of nature while at the same time deducing an obligation from it, a combination of "is" and "ought" characteristic of the social-compact tradition. He creates the impression, however, that physical rather than moral necessity was the dominant motive in the abolition of the Articles of Confederation. By using the passive voice—"all such institutions must be sacrificed"—and referring to no agent in relation to this momentous deed, he implies that there was little choice in the matter.[7] One might conclude that the people and their representatives were acted upon rather than acting themselves.[8]

Madison refers to the same complex of ideas at one other point in *The Federalist*, again in defending the authority assumed by the Federal Convention. But in this case, he suggests that the law of nature and the motives on which it depends are insufficient. His concern is not the *law* that drives men from the state of nature but the *right* that allows them to effect and maintain their separation from it. Quoting directly from the Declaration of Independence (and citing it in a footnote), he writes that the Convention "must have reflected, that in all great changes of established governments, forms ought to give way to substance; that a rigid adherence in such cases to the former, would render nominal and nugatory, the transcendent and precious right of the people to 'abolish or alter their governments as to them shall seem most likely to effect their safety and happiness.'"[9]

Necessity does not make an appearance in this passage. Whereas in the previous passage Madison appealed to the ineluctable decision to reject old forms, here he stresses the freedom to construct new ones. The law of nature seems sufficient for sacrificing or abolishing governments, but its "transcendent and precious right" would appear to be necessary to alter or establish them. Tellingly, the people come to the fore when Madison discusses this right. They are no longer matter to be acted upon, as was implied in his treatment of the law of nature. A right assumes choice, a certain latitude in action and thought. It is distinctively human, separating humanity from the rest of nature and its unchanging course. If necessity is the ground for the law of nature, liberty would seem the basis for natural rights.

It should be noted, however, that the right at issue here is not just any natural right but what I have called the *political* right of nature. This right makes it possible for human beings to leave behind their precarious natural state, to exchange their expansive but demanding natural rights for narrower but more defensible civil rights.[10] For Madison, the political right of nature represented the social compact's defining moment, when political forms began to provide the protection unavailable in the prepolitical condition. As convention took the place of nature and demonstrated its superiority, self-preservation could finally become a less insistent concern. This is what made this particular right "transcendent and precious."

As we shall see, the political right of nature is also unique in another and more troubling way. A defining feature of rights, this one included, is their formality: they provide space for certain sorts of actions but do not dictate the actions themselves. Under the First Amendment of the Constitution, for example, Americans may speak or be silent, pray or blaspheme, assemble with others or keep to themselves. The content of a right is left to its possessor, which makes it possible for a given right to be exercised differently and unequally. Though this might seem to apply as much to the political right of nature as to any other right, Madison assumes otherwise. He takes for granted that those who possess the political right of nature will exercise it widely and well. This explains his popular tone in asserting it. The social compact ascribes to the people as a whole—not to a part of them or to a chosen few—the capacity to make a constitution and the willingness to do so in a public-spirited fashion. Unlike, say, the right of property, which results in various kinds and degrees of property holding, the political right of nature presupposes that it will be used with a rather elevated uniformity.

Madison leaves unsaid, at least in this passage, what makes these assumptions possible. How do the people come to possess the practical wisdom or prudence necessary for establishing a sound government? What is the source of their concern for the common good, or of their disinterestedness? His silence with respect to these questions shows that the political right of nature has certain pretensions. Unlike the law of nature, which has an air of resignation about it, the political right of nature points to itself with a definite if seemingly groundless pride. It claims not just the potential for action but its reality, and not just any action but action of the loftiest sort—the founding of a regime. The rousing, defiant tone of the Declaration of Independence—the very fact that it is a declaration—derives from its high expectation that the people are in fact capable of instituting forms of government that will secure their safety and happiness.

Madison certainly was not the first to make such a distinction between right and law in discussing the social compact. Hobbes differentiated between *jus* and *lex* in describing nature, and his analysis is instructive for our purposes. A law of nature, he wrote, "determineth" and "bindeth." It is best understood as an "Obligation." In substance, it is "a Precept, or generall Rule . . . by which a man is forbidden to do, that, which is destructive of his life, or taketh away the means of preserving the same; and to omit, that, by which he thinketh it may be best preserved."[11] Hobbes proceeds much as Madison later would: he emphasizes first the compulsory nature of the law, then its basis in self-preservation, and finally, the approach that it dictates with respect to available means.

By contrast, the right of nature, as Hobbes would have it, "consisteth in liberty to do, or to forbeare." It is that "Liberty each man hath, to use his own power, as he will himselfe, for the preservation of his own Nature; that is to say, of his own Life."[12] Necessity's reign is less apparent here. Right is the province of liberty, and the mental operation appropriate to this state, says Hobbes, stressing the common root of the two key words, is *de*-liberation. But he considers deliberation a low thing, a seemingly arbitrary process in which appetites and aversions succeed one another until one is acted upon. It is a capacity that human beings share to a large degree with animals.[13]

We should be reluctant, of course, to burden Madison with all this Hobbesian baggage. That he shared Hobbes's basic understanding of the relationship between law and right, necessity and liberty, is fairly clear. Yet in one decisive respect, Madison's account differs from that of Hobbes: Madison presents the social compact's reliance on the political right of nature as a reason to boast, as a source of pride and jealous attachment for the people as a whole. The political right of nature would thus seem to be related to the "honorable determination" that he links with the cause of republicanism elsewhere in *The Federalist*.[14] Nothing could be further from the intention of Hobbes, who well understood the threat posed to self-preservation by such vainglorious claims.[15]

Though Madison speaks of compacts at several different points in *The Federalist*, he refers to the *social* compact only once, in defending the Constitution's specific restrictions on the authority of the state governments. "Bills of attainder, ex post facto laws, and laws impairing the obligation of contracts," he writes, "are contrary to the first principles of the social compact, and to every principle of sound legislation. The two former are expressly prohibited by the declarations prefixed to some of the State Constitutions, and all of them are prohibited by the spirit and scope of these fundamental charters."[16] Madison here suggests the insufficiency of "the first principles of the social compact," which presumably correspond to the law of nature. These principles must be bolstered by the dictates of sound legislation, by the declarations of the state constitutions, and, most obviously, by the restrictions under discussion. Such supports may belong to the social compact in its fullest sense, but they are not to be confused with its first principles. It would seem that these principles only become effective through particular decisions on constitutional matters. The law of nature drives home the urgency of self-preservation, but it requires the political right of nature, with its concern for the *means* of self-preservation, to do anything about it. For Madison, only well-designed political forms—"fundamental charters"—could secure the ends of the social compact.

The division implied in this passage between the early and the later stages of the social compact (that is, between its first principles and the institutions established to give them effect) appears at other points in *The Federalist*. In the lines immediately preceding his discussion of the state of nature in Number 51, Madison refers to justice as the end of both "civil society" and "government."[17] As David F. Epstein notes, this distinction "recalls Locke's account of men's original, *unanimous* choice to form a society, which is the foundation for the *majority's* right to choose a form of government."[18] Madison provides no such elaboration here, but in keeping with this distinction, he does speak of government elsewhere in *The Federalist* as the "political form of civil society."[19] Many years later, Madison would be more explicit about these two stages. "The original compact," he observed, "is the one implied or presumed, but nowhere reduced to writing, by which a people agree to form one society. The next is a compact, here for the first time reduced to writing, by which the people in their social state agree to a Govt. over them. These two compacts may be considered as blended in the Constitution of the U.S."[20] To refine further the difference between the law of nature and the political right of nature, the former seems to apply primarily to the decision to enter civil society (the "social state"), and the latter, to the agreement to form a particular government.[21]

What remains unclear in this account is the specific character of the choice that takes place in each of the two stages. In the passages cited by Epstein, Locke describes these decisions not as choices but as acts of "consent," which suggests simple acquiescence rather than an active consideration of options. Madison was anxious to include the Constitution among those governments established by consent, but in *The Federalist* he pairs consent with deliberation, as if to stress not only the voluntariness but also the quality of the decision.[22] For Madison, deliberation was necessary to elevate consent and give it content. At the same time, however, he nowhere suggests that the people have any special capacity for deliberation. By using consent alone to describe these stages of the social compact, Locke had obscured two crucial issues that Madison would have to confront more directly: the degree to which joining civil society is less than perfectly optional and the actual mechanism by which the people might choose particular political forms.

Madison's presentation in *The Federalist* thus raises several vexing questions about the place of choice in the social compact. Under the law of nature, human action appears to be less a matter of choice than of compulsion, so powerful is the imperative of self-preservation. Under the political right of nature, choice emerges, to be sure, but its grounds and extent are vague. The promise of popularly established government would seem to depend on the people's possession of faculties and dispositions that are rare at best.

God and Nature

Madison's "Memorial and Remonstrance" against religious assessments is easily his most comprehensive statement on the question of religious liberty. Composed in 1785 as part of a campaign to prevent the General Assembly of Virginia from passing a bill that would have established a state "provision for teachers of the Christian Religion," it appeals to a wide range of arguments, both practical and philosophical. Its role in the eventual rejection of the bill is difficult to determine—it was one of many such petitions, and not the most popular[23]—but it has since enjoyed a semi-authoritative standing as a gloss on the religion clauses of the First Amendment, which Madison would draft a few years later.[24]

The opening and closing sections of the "Memorial and Remonstrance" are its most philosophical parts; they deal directly with the social compact's essential backdrop—the condition of human beings outside of government. They also begin to describe the relationship between "nature's God," invoked by Madison in *The Federalist*, and God the Creator, the more traditional formulation that he employs in this earlier writing. By examining these rival understandings of God, we can see what sort of transcendent ground, if any, he considered necessary to maintain the claims of the social compact.

Leaving aside for a moment the specific polemical intent of the first several paragraphs of the "Memorial and Remonstrance," what is immediately apparent is their dependence on the terms of the social compact. In the opening paragraph, Madison uses "civil society," as in *The Federalist*, to describe the initial stage of the social compact. Whereas the formation of civil society seemed before to be associated with the law of nature and the importunings of necessity, here it appears to be a much more deliberate affair. Civil society is something that one "becomes a member of." It is established by "institution," which imposes a duty on its members, not to government (which is presumably still in the offing) but to what Madison calls "the General Authority." This obligation is rather severe, requiring that a member of civil society reserve his ultimate allegiance for the General Authority regardless of "any subordinate Association" that he might enter into. Only at this point is there a glimmer of the urgency that Madison attaches to civil society and its ends in *The Federalist*.

This guardedness with respect to the motives that produce civil society might be related to the central practical argument of the first paragraph: that the claims of civil society are inferior "both in order of time and in degree of obligation" to the duty one owes to the Creator. This argument for the temporal and moral priority of religion replaces what would ordinarily precede a description of civil society, that is, an account of the state of nature. There is no reference to such a state or to the law of nature that governs it anywhere in the "Memorial and Remonstrance." Perhaps for the purpose at hand, Madison required a pacific state of nature, not a realm regulated by "the great principle of self-preservation." His stated premise, taken from Article XVI of the Virginia Declaration of Rights, was that religion, "the duty which we owe to our Creator," can only be directed "by reason and conviction, not by force or violence." In order to defend this right in its utmost latitude, he had to play down the basis of his politics, a condition where force and violence do, in fact, make their presence felt. If religious liberty were seen to *depend* on political liberty rather than *precede* it, its standing would become more precarious. In the "Memorial and Remonstrance," Madison thus slights the place of self-preservation in the state of nature, making it possible for human beings to heed their Creator untroubled by their own vulnerability.[25]

If Madison is not entirely candid about the character of the state of nature, he does grant its generative principle. The fourth paragraph of the "Memorial and Remonstrance" affirms Article I of the Virginia Declaration of Rights in its assertion that "all men are by nature equally free and independent." Accordingly, Madison can speak of their "natural rights," that is, the liberties that they enjoy in their "free and independent" condition. He goes on to describe the implications of this equality, not for the state of nature but for the civil society that emerges from it. If he were instead to consider the insecurity and uncertainty that such natural equality promotes in the prepolitical condition, he would draw into question his own argument about the primacy of religious duty and remind the attentive reader of the social compact's great purposes. Madison avoids this pitfall by discussing the degree to which natural equality must be maintained in the institutions that *succeed* the state of nature: "all men are to be considered as entering into Society on equal conditions; as relinquishing no more, and therefore retaining no less, one than another, of their natural rights."[26] For Madison, as for his contractarian predecessors, natural liberty is incompatible with political association. It must be modified in order for men to come together in a single community. Natural rights must be transformed into civil rights.

First, however, there are what we might call the intermediate rights of civil society. These fall somewhere between the unregulated equality of natural rights and the carefully defined civil rights of a particular constitution. These intermediate rights include, on the one hand, an equal say in the establishment of a form of government and, on the other, a claim to that government's impartial protection. The latter right is the very purpose of the social compact, while the former provides some assurance, though no guarantee, that it will be respected. Madison alludes to both in concluding his discussion of civil society's jurisdiction: "no other rule exists, by which any question which may divide a Society, can be ultimately determined, but the will of the majority; but it is also true that the majority may trespass on the rights of the minority."[27]

In embryonic form, this is the problem Madison addresses in *Federalist* 10: how to combine majoritarianism with impartiality. In this context, however, he is not speaking of *government* by majority so much as *constitution making* by majority; other "rules" do exist by which a government might decide a divisive question.[28] That the discussion still concerns civil society and its "General Authority" is confirmed by the account of legislative power that Madison offers in the next paragraph. Having established that religion is outside the province of "Society at large," he writes that it is all the more beyond the reach of members of "the Legislative Body," who are "but the creatures and vicegerents of the former."[29]

Madison's use of "creatures" is worth noting, since it follows a section whose theme is the duty incumbent on human beings toward their Creator. The word emphasizes the government's dependence on the people and the derivative nature of its authority, but it also suggests a parallel between the people and God. God's creatures imitate the divine by creating the constitution under which their legislators act, "the great Barrier which defends the rights of the people."[30] As Madison sees it, a constitution represents the chief advantage of entering civil society. It does for individuals what they once had to do for themselves: it "defends" their rights.

But these are not the rights of nature. They are civil rights, rights whose standing derives from their place in a form of government. As Madison enumerates them at the end of the "Memorial and Remonstrance," they include freedom of the press, trial by jury, and the suffrage.[31] As the specific rights by which the more general rights of nature and civil society are made operative,[32] they allow the people to delegate the task of self-defense to "an authority derived from them," to establish a "commission" under which their most fundamental needs will be tended to by their "creatures." The constant anxiety of the state of nature is replaced by a "prudent jealousy," which works to ensure that the terms of the commission are obeyed and that "Rulers" are not "guilty of encroachment." Under such an arrangement, the "first duty of Citizens" is "to take alarm at the first experiment on [their] liberties."[33] Vigilance with respect to one's civil rights comes to take the place of the much more onerous superintendence of one's natural rights.

The right of conscience occupies a peculiar place in this scheme. At times, Madison maintains its similarity to other fundamental rights, insisting that they are all held "by the same tenure," by which he seems to mean some combination of natural origin and constitutional enshrinement.[34] But religious liberty does not come into existence with civil society or government, as do trial by jury or freedom of the press. It antedates the social compact and is unmodified by it. Madison contends "that in matters of Religion, no man's right is abridged by the institution of Civil Society and that Religion is wholly exempt from its cognizance." This immunity, as we have seen, comes from a theologico-political principle that asserts the superiority of religion over politics: "It is the duty of every man to render the Creator such homage and such only as he believes to be acceptable to him. This duty is precedent, both in order of time and in degree of obligation, to the claims of Civil Society."[35]

This principle presents several difficulties for the social compact. The first and most obvious is the potential conflict between the two sorts of duty. Some might pay homage to God, after all, by stoning sabbath breakers or destroying private property. Madison's theologico-political principle prevents him from joining with Locke, who says that such "things are not lawful in the ordinary course of life, nor in any private house; and therefore neither are they so in the Worship of God, or in any religious meeting."[36] Indeed, Madison was quite deliberate in eschewing the Lockean term "toleration," with its implication of the mere sufferance of religion.[37] The possibility that conscientious dissent or divine command might conflict with the ends of political life did not seem to trouble him. He paired his overriding concern to prevent the violation of conscience with an apparent indifference to the consequences of its inviolability.

The obvious Protestant subtext of the "Memorial and Remonstrance" helps to save Madison's view from its most destructive political implications. His argument exploits the often-noted compatibility between natural-rights doctrine and dissenting Protestantism. However different their intent, both traditions depend explicitly on the privileges enjoyed by individuals. As Thomas Lindsay writes, Madison presents his demotion of politics in the "Memorial and Remonstrance" as "a means to the realization of true religion, which . . . is achievable only through the meeting of the individual conscience with the word of God, as found in Scripture."[38] Religious belief, so understood, makes for a relatively benign politics. It is highly personal, so it discourages both collective action and deference to religious authority (Madison could speak of people practicing their religion "singly"[39]). And it is resolutely other-worldly, so it manifests itself not in ritual observance or faith-inspired works—messy and quasi-political matters that involve our bodies—but in "conviction," in the "opinions" that depend on our "minds."[40]

Madison's Protestantism, then, does not so much trump the social compact as skirt its basic concerns. By occupying itself almost exclusively with the subjective state of the believer, it makes possible a strict segregation of body and soul. Religious truth becomes a particular sort of experience rather than a doctrine. In this view, sincerity takes the place of right-thinking and -acting. And because coercion ceases to have any religious efficacy, authority over the body can be safely entrusted to the political realm.[41] Duty to God may be "precedent" in Madison's scheme, but it is duty of a particularly innocuous sort.

Madison's confidence in the workability of subordinating politics to religion can also be interpreted in a less pious vein. He may have believed that, in the absence of a religious establishment, the authority of revealed religion would wane, a victim of its own indeterminacy, and that obedience to nature's God would take its place. Although Madison speaks respectfully of the "light of revelation" in the "Memorial and Remonstrance,"[42] elsewhere he questioned its intelligibility and doubted its necessity.[43] Lindsay appears justified in concluding that far from embracing the Protestant "belief in the accessible truth of the Bible," Madison denied the "human capacity to know the nature and existence of the commands of—and thus the duties toward—revelation's God."[44]

The fundamental obligation to political authority, on the other hand, was far less equivocal: "a member of Civil Society, who enters into any subordinate Association, must always do it with a reservation of his duty to the General Authority." Although just a formal requirement at this point (its substance depending on the particular regime), this stipulation presents a clear, binding standard for political rectitude. The obligation to civil society is self-imposed, but it also depends, like one's duty to God, on the persuasiveness of external "evidence." In this case, however, the source of the evidence is the law of nature, which acts on the mind not directly but through the body.

Dominion over the mind was beyond the power and authority of government, according to Madison. The making of "laws for the human mind" was an "ambitious hope" that should be extinguished forever, he wrote to Jefferson upon passage of the Virginia Act for Religious Freedom.[45] As a corollary, we might conclude that Madison regarded laws for the human *body* as a *modest* hope on which to rely. Madison believed that the universally felt promptings of the body were the only legitimate basis for the most authoritative human association. They were undeniable and relatively uncontentious, unlike the ambiguous, historically distorted words of a prophet or apostle. For Madison, nature's God, speaking through "the great principle of self-preservation," was knowable in a way that the God of revelation was not.

Madison's theologico-political principle presents yet another difficulty for the social compact, this one of an opposite complexion to the first. Unlike his philosophical precursors, Madison never contended that the social compact required support in the form of authoritative religious opinion. The civil religions of Hobbes and Rousseau are the extreme instances of such support, but Locke too looks to a belief in the existence of God to uphold the agreements on which society is based.[46] Even Jefferson, wary though he was of religion, wondered if "the liberties of a nation [could] be thought secure when we have removed their only firm basis, a conviction in the minds of the people that these liberties are of the gift of

God?"[47] Madison apparently viewed such divine sanction as unnecessary to encourage citizens to attend to their duties. The Creator whom he invokes in the "Memorial and Remonstrance" certainly does not provide transcendent confirmation of the political order, confined as He is to the private domain of conscience. Nor does it seem that Madison considered popular religiosity of any kind a condition of political health.[48]

If religious belief was not needed to secure popular devotion to the social compact, what was? In the "Memorial and Remonstrance," Madison alludes to alternate grounds. "Rulers who wished to subvert the public liberty, may have found an established Clergy convenient auxiliaries," he writes. "A just Government instituted to secure & perpetuate it needs them not. Such a Government will be best supported by protecting every Citizen in the enjoyment of his Religion with the same equal hand which protects his person and his property."[49] An impartial justice furnishes the strongest and most reliable basis for stable government. If a citizen's claim of equal protection is respected, Madison asserts, he will be content, at least with his own lot.

But what is to protect "*every* Citizen" if the government sees fit to single out some hapless group or individual? What will prompt the secure citizen to rise to another's defense? Madison's answer in the "Memorial and Remonstrance" relies on the pride that he associated with the political right of nature. As his many emphatic references to the Virginia Declaration of Rights demonstrate, he wished to arouse popular indignation at the Virginia legislature's violation of a form of government instituted by the people of the state. Because this "prudent jealousy" was at a considerable remove from any immediate threat to themselves, it could not be described as strictly defensive. Madison depended on the people's willingness to act even in the absence of some pressing necessity, on "principle" rather than on "consequences," a trait that constituted "one of the noblest characteristics of the late Revolution."[50] Unlikely though it may sound, he attributed this nobility to the social compact itself. It was a product of the people's spirited attachment to something of their own making and allowed them to see the constitution as more than a mere instrument. Madison wanted them to feel the righteous anger of a creator with its errant creation, like the God of Exodus with the recalcitrant Israelites. The *imitatio dei* implicit in his account of the social compact thus enlarged and moralized the people's stake in constitutional government. It made them take an interest not just in its performance but also in its forms.

The Durability of Civil Society

I have suggested that Madison's reticence in the "Memorial and Remonstrance" concerning the state of nature was related primarily to the petition's practical aim. His defense of an unrestricted right of conscience, I have argued, would have been compromised by a frank discussion of necessity and its expression in "the great principle of self-preservation." A further reason might also be adduced for his relative inattention to the prepolitical condition in the "Memorial and Remonstrance" and in other writings of this period. Turning to Madison's speech on citizenship, it is apparent that for all the genuine desperation he saw during the revolutionary war, he did not consider the state of nature to be a feature of the earliest days of American political life. The newly independent states had never fully reverted to such a condition. For Madison, the American Revolution took place, so to speak, entirely within civil society—that is, within the first, merely social stage of the social compact.

The occasion for Madison's remarks on citizenship was a petition presented to the First Congress in May 1789. It claimed that the election of one of that body's members, William Smith of South Carolina, was invalid because he had not been a citizen of the United States for the constitutionally required seven years. Although born in South Carolina, Smith had gone to England in 1770, at the age of twelve, to be educated. He had attempted to return during the course of the Revolution but had been thwarted by a series of mishaps. Finally returning to South Carolina in 1783, he had quickly established himself in state politics, serving in the legislature and then winning election to Congress. Like most Americans, he was a British subject by birth, but unlike them, he had not been present when independence was declared nor had he fought in the revolutionary war.[51]

David Ramsay, the petition's sponsor, made a straightforward case for Smith's ineligibility. As he put it in a letter to Madison, "As in the time of [Smith's] absence the Revolution took place I contend that in order to his becoming a Citizen of the United States something must have been done previously on his part to shew his acquiescence in the new Government established without his consent. The lowest test of acquiescence is . . . residence in the Country. Till he resided under the Government of the united States I cannot therefore see how he acquired Citizenship."[52] According to Ramsay, Smith's standing was to be determined not by any prior association with the people who brought about the Revolution but by his relationship to the particular regimes that they established. In this view, citizenship was an exclusively political matter. Having no connection with any American *government* until 1783, Smith's citizenship could only be dated from that point.

In defending Smith, Madison did not challenge Ramsay's premise that a determination of citizenship was primarily a political question, dependent on the qualifications and terms set out by a particular regime. Thus he begins by saying that the decision should be based on "the laws and the constitution of South Carolina, so far as they can guide us." Unfortunately, this was not very far. South Carolina lacked a law "defining the qualities of a citizen or an alien." If such a law had existed, the question would never have come before Congress. Madison asserts that without a clear legal standard it is necessary to follow "principles of a general nature" or, more specifically, "the principles established by the revolution." These were the principles of the social compact, which, Madison emphasized, furnished both the preferred political definition of citizenship and, in its absence, a social definition as well. Madison relied on this second standard of citizenship to conclude that Smith was a citizen of the United States "on the declaration of independence."[53]

As in the "Memorial and Remonstrance," Madison draws attention to the two discrete phases of the social compact. The "particular society of which we are members" is to be distinguished from "the sovereign established by that society." They constitute, respectively, our "primary" and "secondary" allegiances.[54] The basis for such a rank ordering was government's instrumental relationship to civil society. Its offices and powers were just a configuration of means, having no special authority of their own. Consequently, one's duty to a given regime was contingent on its receiving the ongoing support of the society that established it; its abolition left the social bond intact. In such an event, the "General Authority" of civil society—to use Madison's term from the "Memorial and Remonstrance"—reclaimed its prerogatives and erected another regime. More to the point, one's membership in and obligations to civil society were unaffected by the dissolution of government.[55] Accordingly, when Smith's native state declared independence, he "was bound by that act and his allegiance transferred to that society, or the sovereign which that society should set up, because it was through his membership of the society of South Carolina that he owed allegiance to Great Britain."[56] Ramsay's error lay in failing to see the significance of this social relationship.

For Madison, the primary qualification for citizenship was membership in civil society rather than political participation. From this perspective, inclusion in a regime was not dependent on the traditional activities of citizenship, such as exercising the franchise or holding public office. These privileges were only modifications of membership in civil society, allowing some portion of that society to secure the ends sought by all. This permitted politics to be an activity of the few, but without implying any special deprivation for the vast majority, all of whom retained an equal claim to the impartial protection of the regime and the right to resist it should it become arbitrary. No one, Madison believed, could be rightly excluded from this type of citizenship—a view that explains his unequivocal, if still deeply problematic, condemnation of American slavery.[57] In Smith's case, South Carolina might have defined citizenship in such a way as to make him ineligible for public office, but since it had no such restrictions, his membership in civil society was a sufficient qualification.

The account of citizenship presented by Madison anticipates modern usage in its reliance on social membership. Today Americans readily designate as citizens those who take no active part in public life, even refusing the burden of an occasional visit to the polls. This depoliticizing of citizenship is very much in accord with the social compact's low opinion of political activity, a view that sets it apart from premodern thought. Whereas Aristotle regarded politics as an arena for the expression of distinctive (if ultimately partial) claims about justice,[58] under the social compact no such disagreement is possible, since the compact itself represents the definitive solution to the problem of justice. Different regimes are simply alternate means to peace, prosperity, and personal security—the qualities that define a just liberal society. For this reason, kings and aristocrats, while perhaps unreliable guardians of the people's liberties, were not inherently incapable of serving the popular interest, according to Madison. Their competition and mutual suspicion could bring greater security for all.[59]

Such a view of regimes allowed Madison to say that civil society and government, the social and political stages of the social compact, were only different "mode[s] of action,"[60] not discrete aspects of human well-being. For him, the efficient cause of the political partnership—the urgent needs that led men from the state of nature into civil society—was seemingly its final cause as well. The political activity that arose only under government did not in itself constitute an end.[61] By insisting that civil society was the basis for political continuity, Madison disagreed with the Aristotelian notion that "it is looking to the regime above all that the city must be said to be the same."[62] For him, governments would seem to be little more than instruments for achieving certain unvarying ends.

This interpretation of Madison is objectionable in one key respect, for it implies that he was indifferent to forms of government and to the scope of actual (as opposed to merely social) citizenship. Epstein associates this view with "Lockean liberalism" and remarks on its inconsistency with Publius's "repeated and very emphatic insistence on a 'strictly republican' or 'wholly popular' form of government."[63] In chapter 4, I will suggest how Madison's republicanism, rightly seen as an end in itself, was also derived from the social compact. Notwithstanding Madison's remarks here, regimes did matter to him—and not just to the extent that they served as useful tools.

To return, then, to Smith's case, Madison admitted that the destruction of civil society would effectively eliminate any claim of citizenship, but he denied its relevance in this instance. In fact, the "error of the memorialist" lay in supposing that "the separation which took place between these states and Great Britain, not only dissolved the union between those countries, but dissolved the union among the citizens themselves: that the original compact, which made them altogether one society, being dissolved, they could not fall into pieces, each part making an independent society, but must individually revert into a state of nature."[64] Anarchy had not resulted from American independence because civil society had survived the dissolution of government. Nor did civil society's authority become arbitrary in the absence of a constitution. Existing laws remained in force, subject to future amendment by a new government. This was necessary, as Madison had written a few years earlier, "to obviate pretexts" that independence had "abolished all civil rights and Obligations."[65] In sum, the situation had produced desperate uncertainty (as we shall shortly see) but not the lawlessness and violence that the dissolution of civil society would have sparked.

Madison's self-assurance about the continued existence and authority of civil society in the wake of independence was matched by a certain ambiguity about its actual extent. Having suggested that each colony had become "*an* independent society," he goes on to say that "the *colonies* remained as *a* political society."[66] Evidently, both the individual colonies and the nation as a whole had taken on the authoritative aspect of civil society. But this created two "General Authorities," two mutually exclusive wills "capable of substituting a new form of government in place of the old one."[67]

Madison did not address this problem here. Recalling the speech during his retirement, however, he would describe its central issue with greater clarity: "At the period of our Revolution it was supposed by some that it dissolved the social compact *within the Colonies,* and produced a state of nature which required a naturalization of those who had not participated in the revolution."[68] This later summary of the dispute is consistent with Madison's primary claim in his speech on citizenship: that Smith was a citizen by virtue of his membership before the Revolution, not in American society as a whole but in the "particular society" of South Carolina.[69] As we shall find in discussing the Articles of Confederation in the next chapter, Madison had reason to obfuscate about the actual moment when American nationhood came about.

Establishing Government

In looking back on his retort to Ramsay some years later, Madison would reaffirm its statement of the basic principle of civil society: "that the will of the majority [is] to be deemed the will of the whole." The social compact required such a precept because unanimity disappeared after the initial decision to form one society. All might agree that the "whole" should safeguard "the rights, the safety & the interests of each," but the whole dissolved into parts when presented with the question of means. Thus "the objects in view could not be attained, if every measure conducive to them required the consent of every member of the society."[70] Whereas civil society could take but a single form—a reflection of necessity's steady and uniform pressure in the state of nature—government admitted of an enormous variety of forms. Its establishment demanded a choice. In the terms of our earlier discussion, the law of nature reduced human beings to a common denominator, while the political right of nature—the right to form a government that promised relief—invited differences. Unanimity based on equal vulnerability gave way to disagreement over the means to escape it.

The mechanics of such majority constitution-making and the sort of participation required by it did not occupy the early theorists of the social compact. Because their central concern was the nature and scope of government power, their account of its origin could leave many questions unanswered. They could describe the premises of legitimate government without delving into the practical details of its foundation. If the social compact was not exactly hypothetical for them, it was something of a heuristic. The American students of Hobbes and Locke, having overthrown their established governments while appealing to the ends of the social compact, thus found themselves confronting an incomplete account of its beginnings. As a social scientist might put it today, the model was underspecified.

The most insightful of these American students proposed a solution: the constitutional convention. By the early 1780s, when he was composing his *Notes on the State of Virginia,* Thomas Jefferson could write that most of the American states "were of the opinion, that to render a form of government unalterable by ordinary acts of assembly, the people must delegate persons with special powers. They have accordingly chosen special conventions to form and fix their governments."[71] Jefferson had been among the first, in fact, to see conventions, long a part of British and revolutionary American political practice, as something more than an informal (or even illegal) supplement to constituted authority. They were the vehicles through which the sovereign people might exercise the powers to which the social compact entitled them. This view had prevailed in many of the states after independence, but Virginia had been an exception. In 1776 Jefferson had been alone among the leading men of the Commonwealth in opposing the assumption of constituent powers by an assembly elected for other purposes.[72] As the War of Independence drew to a close, Virginia's frame of government, established under dubious authority in Jefferson's eyes, had yet to be put on a satisfactory footing. His *Notes* were, among other things, a call to reform. He urged the meeting of a convention that might place the "ordinance of government" on "a bottom that none will dispute."[73]

Distracted by the death of his wife and then called away by national office, Jefferson was unable to press the Virginia General Assembly to take up his plan. That duty fell to Madison, who returned from service in the Continental Congress at the end of 1783 with an equal desire to see the constitution of 1776 revised. Beyond giving the state constitution an unambiguous standing as fundamental law, both men also wished to effect certain basic structural changes—in particular, a proper balance of powers. In their view, the Revolution-era constitution dangerously concentrated power in the legislature, leaving the executive and judiciary departments defenseless and dependent.

These two objects of reform—the constitution's authority, on the one hand, and its structure, on the other—supply the main headings for the one surviving document from Madison's effort at revision: a set of notes from a speech he delivered before the Virginia General Assembly in June 1784. The first half of the speech falls under the rubric "Nature of a Constitution" and deals with the constituent authority of the people. The second half, which sets aside the question of the "so called" constitution's authority, lists and explains the charter's various structural defects.[74] Although the reformers were ultimately unsuccessful—the Virginia constitution would not be revised until 1829—there are few other places in which Madison spoke so explicitly about the social compact's requirements for constitution making.

Madison's principal aim in examining the "Nature of a Constitution" was to show that the "[Virginia] Convention of 1776 [was] without due power from [the] people."[75] His argument relies on the example of several other states, all of whose constitutions, in his view, were established in a more legitimate fashion. His notes list these states by name along with the page numbers in the recently published *Constitutions of the Several Independent States of America* on which their preambles can be found. Nearly all of these opening declarations appeal to the people's fundamental right to establish a government of their choosing.[76] More to the point with respect to reform in Virginia, most of the constitutions Madison cited emphasize the specific mechanism by which this right was to be exercised—a convention chosen expressly for that purpose.[77] For Madison, the "Nature of a Constitution," strictly understood, would seem to require the popular election of representatives whose exclusive task is the writing of a constitution. At a minimum, the people should know that the representatives they choose, whatever their other duties, are to have constituent powers. Even by this lesser standard, the Virginia constitution of 1776 fell short. Under it, as Madison observes, "power from [the] people [is] no where pretended."[78]

Madison also found another defect in the authority of the Virginia constitution. Not only were those who produced it insufficiently dependent on the people, the people themselves did not have the right to promulgate a constitution at the time. Like New Hampshire and New Jersey, Virginia had enacted its constitution before the colonies had formally declared their independence.[79] Having not yet reverted to a condition of civil society, the people of Virginia were not entitled to establish a new government. They remained bound, at least in part, by their former allegiance.

This did not make the constitution enacted by Virginia illegitimate on its face. It was passed, as Madison writes, "from impulse of Necessity," and this provided some justification.[80] The precise meaning of the phrase is suggested by Madison's reference to the preindependence state constitutions of New Hampshire and New Jersey. In each case, the constitution originated as an urgent matter of communal self-defense.[81] Likewise, the Virginia constitution of 1776 had been a response to pressing public need (for "preventing anarchy," according to Jefferson[82]). Though Madison recognized the dire circumstances that had dictated these assumptions of constitutional powers, he nonetheless insisted on distinguishing between such expedients and the making of a proper constitution. An "impulse of Necessity," which is to say, the law of nature, might give the impetus to constitution making, but it had to be complemented by deliberation, by a genuine act of human choice.

From the standpoint of structure, necessity might also be a defective basis for constitution making. As noted, both Madison and Jefferson considered the Virginia constitution overly simple, a legislative monolith with weak executive and judicial adjuncts. Such a "Union of [the] powers of Gov[ernmen]t," Madison declares in his substantive critique of the constitution, is "tyranny."[83] But was this structural flaw related to the constitution's having been established "from impulse of Necessity"? Madison hints at an answer in his final point about the constitution's questionable authority. The delegates who created the charter, he observes, made "themselves [a] branch of [the] legislature."[84] That is, the convention, having devised a constitution that gave a dangerous preponderance to the legislature, then transformed itself into that very body. Madison does not suggest some sinister motive at work in these events. Rather, he implies that an "impulse of Necessity" militates against complex forms of government. Civil society arises from necessity but attempts to transcend it. It is a simple form intended to make possible the creation of a more complex and effective form. The motive of self-preservation, while strong enough to lead human beings to associate, is not so unrelenting as to keep them from considering various means for escaping their predicament. If the burden of necessity were so overwhelming as to foreclose such deliberation, the natural default would be a form of government that looks very much like civil society—a simple regime based almost exclusively on popular majorities or, in this case, their representatives.

For Madison, this amounted to forgoing the crucial final stage of the social compact, when human convention could finally overcome nature's deficiencies. A comparison to Thomas Paine is instructive, for on this point, his social compact occupies the opposite pole. Paine too made a connection between a unitary, popular regime and civil society, which he called the "first parliament." For him, however, this "natural" condition approximated the best regime: "I draw my idea of the form of government from a principle in nature, which no art can overturn, viz. that the more simple any thing is, the less liable it is to be disordered, and the easier repaired when disordered"[85] For Paine, nature should prevail over art in a form of government, so complex regimes, the product of convention, were not superior to civil society, just more convenient. In this view, so unlike Madison's, a constitution was a compromise not a consummation.

What Madison fails to describe is who must take part in the deliberations necessary to establish a sound constitution, and in what manner they should do so. He leaves undefined, in other words, the relationship between the people and their constituent representatives. He twice states that the fundamental problem with the Virginia convention of 1776 was that it lacked "power" from the people. As his examples from other states suggest, this means an absence of formal delegation. But was such authorization enough? Could the people's constituent representatives act independently of them once chosen, or did their decisions somehow have to reflect the views of those who elected them?

One might reasonably conclude that Madison considered it the right of the people not only to consent to the government under which they lived but also to deliberate over its forms. If consent alone were necessary, the "acquiescence" on which the Virginia constitution rested would be enough, but Madison calls this a "dangerous basis." With the passing of the circumstances that made an emergency constitution necessary, "decency requires [the] surrender of power to the people."[86] Here popular "power" appears to assume a substantive quality. The people's opinions about a form of government had to be taken into account.

For Madison, accommodating this popular right did not demand an ongoing referendum on constitutional issues or even ratification of a constituent assembly's work once completed. The election of constituent representatives *by* the people *for* that express purpose seemed to satisfy the social compact's requirements.[87] He would appeal to this standard four years later, in a speech at Virginia's ratifying convention for the federal Constitution, and give credit for the innovation to the states: "Nothing has excited more admiration in the world, than the manner in which free governments have been established in America. For it was the first instance from the creation of the world to the American revolution, that the free inhabitants have been seen deliberating on a form of government, and selecting such of their citizens as possessed their confidence, to determine upon, and give effect to it."[88] The people's views had shaped their selection of constituent representatives, and the representatives in turn had felt a natural obligation to act in light of, if not in absolute obedience to, the opinions of those who had chosen them.[89]

For Madison, the device of a constitutional convention met a clear need in the social compact. Yet his account only begins to describe the mechanism and the motives required for constitution making, leaving several formidable problems. In the first place, how do the people and their constituent representatives manage to transcend the selfish passions and interests that play such a prominent part in the social compact? Madison's response presents something of a paradox. The establishment of a sound and legitimate constitution would seem to require peace, that is, an escape, however temporary or accidental, from the immediate necessity of self-preservation. But necessity is what reminds human beings of their most fundamental needs and prompts them to unite in political communities. Given a respite from its chastening influence, they pursue their various private aims, indifferent to the consensus that makes this pursuit possible. Madison stated the difficulty well in the speech at Virginia's ratifying convention.

If it has excited so much wonder, that the United States have in the middle of war and confusion, formed free systems of government, how much more astonishment and admiration will be excited, should they be able, peaceably, freely and satisfactorily, to establish one general government, when there is such a diversity of opinions, and interests, when not cemented or stimulated by any common danger? How vast must be the difficulty of concentrating in one government, the interests, and conciliating the opinions of so many different heterogeneous bodies?[90]

For Madison, peace appears to be both the necessary condition and the nemesis of constitution making. Without it, there can be no deliberation, but under it, human beings tend to forget the common ends about which they must deliberate.

In the second place, deliberation itself was a problem for Madison. As his notes on revising the Virginia constitution suggest, he disagreed with Hobbes's assertion that *"Liberty* and *Necessity* are Consistent."* For Hobbes, liberty was no more than unimpeded movement. Accordingly, all human actions, whatever their cause, "proceed from *liberty.*" Hobbes required such a formulation because the notion of causality on which his political thought is based made manifest "the *necessity* of all mens voluntary actions," not least their flight from the state of nature. Liberty could only describe the external conditions for human action, not the human will itself.[91]

Madison, by contrast, refused to dissolve the distinction between the voluntary and the involuntary. For him, a constitution based on an "impulse of Necessity" was both illegitimate and, in all likelihood, inadequate to its purposes. Like Hobbes, Madison associated deliberation with rights, but he assigned to it, at least with respect to the most fundamental political acts, a moral standing and practical efficacy that are foreign to Hobbes. For Madison, the capacity to deliberate emerges as a rather elevated faculty, not the common equipment of all creatures capable of locomotion. He dissents from Hobbes's radically egalitarian account and opens the possibility of profound differences among human beings with regard to political action.

But could Madison reconcile such a notion of deliberation with the prominence of necessity in the social compact? There is evidence that he was conversant with this problem at a more abstract level and had attempted in some fashion to resolve it. In the early months of 1778, while serving on the Governor's Council in Williamsburg, Madison was queried by the clergyman Samuel Stanhope Smith, a friend from his days at Princeton, about the "knotty question of *liberty* & *necessity* that has so much embarrassed philosophers." Smith's letter included a short treatise of his own composition, which made the case for volitional liberty against what he took to be the contrary positions of Locke and others. Smith had discussed the subject before with his former classmate—he wrote "with the utmost conciseness," knowing that Madison was "well acquainted with the subject"—and assumed that Madison was unsympathetic to his arguments.[92] Madison's reply has not survived, but we can surmise its content from a remark made by Smith in acknowledging it. The comment furnishes a neat summary of the tension apparent in Madison's account not only of deliberation but also of the social compact more generally. As Smith put it, "I have read over your *theoretical* objections against the doctrine of moral liberty; for *practically* you seem to be one of its disciples."[93]

Chapter Two

Pride, Property, and American Nationhood

It is hard to quarrel with the renown of Madison's *Federalist* 10. Elegant and penetrating, the essay is rightly credited with bringing to American political thought the important counterintuitive insight that social diversity can be an instrument of national unity. All the same, *Federalist* 10 is hardly the sum of Madison's mind on this subject. What its academic and popular interpreters too often overlook is the extent to which Madison's argument about diversity points to a prior, more practical question: how was such a welter of parties and interests to be brought into a single sphere in the first place? Surely the very problems that called for an extended sphere would make popular assent to its establishment unlikely; factious sorts would have to be willing to participate in a regime whose avowed purpose was to thwart them. Madison spoke of this difficulty elsewhere in *The Federalist,* and with obvious reference to Number 10. Describing the obstacles faced by the Federal Convention, he observed:

> Nor could it have been the large and small States only which would marshal themselves in opposition to each other on various points [at the Convention]. Other combinations, resulting from a difference of local position and policy, must have created additional difficulties. As every State may be divided into different districts, and its citizens into different classes, which give birth to contending interests and local jealousies; so the different parts of the United States are distinguished from each other, by a variety of circumstances, which produce a like effect on a larger scale. And although this variety of in-

terests, for reasons sufficiently explained in a former paper, may have a salutary influence on the administration of the Government when formed; *yet every one must be sensible of the contrary influence which must have been experienced in the task of forming it.*[1]

In short, however useful American diversity might prove to be in maintaining the Constitution once established, it was a formidable hurdle to the task of establishing it.

Such narrow concerns could be transcended in certain circumstances, to be sure. As Madison wrote in *Federalist* 51, "In the extended republic of the United States, and among the great variety of interests, parties and sects which it embraces, a coalition of a majority of the whole society could seldom take place on any other principles than those of justice and the general good."[2] The possibility of winnowing public-spiritedness from more selfish material was an essential aspect of Madison's constitutionalism. But it was just that—an aspect of his *constitutionalism.* It presupposed a "whole society" organized as an "extended republic." For Madison, social diversity had to be arranged in a particular way if it was to be of political advantage. If this were not the case, there would have been no need for a new constitution in the late 1780s. After all, the American people became no more or less diverse in the transition from the Articles of Confederation to the Constitution. It was the form that such diversity took—that is, the regime in which it was allowed to find expression—that was decisive. Again, however, if the Constitution was required to make American diversity safe, how could it arise from that diversity?

To address this question, I will focus on the two sorts of attachments that Madison himself stressed: those arising from the political claims of the states ("marshal[ing] themselves in opposition to each other") and those arising from the "variety of interests" within the states. These two great sets of obstacles to union constituted for Madison yet another qualification of the traditional social compact. If a wartime "impulse of Necessity" threatened the possibility of genuine deliberation, so too did the more pacific side of the social compact, where the special vices of the Articles of Confederation were allowed to flourish.

Madison rejected the idea that the drive for self-preservation alone could bring about a lasting release from the state of nature. Such an escape required the political right of nature as well, a right that confers dignity, supposing as it does that men are capable of devising a political solution to their natural predicament. For Madison, this right found practical expression in America in the sovereign pride of the states, in their "interfering pretensions."[3] The problem, of course, was that such attachments could be misplaced. The most jealously guarded political forms were often defective, serving as a shield against present danger while concealing more distant threats. Pride in familiar political forms, Madison recognized, could interfere with the necessary consideration of new ones.

No less of an obstacle to union were the states' manifold claims of interest, made possible by the security available in what Madison called "civilized nations."[4] Under the Articles of Confederation, such attachments stood as a counterpoint to the fear and anxiety that ordinarily do the social compact's dirty work. Whether understood in terms of Hobbesian "nastiness" or Lockean "uncertainty,"[5] these chastening passions make unanimity and concerted action possible in the state of nature, giving to every compacting individual a reason to join civil society and to establish government. When human beings are more secure—as Americans certainly were in the mid-1780s—the passions connected to property prevail, and these tend to be narrower and less public-spirited than the concern for social peace that fear and anxiety inspire.

Dwelling on sovereign pride and property may seem a peculiar if not a contradictory way to discuss the social compact. Indeed, the state of nature, on which the social compact depends, is usually thought to precede (or exclude) any serious political or economic activity. For Madison, however, the state of nature meant the absence not so much of ordinary political and economic motives as of necessary political forms at some level of society. The failures of the national and state governments had produced in America something of the pervasive unease of the philosophers' state of nature, but the basic institutions of the political and social order had remained intact and thus still allowed the relatively free play of assertive political pride and interested self-regard. These seemingly practical objections to the usual first principles of the social compact represent, in my view, a theoretical revision. One might say, borrowing a term from Michael J. Sandel, that Madison attempted to demonstrate the inadequacy for the social compact of a notion of the self "unencumbered" by all but the narrowest concern for self-preservation.[6]

The Articles of Confederation in Retrospect

The voluminous papers of Madison include a great number of contemporary documents dealing with his specific objections to the Articles of Confederation. His correspondence and speeches from the 1780s, his well-known 1787 memorandum on the "Vices of the Political System of the United States," and several essays of *The Federalist* all catalogue the deficiencies of the Confederation in damning detail. But only much later, in his retirement, did Madison attempt a historical overview of this first effort at American union, from its inception to its unceremonious demise. His brief account, entitled "Preface to Debates in the Convention of 1787," was intended to introduce his published notes from the Federal Convention. The "sketch," though "never finished nor applied," as its first line announces, is a fairly comprehensive summary of the origins and early difficulties of the Articles of Confederation.[7] Of more interest for our purposes, it also presents Madison's analysis of the motives at work during this crucial period.

For Madison, the Articles of Confederation were best understood as an instrument of the struggle against Great Britain. Prepared in the wake of independence, they were to provide for the "future management of the common interests," especially in military matters. What before had been left "to the discretion of Congress, guided by the exigencies of the contest," and "to the known intentions or occasional instructions of the Colonial Legislatures" would be handled more effectively, it was hoped, through a formal, established charter.[8] In form and purpose, the Confederation was intended primarily to achieve the great shared end of its parties, the thirteen distinct states (or civil societies, as Madison referred to them in his speech on citizenship) that had proclaimed their independence from Britain but required mutual assistance to achieve it.

In describing the three-and-a-half years that it took for the articles to win ratification, Madison highlights the tension between the concerns of particular states and their general interest in a successful prosecution of the war effort. Thus, in March 1781, Maryland, the last holdout among the states, gave up its insistence on national rights to the western lands held by its larger neighbors and "yielded to the persuasion that a final & formal establishment of the federal Union & Govt. would make a favorable impression not only on other foreign nations, but on [Great Britain] herself." By "giving a Stable & authoritative character to the Confederation," Maryland hoped that "a successful termination of the contest might be accelerated."[9] Similar considerations had swayed the other states, but only after long persuasion. Though the "motives to hasten the establishment of a regular and efficient Govt." should have been "obvious" to all, Congress still found it necessary to plea for a sacrifice of "local considerations and favorite opinions to the public safety, and the necessary harmony." The "crisis" had finally succeeded in repressing "opinions and pretensions" that might have been "inflexible in another state of things."[10] This is apparently what Madison had in mind when, writing to George Washington just four years after ratification of the Confederation, he remarked, "Nothing but the peculiarity of our circumstances could ever have produced those sacrifices of sovereignty on which the foederal Government now rests."[11] The "necessary harmony" for constitution making could arise, it would seem, only from insecurity.

Madison's explanation of the origin of the Articles of Confederation places him on one side of the dispute among historians about the political significance of this first American constitution. Merrill Jensen has argued that the articles were the self-conscious embodiment of the political ideals of American "radicals," those state-oriented elements that worked most forcefully for independence but would later lose out to the "conservatives" who proposed the Constitution of 1787.[12] Jack N. Rakove, the leading critic of Jensen's hypothesis, concurs with Madison in pointing to the expedience of the articles and their instrumental value in the struggle for independence. As Rakove puts it, "An examination of the conditions and circumstances governing the framing of the Articles of Confederation . . . suggests, more than anything else, the extent to which political exigencies imposed powerful limits on the sweep of formal constitutional thought."[13] Madison, in fact, emphasized the degree to which the war-inspired need for union, as well as sensitivity to the pretensions and interests of the states, prevented essential reflection on the Confederation's character. The priority, he wrote, was "so framing the fedl. system as to obtain the unanimity required for its due sanction."[14] This meant deferring discussions on delicate subjects like the rules of suffrage, western lands, and commercial regulation. Above all, it meant avoiding consideration of what Madison called the Confederation's "radical infirmity": the dependence of Congress "on the voluntary and simultaneous compliance with its Requisitions" by so many independent states.[15]

Like the Revolution-era state constitution of Virginia, of which he was so critical, the Confederation was tantamount in Madison's eyes to civil society, that stage of the social compact in which unity took priority over form. In both cases, war—the impetus for civil society's formation—had fostered institutional simplicity, leaving the wills of the contracting parties largely unmodified. In Virginia, this had meant a failure to properly separate and establish the distinct powers of government; in the Confederation, it had meant insufficient reflection on the means for insuring the cooperation of member states in the execution of national policy. Hence, while the Confederation could answer the purposes of war (and even here, only to a certain extent), it could not serve as an enduring constitution.

The defects of the Confederation, so evident even in wartime, were magnified as hostilities drew to a close after the American victory at Yorktown in October 1781. With the formal end of the war two years later, matters worsened. The political and economic diversity that had almost scuttled the formation of a union in the first place could no longer be checked by the prospect of national defeat. Peace encouraged the states to turn even more resolutely inward. As Madison wrote in his brief history, "The close of the war . . . brought no cure for the public embarrassments. The States[,] relieved from the pressure of foreign danger, and flushed with the enjoyment of independent and sovereign power . . . persevered in omissions and in measures incompatible with their relations to the Federal Govt. and with those among themselves (notwithstanding, the urgency of the national engagements, and the increasing anar-

chy and collisions which threatened the Union itself)."[16] In the
years ahead, from 1782 to 1786, Madison would promote a series
of reforms, all intended to bolster national finances and to bring
needed uniformity to commercial regulation among the states.
One after another, these proposals would fail. None of them could
muster the unanimity among the state legislatures required for
amendment under the Confederation.[17] As Madison had anticipated at the time, the strongest motive for concerted action had receded with American success at arms.[18]

From the point of view of the social compact, it would seem
that the states should eventually have been roused from their indifference to the decline of national institutions. Their situation
can be compared to that of the stronger individuals described by
Madison in his account of the state of nature in *Federalist* 51. Whatever the states' claims of self-sufficiency, one might expect that they
too "would be prompted by the uncertainty of their condition, to
submit to a government which may protect the weak as well as
themselves."[19] Madison himself described the juncture in terms of
"the increasing anarchy and collisions which threatened the Union
itself" and "an impending catastrophe."[20] The states had every reason to be concerned for their continued survival. That they were
not suggests that the analogy between individuals and states is, at
best, imperfect.

Madison admits as much in the opening paragraphs of his
"Preface," where he makes an extended comparison between individuals and states in a state of nature: "As the weakness and wants
of man naturally lead to an association of individuals, under a
common authority, whereby each may have the protection of the
whole against danger from without, and enjoy in safety within, the
advantages of social intercourse, and an exchange of the necessar-
ies & comforts of life: in like manner feeble communities, independent of each other, have resorted to a Union, less intimate, but
with common Councils, for the common safety agst. powerful
neighbors, and for the preservation of justice and peace among
themselves."[21] Lest the unsuspecting reader take this as a description of the Constitution, Madison immediately explains that the
analogy applies to the various confederacies, ancient and modern,
with which he had become familiar in studying the problem of
American union. He introduces this equation of states with com-

pacting individuals in order to put the novelty of the Constitution in full relief: "It remained for the British Colonies, now United States, of North America, to add to those examples, one of a more interesting character than any of them: which led to a system without a precedent ancient or modern, a system founded on popular rights, and so comb[in]ing a federal form with the forms of indiv[id]ual Republics, as may enable each to supply the defects of the other and obtain the advantages of both."[22] The essential contrast is that the Constitution was based not on "feeble communities, independent of each other," but rather on "popular rights," which accounted for its "more interesting" and unprecedented character.

This design entailed a different relationship to subordinate governments. A confederacy was premised on its member states' determination to preserve their own distinctive (if not fully efficacious) regimes. A union founded on "popular rights," by contrast, made possible a greater flexibility with respect to these lesser governments. As Madison's comparison implies, the "weakness and wants" of individuals made them experience vulnerability in a way that even the feeblest of states could not. By drawing its authority not from the states themselves but from their citizens, the Constitution tried to transcend the corporate attachments that usually afflicted confederacies. It brought loyalty to these parochial communities into more direct competition with the concern for self-preservation, leading the "divided individual," as Wilson Carey McWilliams has observed, to "follow the path which interest dictates toward a broader affection."[23] As under a confederacy, member states would continue to exist—the people could combine a "federal form with the forms of individual Republics"—but the states' political independence was no longer presupposed.

Turning now to writings that long preceded Madison's "Preface," I will examine the particular defects that prompted his rejection of the articles. This rejection, it must be stressed, did not represent an unwillingness to accommodate the very real local attachments, political and economic, on which the Confederation was based. Rather, it arose from a wish to integrate these attachments into a constitution that would provide better safeguards for the security of the nation as a whole. For Madison, as we shall see, the failings of the Articles of Confederation demonstrated the unique capacity of a true social compact—one founded on the active consent of *individuals*—to achieve the abiding ends of political life.

The Recalcitrance of States

Madison's first serious reflections on the Articles of Confederation coincided with his entry into national politics. When he arrived to serve his first term in the Continental Congress in March 1780, a year before the articles' ratification, the body was already beginning to lose authority in relation to the states. The broad discretionary powers that Congress had exercised since the war's outset were increasingly drawn into question by the state legislatures. The primary reason for this resistance was the growing financial burden of the common effort, which virtually every state felt itself unfairly put upon to support. The situation was exacerbated by the continuing lack of a formal instrument of national government, a fact that contributed to a general wariness of congressional intentions. By the time Madison took his seat, Congress had already given up a large measure of its financial independence by relinquishing its power to print money. His early efforts to help Congress take advantage of its remaining options—requisitions from the states, impressment, loans from private citizens and foreign governments—left him convinced that an expansion of national authority was the only viable solution to the union's woes.[24]

Like most of his contemporaries, Madison did not expect the Articles of Confederation by themselves to bring about a dramatic change in the nation's situation. Whatever impression their ratification might make on allies and lenders overseas, they did not augment congressional authority in any meaningful way. Under the articles' provisions, the compliance of the independent governments of the states would remain the mechanism for implementing national policy. The establishment of a formal government did, however, present two options to Congress that did not exist before. In the first place, a failure to comply with its legitimate measures could be more easily denounced as a breach of faith. It thus became possible for the national government to contemplate enforcement actions of one sort or another. Secondly, the existence of a charter with limited, specified powers allayed fears of congressional arbitrariness and made the states more willing to consider additional grants of authority. If Congress still lacked independent sources of revenue, proposals to correct this situation now stood a chance of winning the states' assent.

It is significant that, of these two options, Madison preferred the first—a resort to coercion—on principle but accepted the second as the more practical alternative. Less than two weeks after final ratification of the articles, he proposed an amendment that would have authorized Congress "to employ the force of the United States as well by sea as by land" against states refusing to comply with congressional measures. While agreeing that such a power "should be explicitly and precisely warranted," he nonetheless contended that under the articles the national government already possessed "a general and implied power . . . to enforce and carry into effect" its policies against delinquent members.[25]

For Madison, this authority was deducible from the very nature of government. It was such legitimate coercive power that made the social compact an improvement over the state of nature, where force was at the disposal of individuals rather than the law. Without it, the affairs of the Confederation could not possibly be coordinated. His amendment, as he wrote to Jefferson, would make it the "interest" of the states "to yield prompt obedience to all just requisitions of them."[26] When Madison's amendment failed, he turned his energies elsewhere, but he continued to consider the absence of enforcement power the primary defect of the Confederation. More than four years later he would again write to Jefferson about how a "single frigate under the orders of Congress could make it the interest of any one of the Atlantic States to pay its just Quota." As it stood, he insisted, the "present plan of federal Government reverses the first principle of all Government. It punishes not the evil-doers, but those that do well."[27]

As Madison knew, such "evil-doers" could only be punished by their own consent. He never suggested that Congress simply exercise force without the approval of the states. His view was far indeed from the "easy discovery of implied powers" that Irving Brant attributes to him on the basis of this unsuccessful amendment.[28] Like the stronger individuals of his state of nature, the members of the Confederation would have to submit willingly to the powers of the federal government, in full recognition of their own vulnerability. As Madison said in support of his proposal, it was "most consonant to the spirit of a free constitution . . . that the penal consequences of a violation of duty should be clearly promulged and understood."[29] The trouble was that the states were not individuals. They were collections of individuals and, as such, were less subject to the sort of arbitrary violence that made submission to regular political authority a compelling option even for the strongest of men. Moreover, as Madison would later admit to Washington, "difficulty and awkwardness" would always attend "operating by force on the collective will of a State."[30] The national government, in short, could neither expect a grant of coercive authority from the states nor really hope to use it if granted.

Deprived of recourse to the "first principle of all Government," reformers could still entertain the possibility of persuading the states to give Congress lesser powers that might provide immediate relief for the Confederation. In particular, Madison and others sought an explicit national right to lay and collect taxes, a power that would have greatly reduced congressional dependence on the voluntary gifts of the states. A 5 percent impost on imports, earmarked to service the growing national debt, had been proposed in February 1781 but had gone down to defeat by the end of 1782 amid objections about its duration and means of collection.[31] In early 1783, a new revenue plan was proposed, with Madison as its leading advocate. His statements in the course of this campaign reveal an important change in his approach to the Confederation. Having resigned himself to the impracticality of coercion, he reversed his earlier tack and decided it was now advisable to flatter the recalcitrant states. His new appeal for the national cause was based not on force but on revolutionary virtue, not on interest but on character. It was, above all, an exhortation to patriotism.

The principal document from this last attempt to secure an independent revenue for the Confederation is the "Address to the States by Congress," a report written by Madison for a committee under his chairmanship. The report accompanied a proposal for restoring public credit through a modified version of the impost that had been rejected less than a year before. Deference to the states and their proud sovereignty is the keynote of both the plan and the address. Thus, in "renewing this proposition to the States," wrote Madison, "we have not been unmindful of the objections which heretofore frustrated the unanimous adoption of it." Under the revised plan, revenue would be collected by state-appointed officers and only for a limited number of years. Because the yield of the impost was expected to be relatively modest, the second component of the plan was yet another call for the states to be punctilious in observing national requisitions. As if to emphasize the primacy of the states, Madison admitted that these "relaxations" rendered the revenue plan inadequate.[32] In two similar passages, he candidly describes such compromises as "the effect of a disposition in Con[gres]s to attend at all times to the sentiments of those whom they serve."[33] Whereas coercing the states would have implied a national government commensurate to national needs, flattering them meant lowered expectations. Insofar as national ends were to be pursued, it would have to be through the medium of local political attachments.

In his earlier amendment proposal, Madison had sought coercive authority for the national government by arguing that the logic and spirit of a "free constitution" entailed reliance on "the penal consequences of a violation of duty." Though his later promotion of the impost represented a retreat from this position, he continued to refer to the Confederation as a constitution. His emphasis changed, however, from constitutional sanction to constitutional obligation, from penalty to promise as the basis of his appeal to the states. Rather than brandish the national government's implied power to compel cooperation, Madison now urged the states to do their constitutional duty. In the congressional debate on the revenue plan, he insisted that "requisitions . . . were a law to the States, as much as the acts of the latter for complying with them were a law to their individual members; that the foederal constitution was as sacred & obligatory as the internal constitutions of the several States; and that nothing could justify the States in disobeying acts warranted by it."[34]

The parallel between the federal and state constitutions lay not in the capacity of their respective governments to enforce them but in their standing as fundamental law. In the absence of coercive authority, Madison relied on the potency of the plighted word. The provisions of the articles should be obeyed because their violation without cause rendered them meaningless; when the states so openly defied an authority of their own making, it essentially ceased to exist. Such reasoning supported Congress's request to the states for a revenue that would be collected directly by the national government. Because requisitions, made in good faith under the articles, were routinely ignored and the means to compel compliance with them was denied to the Confederation, the states were obliged by the federal constitution to grant some kind of compensatory authority. As a "free gift," the national impost would allow the states to fulfill their obligations while not subverting their "sovereignty & liberty."[35] It would skirt rather than confront their unwillingness to comply with the requisitions of the Confederation. On what grounds, though, would they grant even this power? Simply for the sake of principled adherence to the articles?

One of the more obvious goads for winning the compliance of the states is conspicuous by its absence from Madison's address. Refraining from the rhetorical strategy that would later serve Publius so well in the early papers of *The Federalist*,[36] he made no dark predictions of future strife among members of a dissolved Confederation, despite his very real concerns on this score.[37] Instead he spoke of the American union almost exclusively in terms of past deeds and present duties, inserting only a perfunctory request to the states "to reflect on the consequences of rejecting [the revenue plan]."[38] Madison had apparently concluded that circumstances were not urgent enough to make the future a persuasive weapon and that the states might simply react with their characteristic defensiveness. If they were to cede any new authority to Congress, their gaze would have to be directed elsewhere, not to a potentially dire future but to a shared history and, more importantly, to the transcendent principles that made that history worth recounting.

As presented by Madison, the revenue plan was nothing less than a referendum on the Revolution itself, whose looming debt was the national government's most pressing burden. Interestingly, he did not lay great stress on the pledged faith of the states in the articles, as he did in the earlier debate. It was not constitutional obligation as such that concerned him here but rather the particulars of *this* obligation. The debt, he insisted, must be "referred to the cause in which it has been incurred."[39] Hence, "If other motives than that of justice could be requisite on this occasion, no nation could ever feel stronger. For to whom are the debts to be paid?"

Madison proceeded to catalogue the worthy creditors of the nation: a loyal ally in the French king; sympathetic lenders among the Dutch; the uncompensated soldiers of the Continental Army, "that illustrious & patriotic band of fellow Citizens"; and finally, various American creditors, who gladly relieved their country, relying on "its faith, its firmness and its resources."[40] Madison made no mention of the ruinous consequences of disregarding these obligations. The hostility of France, the destruction of American credit, the mutinous rumblings of the officers at Newburg—these were passed over in silence.[41]

What, then, were the "other motives" to which Madison refers, having apparently decided to forgo an appeal to either constitutional duty or the possibility of imminent harm? The character of the creditors would seem to be the key: they were representatives of the revolutionary cause. Rehearsing their contributions reminded the states that they had not achieved their present self-sufficiency and independence by themselves. Madison wanted the states to see adequate provision for the national debt as a sign of their own strength, as the sort of generosity befitting secure sovereigns: "Altho' this debt is greater than could have been wished, it is still less on the whole than could have been expected, and when referred to the cause in which it has been incurred, and compared with the burdens which wars of ambition and of vain glory have entailed on other nations, ought to be borne not only with cheerfulness but with pride."[42] It was this noble sense of accomplishment that Madison hoped to use to the Confederation's advantage.

Madison made explicit the connection between pride and the cause of natural rights in the extraordinary last paragraph of his "Address to the States": "Let it be remembered finally that it has ever been the pride and boast of America, that the rights for which she contended were the rights of human nature. By the blessing of the Author of these rights on the means exerted for their defence, they [the rights] have prevailed against all opposition and form the basis of thirteen independent states."[43] All human beings could claim to possess such natural rights, but the American revolutionaries had set themselves apart by exercising them. They had made good on a boast that ordinarily went untested, saying to the world (as Harvey C. Mansfield puts it), "you can have what we have, and we are superior only because we have shown this possibility to you."[44] The curious thing about such universal rights, as even this brief passage suggests, is that they are most completely realized in particular regimes. The "rights of human nature" were vindicated by the establishment of "thirteen independent states." As a result, the pride that once belonged to the political right of nature grew narrower, becoming transformed into that peculiarly American species of patriotism, cosmopolitan and chauvinistic all at once. The difficulty was that this fierce attachment was not to the nation but to the states, despite the obligations that the states had as a nation. Only by analogy—and a faulty one at that, as we have seen—could the Confederation hope to inspire similar devotion. As Madison recognized, the fate of the Confederation had to be related in some way to the states' own dignity.

If the "rights of human nature" were so entangled in the claims of particular regimes, how could they be made to serve a broader national cause, one that lacked the unique sanction of the social compact? What could elevate the ultimately selfish character of the state governments? This was Madison's problem in confronting the sovereign members of the Confederation. His reply in the "Address to the States" generates a host of questions. The report closes with what is presumably his final and most persuasive argument: a call to the states to exhibit "justice, good faith, honor, gratitude & all the other Qualities which enoble the character of a nation," or, as he puts it more succinctly, the "cardinal and essential Virtues." Far from a mere rhetorical flourish, this appeal to virtue is the culmination of his account of the national debt's significance. It attempts to exploit the sovereign pride of the states, providing the standard against which such republican governments should "justif[y] themselves."[45]

This emphasis on virtue is of special interest because it seems at first glance to substantiate the claims of the "ideological" school, the dominant (if now often challenged) current of thought in contemporary historiography of the American founding. According to this view, early American political thought, at least until the time of the Federal Convention, was distinguished by an expectation of single-minded devotion to the common welfare. As Gordon S. Wood describes this citizen ideal, "In a republic . . . each man must somehow be persuaded to submerge his personal wants into the greater good of the whole. This willingness of the individual to sacrifice his private interests for the good of the community—such patriotism or love of country—the eighteenth century termed 'public virtue.'"[46] The contrast intended by this "republican hypothesis" is with an older, rival account of the founding, one that assigns pre-eminence in early American political thought to consideration of rights and interests, the selfish building blocks of the social compact.

A chief difficulty with the republican hypothesis is its remarkably crude notion of virtue, a fault that is present even in the work of its most sophisticated proponents. Thus J. G. A. Pocock, while tracing the long tradition of republicanism back to its ancient roots in Aristotle's "science of virtue,"[47] shows an almost willful indifference to Aristotle's treatment of the subject. In Pocock's account, Aristotle understood the virtues to be the "value-goals which men pursued," subject to no limitation other than the "theoretically or traditionally identifiable values which men might prefer and associate to enjoy."[48] He portrays Aristotelian virtue as an expression not of the rational nature of human beings but of their subjective preferences, a serious misrepresentation made possible by Pocock's complete silence with respect to Aristotle's ethical works.[49] Casting aside Aristotelian psychology, Pocock describes virtue in purely formal terms, which allows for a similar formality in relating virtue to politics. Of Aristotelian justice, which unites in activity for the common good the other moral virtues that Aristotle describes,[50] Pocock only retains the common good, understood as "the attainment of all particular goods."[51] This goal provides an appropriate standard for republican politics not because it reflects or intimates the natural order of the human soul but because in striving after it, every citizen becomes a "being in relation with the universal" and thereby, presumably, becomes better able to deal "with particular and contingent events and with time as the dimension of contingent happenings."[52]

Of course, such existential priorities are not what makes Pocock typical of the republican hypothesis. Most of its expositors are of a more strictly historical bent. Rather, he is representative because of his readiness to empty republican virtue of any content that might make it a meaningful alternative to other political possibilities. No regime, whatever its principles, can dispense entirely with devotion to the common good, however understood and promoted. Classical political thought, from which Pocock supposedly takes his cue, is distinguished not just by its emphasis on the common good but by its attention to the various competing accounts of the common good and to the relationship of these, ultimately, to the perfection of human beings as such. Separated from the consideration of ultimate ends, "public virtue" can find a place in virtually any regime, even one based on the social compact.

In the closing passage from his "Address to the States," Madison does indeed link virtue to the cause of republicanism. As a fuller quotation demonstrates, however, he did not find the opposition between virtue and rights nearly so absolute as do most defenders of the republican hypothesis.

No instance has heretofore occurred, nor can any instance be expected hereafter to occur, in which the unadulterated forms of Republican Government can pretend to so fair an opportunity of justifying themselves by their fruits. In this view the Citizens of the U.S. are responsible for the greatest trust ever confided to a Political Society. If justice, good faith, honor, gratitude & all the other Qualities which enoble the character of a nation, and fulfil the ends of Government, be the fruits of our establishments, the cause of liberty will acquire a dignity and lustre, which it has never yet enjoyed; and an example will be set which can not but have the most favorable influence on the rights of mankind. If on the other side, our Governments should be unfortunately blotted with the reverse of these cardinal and essential Virtues, the great cause which we have engaged to vindicate, will be dishonored & betrayed; the last & fairest experiment in favor of the rights of human nature will be turned against them; and their patrons and friends exposed to be insulted & silenced by the votaries of Tyranny and Usurpation.[53]

For Madison, the "cardinal and essential Virtues" were perfectly compatible with a regime based on "the rights of mankind." In fact, far from just adding "dignity and lustre" to the American "experiment," they were crucial to its success, compensating for an excess of political jealousy—the combination of selfishness and distrust that was the specific vice of the members of the Confederation and a necessary hazard of the proud doctrine of natural rights. Justice, good faith, honor, and gratitude provided an indispensable counterbalance to the native tendencies of "the cause of liberty."

This view is confirmed by the best-known passage on virtue in *The Federalist,* in which Madison addresses those "sincere friends of liberty" who display "an indiscriminate and unbounded jealousy" toward officeholders and succumb to the "extravagancies of this passion": "Were the pictures which have been drawn by the political jealousy of some among us, faithful likenesses of the human character, the inference would be that there is not sufficient virtue among men for self-government; and that nothing less than the chains of despotism can restrain them from destroying and devouring one another."[54] Here, as in his address, Madison presents virtue as a leavening element that tempers "political jealousy." It describes a dimension of human nature that is somehow missing from the unadorned teaching of natural rights.

That said, it is also clear that the relationship between virtue and republicanism in Madison's thought is far from classical. Whatever virtue's importance, "the rights of mankind" are precedent in every respect. Thus, as he writes in his address, justice and the other virtues are the "fruits" of governments established within the ambit of "the cause of liberty." Their true worth, however pleasing they may be to the eye, lies in their being "Qualities" that "fulfil the ends of government." They are not to be cultivated simply for their own sake. American government might require certain virtues, but it promotes them only incidentally, as fit instruments of policy. In *The Federalist* as well, the "political jealousy" of "the sincere friends of liberty" obviously remains a more fundamental need than the virtue that provides grounds for its relaxation.

Madison was hardly the first to articulate this basic understanding of virtue. As Michael P. Zuckert has noted, it is present in the influential Whig Opposition writings of Cato and, less explicitly, in Locke.[55] Hobbes, however, was its great originator. In *Leviathan,* after providing a fairly traditional list of the moral virtues, Hobbes announces what sets his own account apart from that of his predecessors, especially Aristotle: "But the Writers of Morall Philosophie, though they acknowledge the same Vertues and Vices;

Yet not seeing wherein consisted their Goodness; nor that they come to be praised, as the meanes of peaceable, sociable, and comfortable living; place them in a mediocrity of passions: as if not the Cause, but the Degree of daring, made Fortitude; or not the Cause, but the Quantity of a gift made Liberality."[56] To emphasize that the moral virtues are not individual excellences but the various means to a single public end, Hobbes proceeds to contract them into "one easie sum, intelligible, even to the meanest capacity; and that is, Do not that to another, which thou wouldest not have done to thy selfe."[57] For Madison, as for Hobbes, it was the needs of this rights-bearing "selfe" as opposed to the requirements of the soul that determined the character and extent of public virtue.

Given this limit, moral education requires special care. Because virtue corresponds to no natural inclination, it must be connected somehow to the selfish concerns of human beings if it is not to be experienced as an imposition. For Hobbes, the command of his terrible sovereign secures virtue's place in the commonwealth.[58] Montesquieu finds a basis for the necessary "self-renunciation" ("*la vertu politique est un renoncement à soi-même*") in the constant mutual supervision of a small, homogeneous republic.[59] Madison, as we have seen, depends on the enduring hold of republican pride, the chief psychological consequence of the social compact's exalted claims about human political capacities. As the close of his address shows, he intended to impress upon the states that they, as well as "the great cause which [they] have engaged to vindicate," would be "dishonored & betrayed" by the Confederation's failure. The states, as "patrons & friends" of the "rights of human nature," would be "insulted & silenced" by such an event, depriving them of the boast of which he spoke earlier. Both here and in the related passage from *The Federalist*, Madison presents virtue as the alternative to despotism and tyranny. Virtue would seem to depend on the pride that human beings take in overcoming their justifiable wariness of one another and on finding a means other than absolute government to restrain themselves. It enhances their self-regard because it shows them to be capable of maintaining something of their natural equality without a constant reliance on fear.

In the context of the Confederation, however, the limits of such an appeal were evident in the very terms Madison used in making it. In the first place, we see in Madison's peroration a change in his addressee. While before the audience was unambiguously the states, he now includes "the Citizens of the U.S." as well. This allows him to speak of the Confederation as a single "Political Society," as opposed to a collection of thirteen independent communities. Although the decision to support the Confederation belonged to the states, Madison knew that it was only through the attachment of individual citizens to the federal government that his exhortations to virtue could be effective, overcoming their pride in the independence of their states. It was here that the absence of a federal constitution with popular authority was most deeply felt, for the people had not *made* the Confederation as they had their state governments and so had not invested their political self-respect in its success.

This deficiency related to another. By Madison's own account, the virtues that he called upon were produced by the particular "establishments" that arose from the universal rights of mankind. But particular establishments made for particular virtues, not a general disposition to all humankind. With only slight exaggeration, we might say that justice, good faith, honor, and gratitude become the exclusive property of the regime capable of inculcating them. This presented a familiar problem for the Confederation. For while Hobbes may have relied too much on strict obedience to sovereign authority as the means to bring about such virtue, law-abidingness in some form would seem to be its necessary condition. And law-abidingness is secured by the threat of punishment, the very power whose absence in the Confederation prompted Madison to declare it in violation of the "first principle of all Government." Madison's appeal to virtue thus comes full circle, back to the problem of coercive authority.

Despite its many concessions, the second impost plan shared the fate of the first, finally going down to defeat three years after it was proposed.[60] It was during this period that Madison came to terms with the full significance of the Confederation's lack of coercive power and the incapacity of its laws. Shortly after leaving Congress in 1783, he wrote to Edmund Randolph that "the relative situation of the U.S. calls for a 'Droit Public' much more minute than that comprised in the foederal articles," one demanding "much greater mutual confidence and amity among the societies which are to obey it." The model to be avoided—and the distinction is decisive—was the type of "law which has grown out of the transactions & intercourse of jealous & hostile nations."[61] Madison would elaborate on this theme in the study of ancient and modern confederations that he undertook upon his return to Virginia and still more in the "Vices of the Political System of the United States," the analysis of the union's defects that he composed before the Federal Convention. In this latter document, he explicitly criticizes the logic of his "Address to the States":

> A sanction is essential to the idea of law, as coercion is to that of Government. The federal system being destitute of both, wants the great vital principles of a Political Cons[ti]tution. Under the form of such a Constitution, it is in fact nothing more than a treaty of amity, of commerce and of alliance, between so many independent and Sovereign States. From what cause could so fatal an omission have happened in the articles of Confederation? From a mistaken confidence that the justice, the good faith, the honor, the sound policy, of the several legislative assemblies would render superfluous any appeal to the ordinary motives by which the laws secure the obedience of individuals.[62]

The conclusion that the Confederation was "nothing more than a treaty of amity" carried serious consequences, both practical and theoretical. In the first place, this "delicate truth" could be used to justify a disregard for the requirements of the articles, as Madison would argue in *The Federalist*.[63] More importantly, this conclusion finally exploded the analogy between states and individuals that had proved so destructive to the Confederation. An "individual independence of the States is utterly irreconcileable with their aggregate sovereignty," Madison told Washington. Yet, at the same time, the pretensions of the states could not be ignored: "a consolidation of the whole into one simple republic would be as inexpedient as it is unattainable." A way would have to be found to reconcile the proud self-regard of the states with "a due supremacy of the national authority."[64]

The Narrowness of Interest

Recalcitrant states were not the only obstacle to the establishment of a sound national government. Just as troublesome were interfering attachments based on property and material well-being—in short, interests. To return briefly to the passage from *The Federalist* which opened this chapter:

> As every State may be divided into different districts, and its citizens into different classes, which give birth to contending interests and local jealousies; so the different parts of the United States are distinguished from each other, by a variety of circumstances, which produce a like effect on a larger scale. And although this variety of interests, for reasons sufficiently explained in a former paper, may have a salutary influence on the administration of the Government when formed; yet every one must be sensible of the contrary influence which must have been experienced in the task of forming it.[65]

In the period following his departure from the Continental Congress, reflection on the question of interest led Madison to radicalize further his stand on federal reform. The issue, as he saw it, was not just a lack of authority in the national government, to be remedied by transforming it from a mere "treaty of amity" into a genuine "political constitution." The country's difficulties could not be attributed solely to relations between the state governments and the Confederation. Rather, he concluded, in "developing the evils which viciate the political system of the U.S.," it was also proper "to include those which are found within the States individually."[66] The state governments themselves, in their treatment of their own people, were responsible for the most serious transgressions against the republican cause.

The lesser of these wrongs was a tendency to "multiplicity" and "mutability" in local laws, depriving citizens of a stable, predictable legal environment. More seriously, the states had brought into question "the fundamental principle of republican Government, that the majority who rule in such Governments, are the safest Guardians both of public Good and of private rights." State majorities, united "by an apparent interest or common passion," had shown themselves unable to refrain from "unjust violations of the rights and interests of the minority, or of individuals."[67] This phenomenon, unnamed here, would become "faction" in *Federalist* 10, where Madison provided a more exact formulation: "By a faction I understand a number of citizens, whether amounting to a majority or minority of the whole, who are united and actuated by some common impulse of passion, or of interest, adverse to the rights of other citizens, or to the permanent and aggregate interests of the community."[68]

The two great motives of faction—passion and interest—also affected the Confederation more directly. In the first place, there was the states' passion for sovereignty, the destructive effects of which we have already explored at some length. Interest, our concern here, reinforced political obstinacy but also presented its own particular impediments to national action. Like the political right of nature, interest too was ultimately rooted in physical well-being. It emerged, however, from the bourgeois side of the preserved self, which looked to the enjoyment rather than the establishment of personal security. Interest was desirous where the political right of nature was spirited. But these differences did not preclude an alliance between pride and interest. As Madison ruefully noted with respect to the Confederation, "Every general act of the Union must necessarily bear unequally hard on some particular member or members of it. . . . [T]he partiality of the members to their own interests and rights, a partiality which will be fostered by the Courtiers of popularity, will naturally exaggerate the inequality where it exists, and even suspect it where it has no existence."[69] Selfish partiality made each state a minority faction with respect to the general government. That is, because the Confederation depended on the voluntary compliance of each state rather than on the "republican principle" of majority rule—the ordinary "relief" for minority faction[70]—every state interest became a de facto faction.

The most obvious example was the states' failure to comply with the requisitions of Congress, the first item on Madison's list of the Confederation's vices.[71] But there was a host of other instances when national action had been foiled or exploited by a self-seeking state. Rhode Island, and then New York, had nixed successive impost proposals, and tiny Delaware had refused to participate in an embargo on exports to Great Britain, "not only defeat[ing] the general object of it," Madison indignantly reported, "but enrich[ing] herself at the expense of those who did their duty."[72] As Madison saw it, the political independence of the states invited such a disregard for the good of the wider community. It allowed them to endow their own interests with a special urgency and presumptive legitimacy, whatever the opinions of Americans outside their borders.

Nor did this exhaust the contribution of interest to the problem of establishing an adequate union. For Madison, interest was multifarious, finding ready agents not only in the state governments but also in the "different districts" and "different classes" within the states. These were the sources of the great variety that he wished to incorporate into the extended sphere of the new Constitution, but they posed severe difficulties, as noted, in "the task of forming it." Needless to say, Madison did not regard interest as such to be illegitimate. Faction was objectionable, after all, because it was, in the words of *Federalist* 10, adverse to the "permanent and aggregate *interests* of the community." The problem with interest was its readiness to reach beyond its legitimate claims. If this "impulse" should find "opportunity," interest would willingly give itself over to "schemes of oppression."[73] Though institutions could constrain and educate interests to some degree, when given the chance, they would seek unfair advantage to the detriment of others.

With respect to the Constitution, this raises the question of why such proto-factions would consent to a regime whose avowed intent was to curb their selfish tendencies. Moving beyond mere consent, as Madison did with his social compact, the matter becomes still more vexing. How could such a regime originate from the considered views of an American people composed of "various and interfering interests"? Would they not be disinclined to elect constituent representatives determined to restrain the influence of faction?[74] Madison's assertion in *Federalist* 51 that even the strongest factions might be "gradually induced . . . to wish for a government that will protect all parties" would seem to require some qualification.[75] As his more candid analysis in the "Vices of the Political System of the United States" reveals, factions are more resistant than individuals to insecurity or its prospect. As in the case of states, numbers give them confidence. In circumstances of relative peace, it would seem that a factious people could only make for a factious founding. How could "the spirit of party and faction," whose involvement in "the necessary and ordinary operations of Government" Madison took for granted, be excluded in this decisive instance?[76]

Guidance would certainly not come from the social-compact tradition's standard accounts of founding. Interest, in its ordinary sense, is not to be found there. The rival claims of creditors and debtors, of landholders, manufacturers, merchants, and bankers—the interests that concerned Madison—did not trouble Hobbes and Locke as they contemplated the origin of government, for reasons that Madison himself grasped. Such interests, after all, were not the spontaneous activity of individuals in nature; they presupposed government. As Madison put it, interests "grow up of necessity in *civilized* nations." They are "everywhere brought into different degrees of activity, according to the different circumstances of civil society," that is, under different sorts of regimes.[77] Hobbes was explicit about the impossibility of interest where

men live without other security, than what their own strength, and their own invention shall furnish them withall. In such condition, there is no place for Industry; because the fruit thereof is uncertain: and consequently no Culture of the Earth; no Navigation, nor use of the commodities that may be imported by Sea; no commodious Building; no Instruments of moving, and removing such things as require much force; no Knowledge of the face of the Earth; no account of Time; no Arts; no Letters; no Society; and which is worst of all, continuall feare, and danger of violent death; And the life of man, solitary, poore, nasty, brutish, and short.[78]

For Hobbes, interest could neither develop nor, once developed, be enjoyed in an atmosphere of "continuall feare." The inability to realize one's interest was a motive for submitting to a common power.

This is not to say that interest is simply conventional in earlier accounts of the social compact. Insofar as they take property to be natural, interest could be said to have a natural basis as well. Locke, unlike Hobbes, argued that property was conceivable in the absence of government and that human labor represented a natural title to it.[79] For Locke, however, the natural diversity of property was considerably less significant than its precariousness in the state of nature, where it was "very unsafe, very insecure."[80] Madison's contention in *Federalist* 10 that the "rights of property" derive from the various human "faculties" of acquiring it would seem to owe something to Locke, but as David F. Epstein notes, Madison emphasized the natural differences among men with respect to acquisition rather than their common stake in protecting the fruits of homogeneous labor.[81] Thus, while a "contrariety of Interests"[82] was among the reasons Locke insisted that government be established by a simple majority rather than by unanimous consent, he did not view these conflicts as an insurmountable obstacle to founding. The desire to preserve property as such would prevail over concerns about particular kinds of property.

Madison was unpersuaded by this Lockean view, and not just because he was more impressed than Locke with the diverse ways human beings obtain property. As suggested earlier, Madison's notion of the prepolitical condition downplayed the urgent quest for security that characterized its Hobbesian and Lockean counterparts. He detected a certain exaggeration in their accounts. For Madison, the principle of self-preservation was less irresistible, existing as it did in perennial competition with the political and economic attachments made possible by peace. It was not that he questioned the centrality of the former as a motive for the social compact, only its reliability in the actual circumstances of political life, where men clung to their political loyalties and their interests with great tenacity, however threatening the situation.

Self-preservation was seldom so insistent—or so clearly at issue—as to suppress entirely these important differences. Danger and complacent diversity could exist side by side. Accordingly, at Virginia's ratifying convention for the Constitution, Madison could rebuke Patrick Henry for ignoring the general insecurity that afflicted the nation: "He informs us that the people of this country are at perfect repose; that every man enjoys the fruits of his labor, peaceably and securely, and that every thing is in perfect tranquility and safety. I wish sincerely, sir, this were true. If this be their happy situation, why has every state acknowledged the contrary? Why were deputies from all the states sent to the general convention? Why have complaints of national and individual distresses been echoed and re-echoed throughout the continent?"[83] At the same time, Madison could recognize the difference between this situation and actual war, when the incentive to set aside divisions would be more keenly felt:

> If it has excited so much wonder, that the United States have in the middle of war and confusion, formed free systems of government, how much more astonishment and admiration will be excited, should they be able, peaceably, freely and satisfactorily, to establish one general government, when there is such a diversity of opinions, and interests, when not cemented or stimulated by any common danger? How vast must be the difficulty of concentrating in one government, the interests, and conciliating the opinions of so many different heterogeneous bodies?[84]

The absence of "perfect repose" might call for a reform of the national authority, but it did not rise to the level of "common danger." Madison gives the impression of an American people brought to attention by the failures of their governments but still very much involved in their narrow political and economic pursuits.

For Madison, it was not just the bare existence of various interests that hampered efforts at national unity. It was also their political assertiveness, a difficulty peculiar to the American situation but implicit in the very terms of the social compact. Interests may indeed "grow up of necessity in civilized nations" and their "regulation" may form "the principal task of modern Legislation,"[85] but this did not in itself require their direct participation in politics. Madison stressed that interests did not have to speak to be known. There was something objective about them. They were a matter of "information" and could be "discerned" by those who did not share them.[86] As a result, a "civilized" nation did not need to be republican. It only had to provide the security and order necessary for the exercise of "unequal faculties of acquiring property," a function that did not require consulting those who were to be protected. Such ends could be achieved by "creating a will in the community independent of the majority," as was done in hereditary governments.[87] That a people might choose to exclude themselves

from government is why Madison can speak of such an independent "will" as "created." From the standpoint of interest, an arrangement of this kind was objectionable not because a "prince"
was incapable of comprehending and discriminating among the
various needs of his people but because the risk was too great that
he would pursue his own interest, sacrificing "their happiness to
his ambition and avarice."[88] It was a problem of public-spiritedness
rather than of know-how.

What a monarchy could not provide, however, was the satisfaction that comes from the political expression of interest. This
was the source of Madison's difficulty. Though he understood that
the disfranchisement of interest was one possible solution for faction, he rejected this option as "unwise": it would be "folly to abolish liberty, which is essential to political life, because it nourishes
faction."[89] Madison did not explain this assertion, but it is implied
in the principles that elevate interest in the first place. As we have
seen, the political right of nature, whatever its instrumental relationship to self-preservation, makes certain claims of its own. It
points to the political capacities of all human beings as a cause for
pride, creating political expectations that transcend the moment
when government is established.

This heightened assertiveness of interest, so troubling for the
establishment of a form of government, might also be explained in
less purely political terms. Madison discovered its origin as much
in the needs of interest itself as in the proud self-regard that insists
on participation in public affairs. For Madison, a nonrepublican
government not only failed to satisfy men's political claims, it also
served as an unreliable guardian of their interests. Only by retaining a say in government could a member of civil society hope to
protect himself, whatever the extent of his property. Interest was
thereby democratized and could even present itself in the form of
propertylessness. This represented an important departure from
Locke, particularly with respect to the political significance of
property. For Locke, property in its most comprehensive sense included all the basic interests of human beings: life, liberty, and estate.[90] Life remained the most fundamental of the three, but the
other sorts of property helped preserve it, providing an early-
warning system against arbitrary government. As Locke saw it, a
subject could gauge the legislative power's intentions toward his

person by its treatment of his liberty and, especially, of his estate. For this reason, the consent of the majority of property owners to taxation—with property taken in its conventional meaning—was a sufficient formal safeguard for life and liberty as well.[91]

Madison, by contrast, anticipated the view of C. B. Macpherson, who argues that Locke's assignment of political rights to estate alone failed to protect those whose only real possession was their labor.[92] This emerges most clearly in Madison's advice to several friends in Kentucky on what form of government that district should adopt upon becoming a state. He seems to speak directly to Locke as he laments the models that were available to Americans at the time of the Revolution: "In all the Governments which were considered as beacons to republican patriots & lawgivers, the rights of persons were subjected to those of property. The poor were sacrificed to the rich."[93] Where Madison parts company with Marxist and progressive critics, of course, is in wishing to provide as well for the just claims of those who create wealth. As he continues, it is necessary to secure "the *two* cardinal objects of Government, the rights of persons, and the rights of property."[94] Accordingly, property might receive some special consideration, in the form, say, of a property qualification for one house of the legislature. But measures of this sort were in disfavor, as Madison told his correspondents. The tendency of Americans had been to reverse the mistaken assumption of Locke: "The two classes of rights were so little discriminated that provision for the rights of persons was supposed to include of itself those of property."[95]

Here was the rub for Madison, for any direct protection of property was likely to offend the "sense of equality" that prevailed in a "free Country."[96] Such expedients might be tried in Kentucky while most of its people still had an interest in property either "in possession or in prospect." But, as Madison observed, in more populous and developed regions, "the smaller part only can be interested in preserving the rights of property."[97] The influence of such a division was already being felt elsewhere in the nation. The "pestilent effects of paper money,"[98] for instance, were not confined to such turbulent outposts as Rhode Island. Even conservative Virginia was not immune.[99] Both the extended sphere and the Constitution's restrictions on the states were intended to protect property against popular excesses. In what way, however, could such constraints be seen to arise from the people's deliberate assessment of their own interests, especially in light of Madison's low expectations for interest as such? Moreover, even if these limits did not originate in the people, what could prompt their popular acceptance?

One could object that these questions are colored by a biased presentation of Madison's view of interest. Indeed, it is easy to find passages in his writings that suggest a more expansive notion, one that includes various public goods. In *The Federalist*, for example, Madison distinguishes between the "true interest" of the country and the "temporary or partial considerations" that distract from it. He contrasts "an enlarged and permanent interest" with "an impatient avidity for immediate and immoderate gain."[100] Drawing on these and other texts, Eugene F. Miller rightly concludes that Madison, in the guise of Publius, conceives of interest "as something broader than the mere pursuit of material gain and more comprehensive than the individual's self-interest."[101] But Miller tends to conflate the existence of this higher form of interest with its political efficacy. For Madison, interest was an objective, observable fact about a person, district, state, or nation. He did not doubt that the United States had "permanent and aggregate interests"; he simply feared that they would not prevail over more proximate interests. This tension is apparent in an illuminating passage from a 1786 letter to James Monroe, provoked by the willingness of the eastern states to barter the American right to navigation on the Mississippi for continued access to Spanish markets:

> There is no maxim in my opinion which is more liable to be misapplied, and which therefore more needs elucidation than the current one that the interest of the majority is the political standard of right and wrong. Taking the word "interest" as synonomous with "Ultimate happiness," in which sense it is qualified with every necessary moral ingredient, the proposition is no doubt true. But taking it in the popular sense, as referring to immediate augmentation of property and wealth, nothing can be more false. In the latter sense it would be the interest of the majority in every community to despoil & enslave the minority of individuals; and in a federal community to make a similar sacrifice of a minority of the component States.[102]

The essential counterpoint is between a properly moralized notion of interest—one that respects rights and recognizes the need for impartiality—and interest in its "popular sense." The people, according to Madison, tend to advance their own material well-being despite their awareness of its incompatibility with the rights of others.

Madison did not dismiss entirely the possibility of educating interest, of broadening its perspective. As we saw in analyzing the "Memorial and Remonstrance," rights could be protected in a principled way by reminding the people of their "ownership" of constitutional protections and stirring their indignation against trespassers. But a constraint of this kind applied primarily to a government that acted without the support of a social majority, not to a social majority itself. Such a majority might be attached to the forms of a particular government, but its interest in them was conventional, requiring a lively belief among the people that constitutional restrictions were a product of their own making. The promptings of property and material well-being were more natural and spontaneous, thus more forceful.

The Federalist also points to a more elevated notion of interest, in which self-regarding impulses could be used to achieve public aims. Under the Constitution, Madison argued, representatives would find fidelity to their constituents advantageous. Senators, by their prominence and duration in office, would come to associate their own standing with that of the nation. And federal officials generally, whose interests would "be connected with the constitutional rights of the place," would help maintain a separation of powers.[103] But again, Madison's expectations for such restraints were modest. He did not suggest that they would be effective against a determined majority. He conceded, in the end, that few would directly seek the "permanent and aggregate interests" of the community.

These enduring interests could still be realized, though, because they were embedded in the very matter of ordinary interest. Combined with appropriate constitutional structures, the extended sphere made it possible to frustrate the factious designs of ordinary interest but also allowed its legitimate claims to be heard. Under such arrangements, as we noted at the outset, "a coalition of a majority of the whole society could seldom take place on any other principles than those of justice and the general good."[104]

Madison's insight is characteristic of the modern approach to interest, in which one is "carried from short-term calculation to true interest by the external action of a system or market that is not under [one's] control."[105] In this way, interest is rendered safe, even salutary, by a disinterested system. Still, the problem with which we began remains: whence the disinterested system?

The political right of nature holds the key to this puzzle, but as we have seen, it is confounded in Madison's account no less by the demands of pride and interest than by the pressing insecurity out of which the right itself emerges. In either case, the conditions for effective deliberation are undermined. In times of relative peace, the people are too attached to their parochial political communities and their property to engage in concerted action. Under conditions of war or potential violence, they are too concerned with immediate self-preservation to consider the requirements of long-term safety. The social compact is overwhelmed by diversity, on the one hand, and by urgency, on the other. The range of possible motives appears to be incommensurate to the task.

Motivation aside, there is also the substantive aspect of deliberation, which was vital to Madison's project. Assuming the willingness and opportunity to consider the good of the nation as a whole, what particular capacity or knowledge was required to bring it about? Who was capable of producing a disinterested system? To maintain its egalitarian premises, the social compact had to assume a certain popular prudence in these matters. According to the Declaration of Independence, government is to be established by the people themselves, "laying its Foundation on such Principles, and organizing its Powers in such Form, as to them shall seem most likely to effect their Safety and Happiness." But if the people were inadequate to this task, who was to perform it? Moreover, what would such an incapacity imply about popular government and about the social compact itself?

Chapter Three

The Paradox of Liberal Prudence

Under Madison's social compact, the political right of nature is a prudential right, a claim to be able to choose the means necessary for realizing the highest political ends. To a certain extent, this is consistent with prudence as it originally comes to sight in political thought. Aristotle describes prudence as the virtue of the practical intellect, the prudent man being one who "can aim well at the things which are attainable by action and are best for man."[1] But a right to exercise a virtue is not the same as the virtue itself—a prudential right is not the same as prudence. Madison charged prior accounts of the social compact with having ignored this difference. In their determination to see that authority was legitimate, he suggested, they had failed to consider that it might not be competent. While he did not deny that the people had the right to establish forms of government, he doubted that they possessed the qualities of intellect and character necessary for the task.

This chapter places Madison's position on prudence against a wider historical and theoretical backdrop. As we shall see, his thoughts about the meaning and purpose of constitutional conventions changed in the period leading up to and immediately following the Federal Convention of 1787. Madison came to view constitutional conventions as a counterpoint to the people and to popular political institutions, as an opportunity to transcend sovereign pride and narrow interest. Such gatherings were a rebuke to the more comprehensive claims of the popular sovereign, demonstrating both its limitations and the conditions of its rule. This was most evident in his description of the relationship between the people and the Federal Convention itself. Though the Convention sprang from the people's discontent and had to meet with their approval in the end, its ability to design an adequate constitution was based largely on its independence from popular views. For Madison, the Convention was not simply an administrative substitute for the unwieldy deliberation of the people as a whole; it represented a qualitatively distinct form of political intelligence.

Various understandings of prudence, both ancient and modern, throw light on Madison's apparent denigration of the people. I begin with Aristotle, whose account bears a certain resemblance to that of Madison, and then present Hobbes's critique of Aristotelian prudence, especially as it relates to those aspects of the social compact that remained fundamental for Madison. For Hobbes and for Locke, prudence was conspicuously absent from founding; embarrassed by its inegalitarian premises, they tried to show how adequate political forms might simply arise from an understanding of the natural condition that was available, in principle, to all men. Finally, I briefly consider Rousseau and Hume, two modern writers who shared Madison's objections to the naive account of government's origin in these earliest descriptions of the social compact. Both recognized the social compact's practical dependence on a founder or legislator and the difficulty of reconciling this need with many of the doctrine's basic assumptions.

Neither Statesmen nor Philosophers

Having completed his service as a delegate to the Continental Congress, Madison returned in December 1783 to Virginia, where he was quickly reelected to a seat in the General Assembly. The next several years would find him increasingly occupied with reform efforts in his own state. Jefferson's proposed "revisal" of the Virginia law code—a set of 126 bills intended to liberalize virtually every aspect of public life in the state—had languished since the late 1770s for want of an able advocate in the legislature. By now a figure of some political prominence himself, Madison took on this vast application of Enlightenment principles. Nor did his efforts stop with ordinary laws. His energies at the time were also devoted, as we saw in chapter 1, to putting the Virginia constitution on a sounder footing.

Still, the worsening national situation under the Articles of Confederation was never far from Madison's mind. Among his first achievements upon returning to Virginia was persuading the General Assembly to comply with federal requisitions and to instruct its delegates in Congress to support coercive action against noncomplying states. But Madison knew that these were little more than temporizing measures. His primary goal remained the vesting of further taxing and commercial powers in the Confederation. To that end, he would go on to promote two state-sponsored gatherings intended to solve the chronic trade problems of the union, first at Mount Vernon in 1785 and then at Annapolis in 1786. These two related meetings led to a third, the Federal Convention, making Mount Vernon a "sort of preliminary to the preliminary," as Clinton Rossiter puts it.[2]

The three gatherings reflect a growing conviction on Madison's part that the required reforms could not occur within the context of ordinary politics. Having failed, at both the national and the state level, to bring about change by the prescribed means, Madison came to see a convention as a necessary alternative, a chance to circumvent popular forms, however temporarily, in order to better secure popular rule. Though a convention began in ordinary politics—it had to be called, or convened—the irregularity of its authority and its ultimate lack of accountability gave it extraordinary latitude. This was a far cry from the standard described in Madison's speech on revising the Virginia constitution. Indeed, with each step toward the Federal Convention, the people's place in constitution making became more problematic for him: his previous insistence on their selection of constituent representatives—that is, on the people's substantive contribution to establishing particular constitutional forms—gave way to mere after-the-fact consent. The possibility of popular reason receded and was replaced by a dependence on popular feeling.

Like the more general critique of the social compact sketched in the preceding chapters, Madison's reservations about popular constitution-making began with a somewhat idiosyncratic view of the state of nature. It was not a condition of anarchy or constant anxiety, as the standard accounts would have it. Rather, it was the absence of necessary political forms at some level of society, a serious constitutional shortcoming of some sort. The difficulty was that such a threat was often several removes from actual arbitrariness or disorder. It could be *discerned* by a few long before it was *felt* by all. However menacing a feckless Confederation might be to Madison, it did not trouble the average American until a Daniel Shays appeared on the scene or trade wars broke out between the states. Even then, as Madison saw it, a consensus for reform was unlikely. Simple aversion to the status quo lacked remedies; the people knew what they disliked but not how to fix it. It was in this respect that those few who were capable of anticipating constitutional crises most differed from their fellow citizens. Because their judgment was based not on feeling but on principle, not on the palpable vices of bad government but on the known standards of good government, they could propose concrete alternatives rather than merely asserting the need for change. Madison's mature view of constitutional reform ultimately relied on both sorts of reaction, on the understanding of the few and the dissatisfaction of the many.

Popular dissatisfaction was the more fickle of the two elements, filtered as it necessarily was through allegiance to the states. Late in 1784, Richard Henry Lee, then serving in the Virginia delegation in Philadelphia, wrote to Madison about the possibility of bringing together the states to revise the Confederation.[3] In his reply, his earliest statement on a federal convention, Madison did not pretend to have any affection for the Confederation, but he was reluctant nonetheless to endorse reform. He claimed ignorance of the delicate political calculus on which such an effort would hinge. On the one hand, there was the "temper" of the people of the different states. His fellow Virginians were well enough disposed to bolstering national authority, but he could not speak for the other states. On the other hand, there were the state officeholders, the medium through which popular sentiments would have to be expressed. Among the members of Virginia's General Assembly, he expected the usual "prejudices & jealousies" against innovation, particularly any innovation as would "derogate from their own power & importance." In summarizing the matter to Lee, Madison suggested that both the people's readiness to consider reform and the specific method to be used in proposing it, especially in relation to the state governments, required careful scrutiny. "The question," he wrote, was "in what mode & at what moment the experiment for supplying the defects ought to be made."[4]

For Madison, popular sentiment and official pride and self-regard became the decisive factors in constitutional reform. Their interaction determined the appropriateness of a given "mode" and "moment." Popular opinion was foremost. For constitutional change to occur, the people had to be deeply unhappy with their current situation, some pressing circumstance having shaken their attachment to the regime under which they lived. The would-be reformer's appeal to principle alone was not enough. Officeholders presented a different and more complex problem. They combined a defensive concern for their own dignity with the people's prejudice in favor of popularly established forms. Though they were the arbiters of constitutional change, they were at the same time creatures of their own particular state regimes. Like the people at large, they lacked distance or detachment from the constitutional status quo. But while hardship might cause the people to reconsider and relax their proud attachments, officeholders were inevitably less tractable. Authority diminished their sense of vulnerability, and interest and self-regard bound them more firmly to present institutions. Depicting reform as an insult to the community as a whole, they could excite the anger and jealousy of the people and turn them against the possibility of change. For Madison, escaping the influence of officeholders became imperative.

As his letter to Lee shows, Madison considered talk of a national convention premature in 1784. The second impost plan was still pending, and the states themselves were beginning to recognize the self-destructive effects of their unregulated and often predatory commerce with one another. He continued to believe that these problems might yet provide a basis for strengthening the Confederation. In the summer of 1784, he persuaded the Virginia legislature to appoint commissioners, himself included, to resolve lingering disputes with Maryland over the use and navigation of the Potomac. Madison thought that such benign cooperation between two states might serve as a reminder of the benefits of union. The forum, one entirely of the states' own making, was also significant. Sensitive questions of sovereignty could be dealt with narrowly, in the tempering light of interest and away from threatening national institutions. The resulting conference, held at Mount Vernon in March 1785, took place without Madison—he was only notified of it after the fact—but managed to resolve most of the major issues between Virginia and Maryland and even recommended a broader scheme of regional cooperation.

On its face, such an agreement, with its seeming assertion of sectional independence, only served to erode further the authority of the Confederation, the terms of which it certainly violated in spirit, if not in fact.[5] But Madison did not view the Mount Vernon conference in this way. He considered it, as he wrote later, an "apt and forceable . . . illustration of the necessity of uniformity throughout all the States,"[6] complementing his own long-standing efforts to give Congress wider commercial powers. When the compact between the two states came up for ratification in the next session of the Virginia legislature, he attempted to turn it to his own purposes, suggesting that it be submitted to Congress "for their sanction, as being within the word *Treaty* used in the Confederation." When this measure failed, he asked that Congress might at least be formally notified of the agreement. This too fell by a large majority.[7] During the same session, Madison suffered a still more serious setback, seeing his proposal for an explicit grant to Congress of modest commercial powers slowly emasculated, though he sought merely "such direct power only as would not alarm." It was in the context of this "extremity" that he finally lent his support to a resolution by John Tyler for "a general meeting of [commissioners] from the States to consider and recommend a foederal plan for regulating Commerce."[8] This meeting, held some eight months later, was the Annapolis Convention.

Sympathetic historians and biographers have long wished to credit Madison with the idea of the Annapolis Convention, thereby giving the appearance of design in the successive conventions, from Mount Vernon in 1785 to Philadelphia in 1787. They have gone so far as to suggest that Tyler was little more than a convenient front for the proposal.[9] More convincing are the critics of this view, who point out that Madison never claimed authorship of the convention and, moreover, that he and Tyler were antagonists in the debate over commercial powers. They argue that Virginia's support for the Annapolis Convention, which was called without reference to Congress, represented a victory for those opposed to increasing national power.[10]

While this latter account better conforms to the facts, it fails to explain Madison's embrace of so seemingly antinational a proposal. The case against his having been the mastermind of the Annapolis Convention would seem to apply with no less force to his eventually supporting it. The solution lies in the fact that both Tyler and Madison saw the proposal for a convention as an opportunity to escape the influence of a distrusted institution. For Tyler, it was the Continental Congress, whose prior approval of amendments was required under the Articles of Confederation; for Madison, it was the state legislatures themselves, whose participation in the convention would be restricted to choosing delegates. As the Mount Vernon meeting had shown, the states were willing to cede some of their authority in this limited way. The Tyler proposal, Madison told Washington, seemed "naturally to grow out of" the Mount Vernon meeting and would have "fewer enemies" than his own measures.[11] What had been intended as an affirmation of state sovereignty became for Madison a relatively untrammeled opportunity to pursue national goals.

In justifying the Annapolis Convention, Madison relied explicitly on the analysis that I have sketched above, emphasizing the interplay of popular sentiment and official reaction. Each presented a discrete obstacle to reform. "If all on whom the correction of these vices depends were well informed and well disposed," he wrote to Monroe, "the mode would be of little moment. But as we have both ignorance and iniquity to control, we must defeat the designs of the latter by humouring the prejudices of the former." As before, Madison saw the people's disposition toward constitutional change as fundamental: it determined all else. If their "ignorance" could be overcome, the "iniquity" of their elected representatives would be of less consequence. Enlightenment would come from the "defects" of the Confederation, which would "force themselves on the public attention" and prepare "the public mind" for change.[12] Hardship could educate the people, freeing them from their attachment to existing forms. Madison thus trusted to "experience and even distress . . . for an adequate remedy" and considered the "present crisis" an auspicious time for the Annapolis Convention, finding in it a concurrence of circumstances likely to produce the needed "unanimity."[13]

Madison confessed that, by the time of the Annapolis Convention, public sentiment had become the only meaningful limit on reform. As he saw it, the public's approval—or presumed approval—had given reformers a free hand, allowing them to set aside the constraints placed on their activities by formal, representative institutions, whether the state governments or the Confederation. With the help of "further experience" of reform's "necessity" in the months leading up to the meeting,[14] the Annapolis Convention had brought about two key developments. In the first place, "public opinion" had advanced "in the desired direction." The "general attention" had been turned "to the Critical State of things," preparing "the public mind" for "a salutary Reform of the pol[itical] System."[15] In the second place, the convention had called forth "the sentiments and the exertions of the most enlightened & influencial patriots," most notably the twelve men (including Madison and Alexander Hamilton) who had gathered at Annapolis.

As Madison made clear in explaining the activities of the convention, the first development was the permissive condition for the fullest expression of the second: "Such had been the advance of public opinion . . . that the Convention . . . *did not scruple to decline the limited task assigned to it,* and to recommend to the States a Convention with powers adequate to the occasion."[16] In this way the Annapolis Convention set a series of important precedents, giving momentum to the "bandwagon effect," as Bruce Ackerman calls it,[17] that culminated in Philadelphia: it violated the forms under which it met, it did so in the name of a public opinion that had not been articulated in any politically authoritative way, and it assigned to itself on this basis a wide discretion in making recommendations for constitutional reform. The act of constitution making—if not the final establishment of a constitution—had been removed from the ambit of popular politics. It was in the hands of the "most enlightened and influencial patriots."

Turning now to the period surrounding the Federal Convention, our primary concern will be this peculiar relationship between the people and their constitution makers. As Madison's account of the Annapolis gathering suggests, he had already begun to doubt the possibility of popular constitution-making. The "public mind" was passive, not active; it acceded but did not propose. In coming to terms with the Federal Convention and its broad assumption of authority, Madison elaborated on this divide, going so far as to see it as a reflection of distinct orders of human beings.[18]

For Madison, public crisis became the necessary backdrop for constitutional reform. It imposed a degree of consensus across the usual array of proud and interested attachments. It brought security to the fore, giving to the otherwise fractious realm of public opinion a single dominant concern. Hence, even while lamenting the deteriorating national situation in 1786–87, Madison could take satisfaction in its salutary effects. In Virginia, "the experience of one year" since the calling of the Annapolis Convention had brought about a "revolution of sentiment." The "evidence of dangerous defects in the Confederation" had "proselyted the most obstinate adversaries of reform."[19] If the Federal Convention were to succeed, the crisis in national affairs would have to produce the same transformation throughout the union. Considering "the probable diversity of opinions and prejudices, and of supposed or real interests among the States," Madison wrote a month before delegates began arriving in Philadelphia, the "existing embarrassments and *mortal* diseases of the Confederacy form the only ground of hope."[20]

The catalogue of public ills was indeed serious in this "critical period" of American history, as some scholars have dubbed it. With payments to the federal treasury coming to a halt and congressional authority widely ignored, there was talk of dissolving the union in favor of several smaller confederacies or perhaps even a monarchy.[21] Shays's Rebellion in western Massachusetts was an event "distressing beyond measure," according to Madison, and an extreme instance of the disorder increasingly felt within the states. It furnished "new proofs of the necessity of . . . vigour in the Gen[era]l Gov[ernmen]t."[22] This spectacle of decline had a singular effect on the American people. As Madison wrote of the period some years later, "The aspect & retrospect of the pol[itical] condition of the U.S. could not but fill the pub[lic] mind with . . . gloom." Nor was this necessarily a cause for regret. With an eye to the Federal Convention, the embarrassments, diseases, and ills of the Confederation could be placed in a different light. They were, as he put it, "ripening incidents."[23]

Madison saw the danger of the national situation as an opportunity for the members of the Federal Convention. The people, vulnerable and anxious, would allow the men gathered in Philadelphia a latitude unknown to ordinary representatives. Early in the proceedings of the Convention, Madison thus urged his colleagues to ignore the fleeting, ill-informed sentiments of the people and to focus instead on their permanent needs. He observed "that if the opinions of the people were to be our guide, it w[oul]d be difficult to say what course we ought to take. No member of the Convention could say what the opinions of his Constituents were at this time; much less could he say what they would think if possessed of the information & lights possessed by the members here; & still less what would be their way of thinking 6 or 12 months hence. We ought to consider what was right & necessary in itself for the attainment of a proper Government."[24] If the Convention succeeded in this task, its indifference to instruction from the people would be forgotten. The people's relief would overcome their wounded pride. "My own idea," he told Jefferson at the Convention's conclusion, "is that the public mind will now or in a very little time receive any thing that promises stability to the public Councils & security to private rights, and that no regard ought to be had to local prejudices or temporary considerations."[25] In short, though the people might insist on fidelity to their own views in ordinary circumstances, in a moment of constitutional crisis they would embrace the first credible response to their troubles.

Madison believed he saw this forecast confirmed in the dispute over ratification in Virginia. There "the mass of the people," though confronted with a question that "surpasse[d] the judgment of the greater part of them," resisted the advice of their "popular leaders," undermining the "popular ground . . . taken by all the adversaries of the new Constitution." Trying circumstances had distanced "the body of sober & steady people, even of the lower order," from their officeholders. Tired of the "vicicitudes, injustice and follies which have so much characterised public measures," they were "impatient for . . . stability & repose" and less susceptible to claims of insulted sovereignty.[26] Self-preservation, with its attendant needs and dispositions, had succeeded in dampening the people's proud attachment to local political forms, and this had occurred, according to Madison, in the absence of any real popular capacity for judgment.

What, then, set the Federal Convention apart from its constituents? Clearly, its reaction to national misfortune could not be so reflexive. A mere willingness to accept change, born of fear and uncertainty, could not produce an adequate constitution. Change had to take a particular form, and this choice was beyond the ken of the people. For Madison, what most distinguished the members of the Convention was not their being "unanimously agreed concerning the end" of a proper constitution, but their capacity to deliberate among "an infinite diversity" of means. This was a task "as difficult as it was desireable."[27] The Convention could evaluate alternative solutions to the national predicament. It possessed the judgment—or prudence—that the people lacked. Consequently, the "public mind," when filled with "gloom" over the "political condition of the United States," had to look beyond itself and take comfort in the "hope that so select a Body would devise an adequate remedy for the existing and prospective evils so impressively demanding it."[28]

These limitations placed the dependence of the people in stark relief. When ordinary politics gave way to questions of social and political survival, the people had no choice but to entrust their fate to those whom they knew to be more capable. With the Constitution's ratification in doubt, Madison shared this impolitic view with fellow Virginian Edmund Randolph. Randolph had refused to sign the new national charter in Philadelphia and was sympathetic to calls for a second convention, one more fully informed by popular views. "Whatever respect may be due to the rights of private judgment, and no man feels more of it than I do," wrote Madison, "there can be no doubt that there are subjects to which the capacities of the bulk of mankind are unequal, and on which they must and will be governed by those with whom they happen to have acquaintance and confidence. The proposed Constitution is of this description."[29]

Here, in a moment of private candor, Madison directly addresses the most problematic assumption of prior accounts of the social compact: the notion that the people's right to devise constitutional forms somehow ensures their capacity to do so. It was a necessary pretense, Madison recognized, but at the same time he knew that the people as a whole could not possess prudence in its most comprehensive sense. The "bulk of mankind" were not, in fact, equipped to take advantage of the political right of nature. They required the instruction and assistance of others, by whom they were inevitably "governed" in these matters. Martin Diamond has pointed out that this dependence, far from impugning the possibility of popular self-government, was the very condition for it. As he summarizes Madison's view, it was only through the elevated act of founding that "the complexity of the governmental art" could be reduced "to dimensions more commensurate with the capacity of the many."[30]

This low estimate of popular prudence is evident even in Madison's insistence that the new constitution be ratified by the people. Rather than make some kind of concession to popular judgment, he invariably casts his argument strictly in terms of authority: ratification by the people was the only way to ensure that the Constitution would be paramount to the states.[31] Madison expresses no special confidence in the ability of the people to recognize the merits of the instrument.

On what, then, would their ratification or rejection be based? As we saw in the case of Virginia, one possible motive was simple insecurity, but Madison recognized its insufficiency. Although the people's initial impulse might be grateful acceptance of the Constitution, their political pride would lead them to reconsider. They would want to demonstrate their right to choose. A second, more political motive was popular deference to "leading opinions." In his own state, Madison argued, opposition to the Constitution could be attributed to the objections of a handful of men. If George Mason, Edmund Randolph, Patrick Henry, and a few others had "seen the Constitution in the same light with those who subscribed to it," he had no doubt that Virginia would have been "as zealous & unanimous [in its favor] as she is now divided on the subject." The "great body" of those on both sides of the dispute would "follow the judgment" of such men, who, like the members of the Convention, possessed "public respect & confidence."[32] This class, which could be found in every state, would decide the fate of the Constitution. Madison went so far as to tell the members of the Convention that this group was, in fact, their primary constituency: "We ought to consider what was right & necessary in itself for the attainment of a proper Governm[en]t. A plan adjusted to this idea will recommend itself. . . . [A]ll the most enlightened and respectable citizens will be its advocates. Should we fall short of the necessary and proper point, this influential class of citizens will be turned against the plan, and little support in opposition to them can be gained to it from the unreflecting multitude."[33] Because such men would mold the people's opinions, the Constitution could be safely entrusted to popular ratification. Judgment would be supplied by the few, but the rights of all would be honored.

Madison was unhelpfully laconic in describing this wider class, from which the membership of the Convention was also drawn. They were, to be sure, gentlemen of a sort, but Madison does not provide a comprehensive account of their character, education, or political and social background. He does little more than credit them with a certain constellation of virtues. They were "influencial patriots," "enlightened and respectable" men worthy of "public respect & confidence." In addition and with some variation, they were "men of intelligence, patriotism, property, and independent circumstances"; "the enlightened and impartial part of America"; "the men of abilities, of property, and of influence"; those who possessed "a rational, intelligent, and unbiassed mind."[34] One might usefully consider this class the potential readership of *The Federalist*. Unlike the people, they were capable of arriving at an independent view of the Constitution that was based on something more than the exigencies of the moment.

As for the Convention itself, Madison presents its members as a refinement of these various qualities. They were, in several instances, "the most respectable characters in the U.S." and "the best contribution of talents the States could make for the occasion."[35] Selected from "the most experienced & highest standing Citizens," they were "pure in their motives" and "anxiously devoted to the object committed to them."[36] These passing remarks, incomplete and exaggerated though they are, help to fill out the profile of Madison's constitution-making gentlemen. He furnishes not only clues to the precise character of their prudence (or judgment) but also some idea of its place in the broader psychology of the social compact—a matter of special importance in understanding the division between the few and the many in Madison's thought.

In the first place, it is obvious that Madison considered prudence an intellectual virtue, even if a decidedly practical one. Its basis is unclear, however, at least from the bare indications of the passages above. It would seem to be a combination of natural mental ability (intelligence, rationality), instruction in relevant theoretical matters (enlightenment), and familiarity with the particulars in question (experience). But Madison does not assign any special order or priority to these different elements, nor do they appear together consistently in his praise of the intellectual excellence of his gentlemanly class.

Rare though the intellectual dimension of prudence might be, Madison suggests that its absence only partly explained the people's deficiency. More important perhaps was the moral disposition necessary for the proper use of the virtue. For Madison, prudence was inseparable from a certain type of character. Like Aristotle in his critique of mere "shrewdness," Madison seems to have held that "a man cannot be prudent if he is not good."[37] Judging by the brief remarks cited earlier, prudence as Madison understood it depended on impartiality, lack of bias, and devotion to public objects—it depended, that is, on the qualities usually associated with the virtue of justice. In the American case, justice insisted on the subordination of particular attachments, based on pride and interest, to the good of the whole. It asked the partisans of sovereign states, both large and small, to relax their more extravagant claims, and it demanded that the country's varied interests—farmers and manufacturers, fishermen and frontiersmen, debtors and creditors, importers and exporters—acknowledge one another's needs. Madison found such a disposition in the members of his gentlemanly class, men who were distinctive as much for their willingness to give priority to the entire nation as for their capacity to do so.

The political manifestation of this virtue was patriotism, which is indeed included in Madison's encomia of the leading advocates of constitutional reform. For Madison, this sentiment was explicitly national, a counterpoint to the jealous parochialism of the states. The Federal Convention was to be a unique opportunity for its expression, a moment in which lesser political bonds might be transcended. He wanted the delegates to be capable of a "superiority to partial views and interests," willing to make "no material sacrifices" to "local or temporary prejudices."[38] They would be the individuals of "extended views" and "national pride" against whom he contrasted "the multitude."[39] George Washington personified these qualities, and Madison saw his attendance at the Convention as vital, "an invitation to the most select characters from every part of the Confederacy."[40]

Such patriotism should not be equated with mere nationalism, however, as if the only concern of the delegates was the locus of political power. The "nationalist" rubric favored by historians of the period requires amplification. For Madison, the impartiality of the Convention extended beyond its relative detachment from the demands of the states. Perhaps more importantly, its members also resisted (for the most part) the partisan claims of their own class. They did not consider the irregular intervention of the few a prelude to the permanent authority of the few. Their patriotism was inseparable from the political principles of the independent republic whose defense had engaged so many of them. They were "real friends of the Revolution," determined to "perpetuate the Union" *and* to "redeem the honor of the Republican name."[41] Though they knew the people's limits, they were committed to the project of popular rule.

Madison never spelled out the reasons for this commitment, but one can safely adduce a range of possible motives. At the lowest rung was simple pride in a cause of their own making, an unwillingness to see their political edifice overturned and their boasts made empty. For most members of the Convention, their names—and their fame—were inextricably linked to the American experiment.[42] Expedience in the face of republican expectations was also a possibility: the country's republican "genius" had to be accommodated. This points to eminently practical founders who were more politic than principled.

Whatever the contribution of these inducements, however, more aristocratic ones also came into play. As Madison's own anguished reflections indicate, part of the attraction of the republican project was its very difficulty, its lack of precedent. A grand experiment in self-government was a worthy enterprise for an exceedingly able man, even if it ultimately deprived him of the preeminence that was perhaps his due. It allowed him to serve less the people, whose political impulses were often destructive, than the principles that justified their rule. In writing of Abraham Lincoln,

Harry V. Jaffa has eloquently summarized this lofty standard: "The true ruler of men, with the highest of all ambitions, sees in the idea of equality the principle which requires, both logically and politically, the highest degree of moral self-government. His own sense of superiority can be vindicated only by the knowledge that he has been responsible . . . for restraints which keep his flock in the paths of righteous endeavor."[43] In a more practical vein, there was the recognition too that gentlemen-founders themselves could not be counted on to stick to "the paths of righteous endeavor." In this regard, one might imagine Madison and his peers congratulating themselves for their self-restraint; few of them pretended that their own class, however indispensable in certain respects, could in the long run be a reliable guardian of the people's rights and interests.

These various motives made the Convention a safe forum for republicanism, but more fundamentally, they made the Convention possible. Without genuine devotion to popular rule, the gentlemanly class would have received neither the "confidence" and "respect" of the public nor the wide discretion that came with the public's trust. The Convention's patriotic bona fides raised it above suspicion and gave it a uniquely broad, if temporary, authority. The presence of George Washington—who arrived in Philadelphia, Madison reported, "amidst the acclamations of the people, as well as more sober marks of the affection and veneration which continue to be felt for his character"[44]—and lesser figures with impeccable republican credentials allowed the Convention to rebut the charge of being an aristocratic conspiracy while conferring on it the opportunity to behave like one.[45]

In addition to being somewhat removed from the political recalcitrance of the states and their loyalists, the gentlemanly class also resisted the other great nemesis of reform—narrow interest. As Madison would have it, its members were not economic partisans. They did not understand interest in what he called "the popular sense"—as being concerned with the "immediate augmentation of property and wealth." Presumably, they were the all-too-frequently overruled minority that wished only to act upon the "just and extended maxims of policy" and thereby "effectuate the durable prosperity of the Union."[46] Without denying the influence of enlightenment as such, it seems that their distance from the short-sighted economic impulses of the people derived in large part from their own material security. Madison called them men of "property" and "independent circumstances," and their "respectability" appears to have been economic as well as political.

Though Charles Beard credited Madison as the source for his own quasi-Marxist interpretation of the founding, Madison himself believed that wealth could serve as a badge of political integrity; it freed men from the urgent demands of want and need and endowed them with a certain detachment. They surely could not be bought, in the crude electioneering sense, but neither could they be swayed by every prospective fluctuation in their fortune. Gordon S. Wood argues persuasively that such "disinterestedness," taken in its most literal meaning, was a standard of political rectitude for Madison and the other Federalist constitution-makers. It set them apart from ordinary people, whose primary concerns were in the entrepreneurial bustle of the widening American marketplace. Wood is mistaken, however, in presenting this as a reactionary vestige of classical republicanism, a protest against modern politics and economics.[47] Rather, it was the *precondition* for these modern developments and for the Constitution that made them possible. Madison did insist that a successful politics of interest depended ultimately on disinterestedness, but he did not present the latter as a genuine alternative. He was anything but a nostalgic American Cato. Madison's constitutional activism was an effort to translate the impartiality of this gentlemanly class into a frame of government, to turn the virtues of men into the qualities of a system. The "great desideratum," as he put it, was a "disinterested & dispassionate umpire."[48]

But what of the class itself? What was to be its role in a republican regime? The difficulty is suggested by Madison in a letter to Jefferson, rehearsing the argument of *Federalist* 10, in which he writes of the "various and unavoidable" distinctions to be found in civilized societies. Those based on property were "natural" because they arose from "unequal faculties of acquiring it." Others were "artificial," based as they were on "accidental differences" concerning such matters as politics and religion. These various distinctions had a strong influence on popular politics, but not on every citizen: "However erroneous or ridiculous these grounds of dissention and faction, may appear to the enlightened Statesman, or the benevolent philosopher, the bulk of mankind who are neither Statesmen nor Philosophers, will continue to view them in a different light."[49]

Accustomed though we are to refer to founders like Madison and Jefferson as philosopher-statesmen, this appears to be Madison's sole allusion to the notion. Leaving aside its precise meaning, what is unmistakable is the divide that it suggests between such types and their fellow citizens. Philosopher-statesmen possessed a kind of rare detachment, allowing them to look with dispassion upon the things that others took with utmost seriousness. If the context is any indication, such individuals were needed to overcome the preeminent vice of republicanism—faction. They were at once distant from its causes and aware of its potential remedies. Men of this sort reflected a "natural" distinction for Madison— they clearly possessed "unequal faculties"—but like citizens who were prominent for their property, they posed a problem for a regime of equal political rights.

I have suggested that Madison's idea of prudence demonstrates a certain affinity with Aristotle. At the very least, it is a departure from the broad principles of Hobbes and Locke, from whom Madison otherwise took theoretical guidance. Neither of these thinkers wrote at any length on the problem of founding or, for that matter, seemed to consider it a problem. They let the state of nature do the work for them, implying that satisfactory forms of government could emerge almost spontaneously from the need for them. This notion Madison rejected. Moreover, Madison recognized the provenance, at least historically, of the rival view of prudence. At the Virginia ratifying convention, he spoke of the origins of various confederacies. The ones of ancient times "were brought about by the wisdom of some eminent sage." Those of modern times: "By danger."[50] The new American government sprang from a combination of these principles. But was such a hybrid possible? After all, the claims of Madison's gentlemen were an affront to those of the people. They were, in fact, a potential threat to the rights and interests of the people. Before moving on to the Federal Convention itself, then, we must explore more deeply what is at stake in the opposition between the ancient and modern understandings of this highest of political faculties.

Prudence High and Low

Like so many other words from the moral vocabulary of the past, prudence has lost much of its meaning in our day. It tends to be associated with ambivalence, timid reserve, or lack of principle. But prudence was once considered a virtue, and a rather unique one at that. It was thought to bridge the gap between character and intellect, providing the rational element in moral action. This much was common ground among the great ancient and medieval thinkers. With the advent of modern political thought, prudence underwent a thorough transformation, attributable in large part to the increasing prominence of equality as a political principle. The character and scope of prudence changed: its place in a broader human psychology, its appropriate objects, the degree to which it might be perfected, and, uniting all these, its significance for politics, especially for the outstanding practical problem of politics—founding. The exemplars of this disagreement are Aristotle and Hobbes, who articulate its basic issues with unrivaled force and clarity.

We find Aristotle's only systematic discussion of prudence—what he calls *phronēsis*—in the sixth book of the *Nicomachean Ethics*. As the distinctive excellence of the practical part of the intellect, prudence is concerned with deliberation, with choosing the right course of action in a given situation. Its home is the varied, transitory world of human *praxis*, or action, setting it apart from theoretical and technical reason, which possess far more certainty and precision. Prudence deals with particulars. For this reason, it can be developed fully only in the course of time, as one acquires experience. Thus a young person might be a brilliant geometer or a skilled carpenter but is unlikely to be prudent.

For Aristotle, prudence takes two quite different forms. The first, narrower form is what might be called personal prudence. It consists of "knowing what is good for oneself" and is concerned "with matters relating to the person in whom it exists and with him only."[51] This is prudence as it appears in the exercise of the various ethical virtues, such as courage and moderation.[52] The deliberate choice (*prohairesis*) necessary for such virtue is not undone by the importunings of pleasure and pain, especially of the bodily sort. While acknowledging certain instances in which force or ignorance might render one's actions involuntary, Aristotle is anxious to defend the view that the choices made by human beings are not somehow determined by causes external to them. As he summarizes the matter, "It seems that man is the first principle *(archē)* of his own actions."[53] Since good character is not, for Aristotle, the exclusive preserve of the few, prudence emerges in this account as a fairly democratic intellectual virtue.

The second, more comprehensive sort of *phronēsis* is that "concerned with the city" and "with other people's affairs."[54] Aristotle divides this faculty into two parts. The first part, which he simply calls "political prudence," applies to "particular actions and deliberations." Its subject matter, as described more fully in the *Rhetoric,* includes the usual areas of public policy: revenues and expenditures, war and peace, territorial defense, and trade.[55] The other part of this more comprehensive type of prudence is "legislative" and "architechtonic." It too is based on experience and involves deliberation over particulars, but it differs from its partner in scope. It takes up the "universal"—that is, it is concerned with the ordering of the whole, the regime.[56] Accordingly, Aristotle recommends, both in the *Nicomachean Ethics* and in the *Rhetoric,* that legislators undertake the study of regimes—their number and kinds, what preserves and destroys them, and which are advantageous to which sorts of city. He recommends, in short, an inquiry like the *Politics.* Political science *(politikē),* which he also characterizes as "architechtonic" in the *Nicomachean Ethics,*[57] complements legislative prudence by providing it with alternatives unavailable to experience alone.

When taken in either its political or its legislative sense, prudence is no longer so humble or potentially common an intellectual virtue. As described in the *Politics,* it is a mark of distinction. *Political* prudence is the criterion that Aristotle uses to separate the good man from the good citizen. The two coincide only when the citizen rules.[58] Otherwise, the citizen only executes the decisions of the ruler: "Prudence is the only virtue peculiar to the ruler. The others, it would seem, must necessarily be common to both rulers and ruled, but prudence is not a virtue of one ruled, but rather true opinion; for the one ruled is like a flute maker, while the ruler is like a flute player, the user [of what the other makes]."[59] The citizen is politically "prudent" only to the extent that he implicitly accepts the views of the ruler, who actually understands the requirements of policy. Like a flute maker, the citizen takes instruction, in the form of "true opinion" *(doxa alēthēs)*, from someone of comprehensive expertise.

Legislative prudence is the province of even more extraordinary individuals. At the beginning of the *Politics,* Aristotle suggests that while all human beings possess the "impulse" toward the political partnership, a founder is its efficient cause. Thus "the one who first constituted [a city] is responsible for the greatest of goods."[60] The act of founding is the peak of practical virtue, followed closely by the achievements of eminent reformers such as Solon and Lycurgus.[61] Significantly, Aristotle does not attribute political science to these legislators of the past, though he regards it as the necessary complement of legislative prudence. Their virtue, impressive as it was, resulted not from "thought" but from "some sort of capacity or experience."[62] Aristotle's intention in the *Politics* is to perfect this uncommon, architechtonic faculty. He wishes to use his science, his *politikē,* to refine and expand the practical understanding of the great political man.

In turning to Hobbes, one is immediately struck by the relative simplicity of prudence in his account. For Hobbes, prudence does not assume various forms—personal, political, and legislative. It is a single, rather modest faculty, exercised when "the thoughts of a man, that has a designe in hand, running over a multitude of things, observes how they conduce to that designe."[63] It is little more, in short, than straightforward instrumental reasoning. As in Aristotle's presentation, such practical wisdom is decisively related to experience. For Hobbes, however, there is this difference: prudence is not so much dependent on familiarity with particulars in all their variety as constituted by it. As he would have it, "Prudence is but Experience; which equall time, equally bestowes on all men, in those things they equally apply themselves unto."[64] This is the key proposition of his teaching, and its effect is to collapse the several distinct sorts of prudence found in Aristotle. Whereas for Aristotle, only very capable individuals stand to benefit from certain types of experience, Hobbes argues that exposure alone is the great equalizer. All practical wisdom is the same, differing only in its specific objects.[65]

Hobbes's argument is not intended to raise the aspirations of the commoner, of course, but rather to deflate the pretensions of the aristocratically minded. The self-styled disciples of Aristotle are his target, men with "a vain conceipt of [their] owne wisdome," which they think they possess "in a greater degree, than the Vulgar."[66] Of special concern are those who, taking Aristotle's advice, move beyond the lessons of experience and attempt to make practical use of the general study of political things. Men who "love to shew their reading of Politiques and History" in the councils of state know in their hearts that such learning is a foolish basis for decisions. In their "private affaires," where their "particular interest" is at stake, they invariably rely on untutored prudence.[67] Prudence thus emerges in its truest light for Hobbes under the democratizing influence of interest.

This reassessment of prudence rests on new first principles, both psychological and political. To begin with, Hobbes insists that deliberation cannot be understood as an exercise in detached, rational choice. Men do not stand apart from various possibilities for action and evaluate them. Instead, these possibilities course through the human mind in the form of certain elemental passions—appetite and aversion, hope and fear—which, in their "alternate Succession," make up the items in a running "summe."[68] Deliberation is the process by which these rival motives are resolved into a single vector. Men are *de*-liberated not by making a choice, and thereby foreclosing alternatives, but by the relative intensity of their various passions, whose promptings are irresistible.

Hobbes's fundamental political principles further challenge the traditional understanding of prudence. As his psychology suggests, Hobbes rejects the view that political life represents some sort of human consummation. Such striving for perfection corresponds to nothing in human nature, so it always results in insoluble disagreement and, ultimately, strife. Government has to be understood in relation to the passions, the real motor of human action. There, he argues, lies the possibility of consensus, because all human beings, whatever their other passions, share a single clarifying fear: that of violent death. This makes the pursuit of peace—with its attendant goods of security, self-preservation, and material satisfaction—the first law of human nature.[69] More to the point, it makes pride, the passion for preeminence and distinction, the most destructive of vices. Pride teaches that the proper foundation for government is not the agreement of the many but the excellence of the few. Prudence becomes a title to rule.

For Hobbes, the "question who is the better man" can have "no place in the condition of meer Nature," where "all men are equall" both in their insecurity and in the means available to them to overcome it. Aristotle was mistaken in his *Politics* to make as "a foundation of his doctrine" the idea that some men are by nature "more worthy to Command, meaning the wiser sort," while others are more worthy "to Serve."[70] This precept made the *Politics* "repugnant to Government."[71] It challenged the necessary premise of the social compact: that all men are equally capable of self-preservation. Only if this were true could the state of nature be a place of intolerable vulnerability and government by agreement so plausible an escape from it. If men's capacities varied according to the Aristotelian scheme, there would be no need to create an artificial political order; ruler and ruled would exist by nature. Hobbesian nature provides no grounds for such distinctions. Men are enough alike in passion and intellect to recognize the need for a government that can suppress their pride and dictate peaceful coexistence. For the Leviathan to emerge, Hobbes had to assume that every man is competent to judge whether "the means which he is about to use and the action he is performing, be necessary to the preservation of his life and members or not."[72] Under the tutelage of this universal faculty, human beings are capable of winning a reprieve from the state of nature.

But how can such an expectation be squared with Hobbes's fierce critique of prudence? If practical reason is so modest a faculty, what can it contribute to solving the problem of the state of nature? The answer lies in the peculiar character of the Leviathan. For Hobbes, the establishment of an adequate government requires nothing more than the surrender of the right of nature in all its breadth; it need not be modified, distributed, or restricted in any way. What matters for him is not the form that government power takes but rather its basic property as power.[73] A simple, uniform sovereign can arise from a simple, uniform fear. In this way, prudence, with all its concern for particulars, can be dispensed with. Hobbes presents the novel possibility of ordinary men making

a commonwealth without the intervention of a supremely prudent legislator. The problem of founding, it would seem, had been
solved.

The difficulty comes when the sheer fact of sovereignty does
not prove to be an adequate remedy for the state of nature, when
the people need not just to transfer their natural rights but to do so
in a certain way. Hobbes himself concedes that the *form* sovereignty
takes is of great importance. Monarchy, aristocracy, and democracy
differ in their "Convenience" and in their "Aptitude to produce the
Peace, and Security of the people."[74] He hesitates, however, to express his strong preference for monarchy; his partiality is suspi-
ciously prudential, in the Aristotelian sense, and is, he says, the
"one thing alone" in his political science that is only "probably
stated" rather than "demonstrated."[75] Hobbes thus undermines his
own indictment of those that "thinke themselves wiser, and abler
to govern the Publique, better than the rest."[76] Contrary to his every
intention, he implies, by his own informed preference for monarchy over other possible regimes, that there are politically decisive
differences among men with respect to prudence.

Locke was driven to make similar distinctions in trying to deal
with the social compact's indeterminacy. His problem was compounded by his rejection of absolutism, a solution that Hobbes
could at least credibly relate to the capacities and psychological
motivation of the parties to the social compact. For Locke, sovereignty has to be qualified in important respects if it is to serve its
ends, though he does not go so far as to dictate a form of government. For him, as for Hobbes, it is up to the social majority, "having
the whole power of the Community, naturally in them," to place
the authority to make laws in a democracy, oligarchy, monarchy, or
some combination of these, "as they think good."[77] But Locke does
impose conditions on the constitution making of the social majority. Whatever the particular form of government, laws have to be
established and promulgated, judges have to be impartial, property
cannot be taken without consent.[78] These are prudential conclusions of considerable sophistication, and though based on the dis-
advantages of the state of nature, they hardly represent common-
sense maxims obvious to all. In this way, Locke exacerbates the
problem of founding: he presents a social majority that has the
authority to establish a form of government and an unnamed few,

perhaps the enigmatic "studiers" of the law of nature,[79] who actually possess the capacity to do it well.

Rousseau and Hume differed greatly in their criticisms of these first theorists of the social compact, but both objected to the possibility of a founderless founding. Like Madison, they took the account of government's origins in Hobbes and Locke to be implausibly egalitarian. For Rousseau, the critical error of these modern proponents of natural law is that they have to make every participant in the social compact "a great reasoner and a profound metaphysician." Whether taken historically or normatively, this view is paradoxical. It requires "for the establishment of society . . . enlightenment which only develops with great difficulty and in very few people in the midst of society itself."[80] Hence, despite his profound devotion to human equality, Rousseau could not bring himself to attribute the capacity to form a government to the people: "How will a blind multitude, which often does not know what it wants because it rarely knows what is good for it, carry out by itself an undertaking as vast and as difficult as a system of legislation?"[81]

Rousseau's own solution was the godlike legislator, a superior being whom he describes as having "no relationship at all to our nature." Behind this apotheosis, however, is an exaggerated account of the very traits of character and intellect that Madison claimed for the Federal Convention. The legislator is a person of "superior intelligence," someone "who [sees] all of men's passions but [experiences] none of them." Such men are rare—Rousseau cites Moses, Lycurgus, Numa, and Mohammed—and have to act in the name of the divine to achieve their purposes. But their talents are prudential not prophetic: their "sublime reason" rises above "the grasp of common men" and has to be draped in religious authority to convince "those who cannot be moved by human prudence."[82]

Unlike Rousseau, Hume was sympathetic by and large to the project of Hobbes and Locke. Drawing conclusions from the passions, he too made security and prosperity the touchstones of political right. His objections to the social compact concerned not its ends but its beginnings, a stance that allies him with Madison. To the degree that popular consent is ever involved in the founding of government, one has to turn, Hume held, to the "original contract," the simple and voluntary surrender of liberty by which "the ancient rude combinations of mankind" were formed. He doubted, however, that consent was typical even at this stage of human development. It is precisely when new governments are established that the people are "least regarded in public transactions." In part, this is just a matter of historical record: founding ordinarily takes place at the point of a bayonet, and conquerors are notoriously uninterested in consulting popular opinion. More fundamentally, the people, even offered the opportunity, are incapable of the task. The "wise man" looks with trepidation on the "total dissolution of government"—an event that gives "liberty to the multitude" to make "the determination or choice of a new establishment"—and must hope in the end that a great military commander will rise up to give the people a "master," since "they are so unfit to chuse for themselves." For Hume, the idea of popular deliberation on forms of government was nothing less than "chimerical."[83]

As these brief summaries suggest, Madison's critique of popular constitution-making is hardly unique in its basic thrust. Rousseau and Hume were also wary of the claims of universal prudence and found it necessary to return to the form, if not the substance, of the older tradition. They could not assert such distinctions among human beings in good philosophical conscience, however, as their rhetorically overheated presentations suggest. Because Rousseau and Hume, like the writers they criticize, rejected reason as the ordering principle of the soul, they found it difficult to assign supreme practical rationality to ordinary mortals. This pushed them to opposite extremes in describing the legislator.

Rousseau's portrait anticipates the modern revolutionary. His legislator is a demigod, someone who supposedly transforms human nature and yet resists its most destructive temptations, a "genius" who stands above mere "human dominion."[84] We see in his account a preview of the remorseless megalomania of a Robespierre, Lenin, or Hitler. Hume sets forth the conservative alternative. Though he recognizes decisive differences in the political capacities of men, his real interest lies in deflating the claims of the many, not in lending support to the few. He does not wish to concede to anyone the know-how to make a constitution. As he wrote, in stark contrast to Rousseau, "no human genius, however comprehensive," can achieve a general system of legislation by "mere dint of reason and reflection." For Hume, time and experience were the engines of political progress, and the "wise magistrate" did not allow innovations to disturb "the ancient fabric" of a constitution.[85] In their attempt to compensate for the social compact's rejection of classical prudence, Rousseau and Hume thus provided two distinctly modern remedies: revolutionary action, on the one hand, and the historical sensibility, on the other.

Madison posed an alternative, one more in keeping with the Aristotelian original. While his account of the legislative type is far from complete, it is clear that he believed himself and his counterparts to be capable of rational *praxis*, even with respect to the most comprehensive political questions. Contra Rousseau, he considered the necessary qualities to be rare but hardly superhuman. Contra Hume, he understood the intelligence involved to be practical, even scientific up to a point, but not historical.

Yet as we shall see in the following chapters, what most distinguishes Madison's idea of prudence is its relationship to the republican view of justice—that is, to the claims of the people to self-government. Though Madison took such popular pride to be misplaced to some extent, he also saw it as a source of dignity, much as Aristotle gave credit to the freedom that is the end of democratic regimes. For Madison, the social compact promoted a certain sort of character, a kind of hardy independence and self-respect. This was not to be mistaken for gentlemanly or philosophical excellence, but it was a moral ideal worth trying to vindicate. Rousseau attempted to do away with such pride, hoping to "denature" man so as to destroy his amour-propre.[86] Hume simply ignored the demands of political vainglory, asserting that government by consent gave the people "a great deal more honour than they deserve, or even expect and desire."[87] Madison avoided these extremes: he wished both to accommodate the people's pride and to seek its best possible justification.

Chapter Four

The Federal Convention as Founder

The eighty-five essays of *The Federalist* divide neatly into two thematic parts. The first, comprising numbers 1–36, lays out the broad principles to which any adequate constitution for the United States would have to conform. In these early essays, Alexander Hamilton, James Madison, and John Jay are primarily concerned, as David F. Epstein points out, with "fundamental issues of liberalism."[1] By focusing on certain uncontroversial ends—national defense and internal order, prosperity and personal security—and the basic governmental qualities necessary to achieve them, they hoped to prepare their readers for a discussion of the Constitution's particulars. They wanted, in short, to establish their major premise: that the states, having suffered for years under the Articles of Confederation, required a far more energetic union—but of an as-yet-unspecified sort.

The second part of *The Federalist*, which Madison introduces with Number 37, attempts to complete the syllogism. Its object is "to determine clearly and fully the merits of *this* Constitution."[2] But Madison does not turn immediately to an exposition of the proposed government's powers and structure, to the detailed arguments supporting, say, the "supremacy" clause or the division of the legislative branch into two houses. By his lights, it was first necessary to explain the *nature* and *source* of the reasoning behind the Constitution. Accordingly, in numbers 37–40, Madison considers the means by which the liberal priorities described by Publius in numbers 1–36 were translated into specific institutional forms. His subject in these four essays is the Federal Convention, the bridge between the two parts of *The Federalist*.[3]

This quartet forms a discrete unit that is structured much like *The Federalist* itself. The general movement is from the theoretical to the particular. In Number 37, Madison offers his famous meditation on epistemology. Although these passages are often regarded as a digression or a rhetorical flourish, I believe that they reflect his fundamental stance toward the modern science of politics, especially as presented in the writings of Hume and Montesquieu, two writers whose relative influence on him remains a matter of controversy. Like Aristotle, Madison views political science—even with its celebrated modern innovations—as an essential complement to prudence but not as a substitute for it. Number 38 elaborates on this theme, asserting the indispensability of prudence to constitution making. Because of the social compact's inadequacy in this regard, Madison turns to the ancients for a remedy and finds it in their radical understanding of founding. Number 39, though dealing only indirectly with the Federal Convention, plays a vital role in the series. Its principled defense of the Constitution's republicanism is plainly intended to soften the antiegalitarian harshness of the surrounding essays and to show the exceptional character of founding. Finally, Number 40 takes up the question of the Convention's authority in relation to its specific mandate and to the principles of the Confederation. In defending the latitude assumed by the men who met in Philadelphia, Madison exploits the problematic place of political forms in the social compact, which treats them as mere means to the unchanging ends of civil society.

In this chapter, I attempt to complete the portrait of Madisonian founding begun in chapter 3 and to substantiate my claim that it is best seen in Aristotelian terms. The chief obstacle to this claim is the necessary relationship between Aristotelian prudence (in all of its forms) and moral virtue. In the classical account, reasoning about means amounts to prudence only to the extent that it is guided by a complete notion of the human good. The apparent absence of such a final end in Madison's thought has led Richard K. Matthews to characterize his idea of rationality as purely instrumental, as an early expression of the technological, bureaucratic mind.[4] While there is some truth to this view—insofar as liberalism, Madisonian or otherwise, is concerned with means or "primary goods" as opposed to ends—it fails to account for his devotion to the republican cause, a devotion that is based, I would suggest, on his insight into the full political implications of the social compact. As I hope to show in my analysis of *Federalist* 39, Madison's prudence, informed by the political science of his day, is not simply an ordering mechanism that secures the permissive conditions for the pursuit of other ends. It is directed toward the achievement of a certain kind of human dignity, a rational refinement of the spirited insistence on self-government.

A treatment of the Federal Convention based solely on these few essays invites the charge of naiveté. Earlier this century, when scholarship on the Constitution was dominated by Progressive debunkers like J. Allen Smith, Charles Beard, and Vernon Parrington, so textual an approach would have been denounced for failing to recognize the class interests at work in the movement for a new national government. In the view of these writers, the public-spirited words of the founders were little more than window dressing for a proto-capitalist coup d'etat. In the late 1950s, a more sophisticated form of economic analysis (especially in the work of Forrest McDonald) discredited such class explanations, pointing instead to the influence of a wide and varied range of commercial interests on the politics of the period. The essential question remained, however: how to explain the motives of the Federalist leadership itself. As Stanley Elkins and Eric McKitrick neatly summarized the problem at the time, "When all is said and done, we do not exactly refer to the 'interests' of a James Madison."[5]

In more recent times, with economic determinism so out of fashion, Madison's account of the Federal Convention has been dismissed for contributing to the political mythology of the founding. Hard-headed realism is the order of the day when it comes to interpreting constitutional history. The members of the Convention are to be given their due as "superb democratic politicians," according to John P. Roche in a widely cited article, but their achievement should not be exaggerated, particularly in light of the very real horse-trading that took place in Philadelphia and the dissatisfaction with the final product felt by many of the participants, including Madison. The Convention was not "a College of Cardinals or a council of Platonic guardians," he observes, but "a reform caucus in action."[6] In the more social-scientific language of Calvin C. Jillson, the Convention, like any other democratic "decision-making situation," was a "complex interaction among independent and self-interested agents."[7] By describing it in a more exalted way, argues Judith N. Shklar, scholars only perpetuate the destructive Plutarchian myth of the "legislator-superman."[8]

The chief objection to demystification of this sort is that it is so much at odds with Madison's own understanding. The Federal Convention that he presents in *The Federalist* is not an invention for purposes of propaganda; it reflects his view, expressed repeatedly in private correspondence, that the makers of the Constitution were individuals of extraordinary merit. His deep disappointment with certain aspects of the document did not prevent him from describing the Convention as "a miracle" for the degree of concord that prevailed there in the face of so difficult and complex an assignment.[9] For an observer of political things as unsentimental as Madison, this is high praise indeed. It should not be discounted just because it finds no place in the range of human motives and capacities that today are held to be authentic.

Theory, Prudence, and Science

In *Federalist* 37, Madison offers a précis of the moral and intellectual qualities that together define prudence. Though the essay's renown rests on its central passages, which concern men's capacity "to contemplate and discriminate objects, extensive and complicated in their nature,"[10] the broader context of this discussion is often overlooked. It is framed by a second and equally important theme: moderation. This too is the subject of the "reflections" that Madison asks to be "indulged." It is, in fact, what he takes up first: "It is a misfortune, inseparable from human affairs, that public measures are rarely investigated with that spirit of moderation which is essential to a just estimate of their real tendency to advance or obstruct the public good; and that this spirit is more apt to be diminished than prompted, by those occasions which require an unusual exercise of it." Madison begins with the question of character because information and understanding are not enough for deciding on public measures. A person might be able to identify the public good but be disinclined to seek it. Thus a "just estimate" requires a certain "spirit." This is especially the case with constitutional matters, which touch "the springs of so many passions and interests."[11]

Toward the end of the essay, Madison specifies the destructive motives he has in mind. He returns, after his epistemological observations, to the subject of moderation. The culprits are familiar: "the interfering pretensions of the larger and smaller states" and the great "variety of interests" present within them. Only those enjoying a relative "exemption" from such "pestilential influence[s]" could hope to put them to good use by bringing them within a single, extended sphere. What might be "salutary" in the administration of government "when formed" clearly exerted a "contrary influence . . . in the task of forming it." The work of the Convention was hardly faultless, but it had been free to an astonishing degree of the usual concessions to jealousy and interest. Unlike so many of its historical counterparts, it had resisted "the infirmities and depravities of the human character."[12]

But disposition alone does not ensure the "just estimate" to which Madison refers. It is a matter of intellect as well, and here Madison plunges into the heart of the essay. The Federal Convention faced two types of intellectual difficulties. Some related to the theory of the new government, others to the particular institutions designed to meet the requirements of that theory. As Madison puts it, "It has been shown in the course of these papers, that the existing Confederation is founded on principles which are fallacious; that we must consequently change this first foundation, and with it the superstructures resting upon it." This distinction, between "principles" and "superstructures," is fundamental to *Federalist* 37 and to Madison's thought as a whole. It corresponds to two related domains: that of theory, on the one hand, where the doctrine of the social compact makes possible a degree of certainty about government's ends as well as its general properties; and that of prudence or practical wisdom, on the other, where the variety and complexity of human things require some tentativeness with respect to institutions and invite the recommendations of the modern science of politics.

Madison does not elaborate on the "fallacious" principles in question, except to say that they are evident in previous confederations. He uses identical language in *Federalist* 18, however, and goes into greater detail. The "fallacious principle" behind the downfall of the Amphyctionic Council of ancient Greece lay in treating its member cities in their equal "political capacities"—as sovereigns in their own right—for purposes of membership and administration. Three times he calls this the "theory" of their system.[13] In *Federalist* 20, Madison's last essay before Number 37, he concludes his historical overview of the relevant ancient and modern attempts at confederation and gives his clearest statement of the theoretical difficulty that afflicted all of them: "The important truth, which [experience] unequivocally pronounces in the present case, is, that a sovereignty over sovereigns, a government over governments, a legislation for communities, as contradistinguished from individuals; as it is a solecism in theory; so in practice, it is subversive of the order and ends of civil polity, by substituting *violence* in place of *law,* or the destructive *coertion* of the *sword,* in place of the mild and salutary *coertion* of the *magistracy.*"[14] For Madison, confederations fail because they do not rely on the individual as the basic unit of politics. They neither arise from the vulnerability of isolated men nor properly serve the ends dictated by such a situation. They do not, in short, meet the requirements of the social compact. According to theory, then, a well-constituted national government would exclude the American people in their "political capacities" (that is, as states), a position that he strenuously defended at the Federal Convention.[15]

Madison gives a further idea of theory's clarity by enumerating the other principles by which the Convention was guided. Not only should government be based primarily on individuals rather than on states, it should also possess the "requisite stability and energy" and reflect the "inviolable attention due to liberty, and to the Republican form." Madison does not present these principles as hypotheses, as propositions to be tested and reconsidered. They are authoritative, even axiomatic: "Energy in Government is essential to that security against external and internal danger, and to that prompt and salutary execution of the laws, which enter into the very definition of good Government. Stability in Government, is essential to national character, and to the advantages annexed to it, as well as to that repose and confidence in the minds of the people, which are among the chief blessings of civil society."[16] Madison offers no similar statement of what is "essential" about

"Republican liberty." He instead lists its requirements—that all power be derived from the people, that officeholders be dependent on them, and so forth—and shows them to be contrary in certain respects to the dictates of energy and stability.

Whatever the tension among these principles, however, Madison treats them as given and invokes them as assumptions. All, I would suggest, derive in a very immediate way from the social compact. This is obvious enough in Madison's brief defense of energy and stability, in which he appeals to typical liberal priorities, but it is equally apparent in his treatment of republicanism, as we shall see in *Federalist* 39. For Madison, these principles define the political task, describing its contours with genuine precision. Contrary to Epstein's reading of Number 37 as a whole, the theory on which Madison relies is not the source of the "uncertainty" that occupies so prominent a place in the essay.[17]

This is not to say that Madison considered a firm grasp of theory to be sufficient for the task of founding. Though he often claimed theory as his guide, he could also refer to its more enthusiastic practitioners as "theoretic politicians" or Swiftian "projectors."[18] For Madison, theory's necessary counterpart was prudence or practical wisdom, which concerned itself with particulars. This meant, in the first place, a proper regard for the limits imposed by political circumstance. Prudence determined when theory had to yield to one or another strong attachment—of the states to their sovereignty, for instance, or of the South to the institution of slavery. Such compromises had a profound effect on political forms. They explained why the Constitution could not possess that "artificial and regular symmetry" that arose from "an abstract view of the subject."[19]

But the primary relationship between prudence and institutions was more direct: prudence translated theory into a constitution, into a specific distribution of offices and powers. It was this practical task that elicited Madison's observations in Number 37 on the fallibility of the human mind. The difficulty lay not in recognizing principles—these were well known—but in "combining" them, in "mingling them together in their due proportions." It was the *application* of theory that "could not be easily accomplished."[20] Stressing the obstacles to practical wisdom, Madison wished to give some idea of its special office and, in so doing, to stir appreciation for the accomplishments of the Federal Convention.

This purpose is evident in his discussion of the "line of partition" between the federal and state governments, a subject that leads first to his comments on epistemology and then to some thoughts on political science, the handmaiden of prudence. Madison's concern is with the problem of setting boundaries, and his argument takes the form of a comparison between the natural and the political. Readers of *The Federalist* will appreciate the difficulty of the Convention's assignment, he writes, "in proportion" to their experience in "contemplat[ing] and discriminat[ing] objects, extensive and complicated in their nature," by which he means their familiarity with rigorous, modern science. Madison goes on to provide two instances of unresolved boundary disputes in the study of natural objects: that among "metaphysical Philosophers" concerning the "faculties of the mind" and that among "naturalists" concerning "the great kingdoms of nature" and their "various provinces."

What is most striking in Madison's description of both fields is his unwillingness to concede achievement or progress. Focusing on their failure to establish definitions "with satisfactory precision" and to trace lines "with certainty," he seems bent on dampening scientific optimism.[21] Still more interesting is the fact that elsewhere Madison gave every indication of holding both psychology and natural classification in considerably higher regard. He declared Locke the author of an "immortal system" with respect to "mind," and he was confident of his own ability to fit various American fauna into the taxonomic scheme of the French naturalist Buffon.[22] Despite his reservations in Number 37, Madison apparently considered these two sorts of inquiry to be exemplary sciences—and that may be his point. If these great models of human understanding fell short of perfect clarity, then in moving on to the "science of Government" (or "political science"), "we must perceive the necessity of moderating still farther our expectations and hopes from the efforts of human sagacity."[23] The soundness of the Constitution, Madison intimates, cannot be demonstrated in a formal proof or strict system.

For Madison, political science is not just a less developed science but a different kind of science altogether. In the first place, it is concerned with the "institutions of man" rather than the "works of nature," which means that much of its obscurity arises from "the object itself." Madison makes the unexpected claim that natural things are "perfectly accurate" in "all [their] delineations" and appear otherwise only "from the imperfection of the eye which surveys them."[24] The basis for this assertion is unclear, particularly in light of his preceding remarks on the inscrutability of the "works of nature." It either betrays his genuine confidence in the sciences whose authority he has just challenged or suggests some other, more intelligible category of natural things. A candidate for this second possibility might be the very principles—energy, stability, republicanism—that he cites with such assurance earlier in the essay. As we have seen, they derive from the social compact, which is to say, from "the transcendent law of nature and of nature's God."[25]

Political science also differs from natural science because it is directly concerned with human action and choice. Its object is not knowledge as such but the securing of certain ends. This lends a provisional character to its conclusions, which are made and remade as circumstances warrant, not discovered once and for all. Thus political science is "instructed" by "experience," must deal with new questions "daily . . . in the course of practice," and relies on "the continued and combined labors of the most enlightened Legislators and jurists." Though the Convention's attempt to mark a proper boundary between state and federal authority was a novel undertaking, it was typical of political science in its resistance to precise treatment (Madison compares it to the long and unsuccessful effort of the British to determine the exact jurisdictional limits of their own various tribunals and codes of law).[26] Taken as a whole, Madison's account of political science protects it—and the prudence informed by it—from an inappropriate comparison to the more conclusive inquiries of natural science.

It should be stressed that political science is not identical to prudence for Madison. Rather, it is a sort of knowledge on which practical wisdom can draw. As he wrote in a letter that anticipates the themes of Number 37, disagreement over the new Constitution gave proof of both "the fallibility of the human judgment" (here an unmistakably practical emphasis, omitting any wider epistemological argument) and "the imperfect progress yet made in the science of Government."[27] Despite Madison's disparaging tone, he presents political science as a complement to prudence, a refinement in the direction of system and comprehensiveness. In form, this approximates the relationship between *phronēsis* and *politikē* described by Aristotle.

What sets Madison's political science apart from its Aristotelian predecessor is its content, signaled by his reference to its "progress." Madison agreed with Hamilton that the "science of politics" had undergone "great improvement" in his own day, based on innovations "either not known at all, or imperfectly known to the ancients." Institutions like the separation of powers, checks and balances, representation, and the extended sphere promised to secure good government and to do so on republican terms.[28] These were not simple mechanisms to be copied from a manual for legislators, however. Political science might inspire the general form of such "superstructures," but it remained to practical wisdom to give them a particular shape and adjust them to circumstances. It is for this reason that Madison speaks elsewhere in *The Federalist* of the "inventions of prudence" in assigning credit for the Constitution's various devices.[29]

Considering his obvious debt to certain Enlightenment writers, Madison's elevation of prudence over political science may seem the height of ingratitude. That Hume influenced his ideas on faction, representation, and the extended sphere is beyond dispute,[30] and he himself proclaimed his reliance on Montesquieu's doctrine of the separation of powers.[31] Yet Madison was no slavish follower. His borrowings were selective, and he refined them to suit the distinctive situation of the United States. For him, political science had to be mediated by judgment and by historical and personal experience, "the oracle of truth" in these matters.[32] Only under such direction could it be both practical and safe.

It is thus unsurprising that the more extreme claims for Madison's dependence on the institutional advice of others do not withstand scrutiny. Close analysis of Hume's "Idea of a Perfect Commonwealth," the supposed source of *Federalist* 10, reveals him to be more sanguine about the possibility of disinterested representation and far less keen on popular political participation than was Madison.[33] Moreover, with vast authority given to the localities and a weak, indirectly elected national legislature, Hume's scheme bears a striking resemblance to the Articles of Confederation, the system that Madison worked so assiduously to reform.[34] Madison may have been unduly harsh when, in a letter written during his retirement, he singled out Hume among the "bumbling lawgivers" who were surpassed in practical wisdom by "the founders of our Republics,"[35] but his comment should give pause to the tracers of influence.

Similar qualifications apply to the "celebrated" Montesquieu, whose too rigid treatment of the divisions in the British constitution was embraced by the Anti-Federalists and caused Madison and his allies no end of grief. *Federalist* 47, which draws on the state constitutions to show that the departments of government need not be absolutely separate and distinct, is plainly meant as a corrective to the work of the "great political critic."[36] The objections were again practical. The political science of Montesquieu, though valuable as a general guide, did not deal with the most urgent questions faced by a legislator. As Madison put it a few years later, "Montesquieu . . . has rather distinguished himself by enforcing the reasons and the importance of avoiding a confusion of the several powers of government, than by enumerating and defining the powers which belong to each particular class."[37] For Madison, political science was a useful aid to constitution making, but the exercise itself was inescapably prudential.

Still more insupportable is the contention that these writers deserve credit not only for Madison's institutional insights but also for his first principles. In this view, Madison was a liberal of historical/sociological bent, free of the questionable presuppositions of the social compact. Garry Wills declares that Madison, in opposition to Locke, made "Hume's doctrine on opinion . . . the basis of government."[38] Anne M. Cohler, in a similar vein, sees Montesquieu as the presiding spirit of *The Federalist:* "The circumstances considered are the institutions and life of Americans in 1787 and the foreseeable future, not those of men in a state of nature. Americans require a powerful free government, but not one that is explicitly limited by the natural rights of individuals."[39] Such arguments have a certain plausibility so long as they focus on one or another suggestive document. *The Federalist* itself is a convenient source of evidence because it is more concerned with specific institutional forms than with the grounds of political life. But when a wider view is taken of Madison's work, there is no avoiding his constant resort to the social compact and the ideas associated with it. Like the other members of the founding generation,[40] he saw Hume and Montesquieu primarily as political scientists, authorities to be consulted on the instruments of government but not its origins or ends.[41] As Madison stated in the letter from his retirement cited above, "the rights of man as the foundation of just Government had been long understood" when Americans began making their constitutions. What was "sadly defective"—this being the occasion for his slight of Hume—were the "superstructures projected" from these rights.[42]

More than forty years after writing *Federalist* 37, then, Madison still sharply distinguished between practice ("superstructures") and theory ("the rights of man"). Hume fell on the practical side of this divide, supplying what Morton White aptly calls "political technology."[43] On foundational matters, the "sagacious and skeptical Hume," as Madison referred to him in a more generous moment,[44] was not to be consulted. Madison likewise discounted the theoretical contributions of Montesquieu. He was not the great system-builder in politics that Isaac Newton was in matter and Locke was in mind. In his "particular science," Montesquieu's contributions were critical, not constructive: "He lifted the veil from the venerable errors which enslaved opinion, and pointed the way to those luminous truths of which he had but a glimpse himself."[45]

For Madison, the social compact might stand in need of certain modifications, but it was always the source of his first principles. Political education at the University of Virginia, he told Jefferson, should begin with the works of Locke and Algernon Sidney, writings "admirably calculated to impress on young minds the right of Nations to establish their own Governments," and with the Declaration of Independence, "rich" as it was "in fundamental principles."[46] Whatever their merits as ingenious commentators on government and legislation, Hume and Montesquieu, the great critics of abstract natural rights, did not find a place on Madison's core syllabus.

Classical Lawgiving

Having lowered the expectations for modern political science in Number 37, Madison argues in *Federalist* 38 for the primacy of prudence in constitution making. To do so, he turns to the classical teaching on founding as "reported by antient history."[47] In contrast to his procedure in numbers 18–20, where he provides a broad historical survey of other confederacies, he offers here no modern cases of the establishment of constitutions. Even among the ancients his focus is narrow. Dwelling on the extraordinary deeds of Solon and Lycurgus and making only passing reference to the leading figures of pre-imperial Rome, Madison appears to concur with Cicero that only among the Greeks did the highest expression of statesmanship take the form of a singular act of founding.[48] He presents these examples as evidence of "the improvement made by America on the ancient mode,"[49] but his account implies that the similarities between the Federal Convention and its classical predecessors are much more impressive than the differences. Those given the responsibility of creating modern regimes would seem to require instruction from the ancient Greeks.[50] Bernard Bailyn's wide-ranging readings notwithstanding, *Federalist* 38 points to a classical influence on early American political thought that is neither nostalgically Roman nor merely "illustrative."[51]

Madison begins the essay with a seemingly superficial difference between the ancient and modern modes of "preparing and establishing regular plans of government": the number of men assigned to the task. It is "remarkable," he asserts, that among the ancients the job was performed not by "an assembly of men" but by "some individual citizen of pre-eminent wisdom and approved integrity." To illustrate, he proceeds to list the renowned lone founders of antiquity, starting with Minos and concluding with Solon and Lycurgus. The latter cases appear to warrant special attention with respect to number, Solon having had "sole and absolute power of new modelling the Constitution" of Athens, Lycurgus having reformed the Spartan regime through his "single efforts." According to Madison, a plural founding, executed by "a select body of citizens," is obviously superior in terms of safety and wisdom, for it provides better insurance against both "treachery" and "incapacity."

What, then, inspired the freedom-loving Greeks "to place their destiny in the hands of a single citizen"? Madison's answer: fear of "discord and disunion among a number of Counsellors."[52] This is hardly an incidental concern. In Number 37, Madison himself detects nothing less than divine intervention—"a finger of that Almighty hand which has been so frequently and signally extended to our relief"—in the unanimity that prevailed at the Federal Convention; it was a cause for "astonishment."[53] By having a single outstanding man frame a constitution, the ancient Greeks showed that they took the possibility of factious disagreement very seriously. Moreover, as Madison acknowledges, their resort to the superlative virtue of an individual did not turn out to be especially reckless. Solon and Lycurgus proved, in fact, to be men of unsurpassed wisdom and integrity. These advantages may not impugn the American mode, which risks disharmony in order to secure a wider selection of talent, but they do weaken considerably the case for declaring it an "improvement" to be "admire[d]." In Madison's account, both the ancient Greeks and the Americans gave due attention to "the hazards and difficulties incident to such experiments."[54]

Madison's emphasis on this difference in number becomes still more curious when one realizes that it is the only clear distinction that he makes between the ancient and modern modes of constitution making. There is some suggestion that the "celebrated reformers" of antiquity differed from their American counterparts in the "expedients" that they had to employ to establish their legislation. But Madison never says this outright, and he appears to note these instances only to show the difficulties inherent in any act of founding. "Solon, who seems to have indulged a more temporising policy, confessed that he had not given to his countrymen the government best suited to their happiness, but most tolerable to their prejudices," Madison observes. "And Lycurgus, more true to his object, was under the necessity of mixing a portion of violence with the authority of superstition; and of securing his final success, by a voluntary renunciation, first of his country, and then of his life."[55]

Far from separating the two modes, these examples drawn from Plutarch can even be seen to illuminate the American case. As Madison was aware, having been the self-appointed notetaker at the Federal Convention, Solon's famous statement was cited twice at Philadelphia to warn members not to disregard their constituents' very real attachments to the states.[56] In a slightly more fanciful vein, there were American parallels to Lycurgus as well. The Federal Convention certainly did not send armed men into the agora to secure its reforms—the "portion of violence" to which Madison refers[57]—but Publius does depend on coercion of a sort in *The Federalist*, particularly in its first half, when he describes at length the factious, war-torn future that awaits the country if the Constitution is rejected. Moreover, his appeals to the saving power of Providence and the Almighty might be classed as superstition.[58] Finally, as Epstein notes, the Federal Convention resembled Lycurgus "in renouncing its official life": it ceased to exist with the making of its recommendations and had no authority under the regime that it devised.[59]

Madison's discussion is calculated to obscure the most obvious difference between the ancient and modern modes of constitution making—not their reliance, respectively, on the abilities of the one or the few but the relationship of both of these to the many, to the people. Indeed, the Declaration of Independence seems far from Madison's mind in *Federalist* 38. What is "remarkable" about the ancient lawgivers is the fact that they acted alone, not that it is difficult to ascertain "how far they might be cloathed with the legitimate authority of the people." Only in "some" instances—those of Draco and Solon—were the proceedings "strictly regular." Since Madison's overriding interest remains number, he does not comment on the "less regular" proceedings under Lycurgus—that is, his use of violence, superstition, and suicide—but instead contrasts his single-handed intervention with that of a body of citizens.[60] Throughout, the question of authority is secondary to that of capacity. That "irregularity" is not an insuperable objection to constitution making can be gathered from Madison's sole reference to any of these ancient legislators later in the essay, when he asks "whether the Constitution, now before the public, would not stand as fair a chance for immortality, as Lycurgus gave to that of Sparta."[61]

Though Madison appears to say that formal authorization is not essential to the relationship between a people and their founder (whether one or a few), he does recognize that consent and wisdom must come together in some fashion in the establishment of a constitution. He finds a fitting extended analogy in medicine: "A patient who finds his disorder daily growing worse; and that an efficacious remedy can no longer be delayed without extreme danger; after cooly revolving his situation, and the characters of different physicians, selects and calls in such of them as he judges capable of administering relief, and best entitled to his confidence."[62] The first thing to note about the analogy is its ancient pedigree. Plato and Aristotle often compare the ministrations of a doctor or a trainer to those offered by a supremely prudent statesman, as does Plutarch in the very passage where he recounts the "expedients" of Lycurgus cited by Madison.[63] Like the combination of *politikē* and *phronēsis* described by Aristotle, medicine relies on both a general, theoretical understanding and a knowledge of particulars based on experience.[64]

Madison modernizes the analogy by adjusting it to the terms of the social compact. Whereas the ancient comparison ordinarily emphasizes the expertise of the physician and the ongoing maintenance of health, Madison stresses the choice of the patient and the urgent, even life-threatening nature of his situation. Moreover, the usual counterpart to medicine—the care of the soul—is missing. Like Madison's physicians, the makers of the Constitution deal with the body and its most serious needs, offering advice ultimately aimed at self-preservation. But their know-how is no less rare. What the analogy makes clear, in its ancient as well as its modern garb, is that the patient is ignorant of what is required for his own well-being. We see here a softened, more politic presentation of Madison's blunt private views about the constitution-making capacities of "the bulk of mankind."

Only by appreciating the extremity of this position—of architechtonic prudence in something close to its original form—can we see its great distance from the constitutional order to which it gave rise. However aristocratic Madison's self-understanding might have been, he nowhere proposed that founding should serve as a model for everyday politics. Gordon S. Wood and Garry Wills have suggested otherwise, finding a supposed similarity between the movement for the Constitution and Madison's account of representation under the new regime. In both instances, they contend, it was his intention that virtuous, disinterested gentlemen would prevail over their popular inferiors.[65] Such arguments are usually based on a selective, if not tendentious, reading of *Federalist* 10, where Madison does indeed express the hope that the extended republic will encourage the election of the wise and the virtuous, thereby refining and enlarging the public's views by "passing them through the medium of a chosen body of citizens."[66] As Paul A. Rahe and others have pointed out, however, Madison regarded this as a secondary and rather uncertain safeguard. In his own memorable formulation, "Enlightened statesmen will not always be at the helm."[67]

For Madison, the chief bulwark against factious oppression was to be the number and variety of parties, interests, and sects that could be brought within the sphere of an extended republic. In "this circumstance principally" was security to be found, for it would place serious obstacles in the path of any part of the people that might aspire to an unjust or interested majority.[68] The premise of such a scheme, of course, was that representatives would be responsive to their constituents—attached to them, dependent on them. As Madison argues in a subtle psychological profile of the republican representative in *Federalist* 57, members of the House of Representatives would be bound by the strongest of motives— duty, gratitude, interest, and ambition—to "the great mass of the people." Frequent elections would ensure their "proper responsibility."[69] Though Madison hardly meant to foreclose the possibility of disinterested deliberation on the public good, especially in the more select offices, his general expectation for political life under the Constitution was more modest and did not include a reliance on prudence in its most elevated sense. As Martin Diamond has observed, one finds in *The Federalist* "a profound distinction . . . between the qualities necessary for Founders and the qualities necessary for the men who come after."[70] If the American republic was to endure, it could not depend on the fragile, fleeting resources of its founding. Once given a sound regimen, the patient would have to tend to himself.

Republicanism

Though Madison introduces *Federalist* 39 as the first essay to examine the plan of government itself, it too belongs to his series on founding. Direct discussion of the Federal Convention is put aside for a moment, but the two primary points of the essay—that the Constitution is both republican and, to a considerable extent, federal—are critically related to the troubling problem of authority raised in the surrounding numbers. Here Madison provides a palliative. The people are assured that the basis of the government (unlike the Convention that designed it) is to be "strictly republican," which is to say, "derived from the great body of the society, not from an inconsiderable proportion, or a favored class of it."[71] In addition, they are shown the various ways in which the Convention did in fact comply with its mandate by maintaining the confederate character of the union.

Madison recognized that this second point was the less satisfactory of the two, considering the many elements of the Constitution that made it a truly national government. The obvious question—"by what authority" was "this bold and radical innovation undertaken"?[72]—is raised in the essay but is saved for Number 40, where Madison finally deals forthrightly with the latitude assumed by the Convention. The intent of Number 39 is to show respect for popular claims and to soothe popular fears. Madison tries, in the words of Charles R. Kesler, both "to reestablish his republican bona fides" and to separate discreetly the two parts of his "rather undemocratic account of the problem of founding."[73]

Though republicanism was paired with other, equally essential concerns in Number 37—the Convention had faced the daunting task of combining "the requisite stability and energy" with "the inviolable attention due to liberty"[74]—it is now singled out for special attention, being the "first question that offers itself" in evaluating the new Constitution. Why this premium on republicanism? The first of Madison's three tightly strung reasons points to politics over principle: "It is evident that no other form would be reconcileable with the genius of the people of America."[75] It is important to recall that "genius" had a technical, almost scientific meaning for Madison. A term of art borrowed from Montesquieu, it corresponded to the idea of ethos and, despite its laudatory connotation today, did not necessarily signify approval. Spain too had a "genius," Madison wrote elsewhere, and it was decidedly unrepublican.[76] In this view, his proclaimed devotion to republicanism could be seen as little more than rhetorical—a concession to the prejudices of his audience.

In a similar vein, one could attribute Madison's attachment to the republican form to simple expedience. Recent political events had demonstrated the incapacity of mixed regimes to secure the ends of the social compact, so he perhaps felt compelled to seek alternatives. As he wrote in *Federalist* 51, in unmistakably instrumental language, the Constitution represented the substitution of one "method" for another: having rejected the "precarious security" provided by "a will in the community independent of the majority," the United States would make an experiment of the extended republic with its safely dispersed interests and parties.[77] Perhaps *this* method would work.

Rationales of this sort for Madison's republicanism serve as useful reminders of his political lodestars, those liberal priorities on which he would not compromise. In the end, though, they cannot account for his insistence on a "wholly popular" form of government.[78] Madison's prudential detachment, an attitude dictated by the social compact, prevented him from being an uncritical partisan of republican government, but he was a partisan nonetheless. Regimes mattered to him, and not just for their capacity to maintain peace and security. The "propensity towards Monarchy" among those unsettled by the "turbulent scenes" preceding the Federal Convention, for instance, inspired not his sympathetic understanding but a determination "to redeem the honor of the Republican name." This was the course of "all the real friends of the Revolution."[79]

In Number 39, Madison enlarges on this theme. The genius of the American people aside, only the republican form could be reconciled "with the fundamental principles of the revolution; or with that honorable determination, which animates every votary of freedom, to rest all our political experiments on the capacity of mankind for self-government."[80] As Epstein interprets this passage, it appears to be Madison's intention "to move beyond the explicit revolutionary doctrine and assert a kinship between the Revolution's principle that the people are entitled to choose and judge their form of government, and the republican principle that the people are entitled to choose and judge their rulers."[81]

Epstein does not elaborate on this kinship, but I would argue that it is a plain implication of the social compact, one that Madison understood better than did either of his great teachers. Hobbes and Locke assumed, naively perhaps, that conventional inequality could be made morally and politically consistent with the natural equality they claimed to discover. They believed that most human beings would be satisfied with "a will in the community independent of the majority" (in Madison's words) so long as that will—whether a king, aristocracy, or some combination of the two—protected them from the many dangers and inconveniences of the state of nature. Madison disagreed. While conceding the urgency, even the primacy, of the needs described by the social compact, he found in the doctrine a certain proud self-reliance, a jealous and irascible attachment to the rights of nature. Hobbes completely suppressed this aspect of the social compact, but it is visible, as Thomas L. Pangle notes, in Locke's right of revolution.[82] A fuller expression of it, however, lay in "the vigilant and manly spirit" that Madison saw among his countrymen, a spirit that "nourishes freedom" and was "nourished by it" in turn.[83] This political claim may have been secondary to "the great principle of self-preservation,"[84] with its necessity-driven indifference to matters of pride, but Madison recognized its importance nonetheless.

According to Madison, such spiritedness could not be gratified in the practice of high politics; human beings, on the whole, were incapable of contributing to the establishment of adequate regimes. But it could find a place in everyday politics, and it was this insight that explains his republicanism. Madison thus inverted previous accounts of the social compact: the human desire for self-rule was to be vindicated not in the founding of government—the only fully popular moment in the narratives of Hobbes and Locke—but in the ongoing activities of government, where it could be more safely realized. Citizenship, he was convinced, could not be merely social. If civil rights reflected nothing of the proud self-reliance inherent in the social compact, the members of a society, however prosperous and well protected, would not be fully content with their political arrangements.

But what is it precisely that Madison considered "honorable" about the "title of republic," as he writes in Number 39?[85] The mere accommodation of human spiritedness is hardly of self-evident worth. As Madison stressed in his critique of the Articles of Confederation and the state governments, this disposition could find expression in any number of destructive or vicious ways. Spiritedness became praiseworthy, he clearly held, only through its refinement or education.

For Madison, the Constitution achieved this aim through its

forms, the careful handiwork of the Federal Convention. In various ways, its institutions brought an element of reason to the self-assertiveness of the people. In the first place, they imposed a certain instrumental rationality on the proceedings of the whole, allowing the people, despite their insistent parochialism, to participate in a government capable of pursuing national ends. Though the Constitution did little to moderate directly the passions and interests that were the substance of faction, it did make it possible for the "mild voice of reason" to plead "the cause of an enlarged and permanent interest."[86] Thus, for instance, the extent of the republic diluted the influence of individual factions and so provided an opportunity for a coalition based on "justice and the general good." The moderate size of the House of Representatives made it less likely that "passion" would "wrest the sceptre from reason." And the relative permanence of the Senate gave it the standing to check an "irregular passion" among the people "until reason, justice, and truth, [could] regain their authority over the public mind."[87] In this way, popular government was elevated by demonstrating its capacity to be "good Government."[88]

The Constitution also lent rational direction to spiritedness in a more profound way. Though it was not a common theme for Madison, he did at times allude to a certain order of the soul that republican institutions produced. Reason manifested itself in this regard not in problem solving or calculation but in character, as a kind of self-control and independence. To some extent, a proper republican constitution created the social circumstances for this development. The yeoman farmer, Madison believed, could count virtue, "the health of the soul," as part of his "patrimony."[89] Such character formation was also political, however, and related directly to the influence of the Constitution and its forms. The archetype for this aspect of Madison's republicanism was classical. Indeed, Epstein sees a parallel between Aristotle's emphasis on speech in his description of man as a political animal and Publius's wish to give a wide berth to citizens "to express and act upon disputable opinions." Epstein misses the real affinity, though. What is characteristically Aristotelian is not the mere fact of such assertive opining but rather its role in promoting human virtue when it corresponds to the authoritative opinions of a regime.[90]

Madison assigned a similar role to opinion in *Federalist* 49, where he objects to Jefferson's proposal for resolving constitutional disputes by appeal to the people. Such a practice succeeded during the revolutionary struggle, he writes, because "danger . . . repressed the passions most unfriendly to order and concord." In peacetime, "veneration" and "reverence" for the laws would have to bring about the "requisite stability." It was in these sentiments— "the strength of opinion in each individual" and "its practical influence on his conduct"—that a substitute would be found for the reasoning that could convince "a nation of philosophers" to submit to a wise and free government.[91]

When such allegiance was given to a constitution whose forms were subject ultimately to popular review, there was no taint of ignorant acquiescence. By contrast, Madison nowhere suggests that this same type of respect be given to any public official or ruler. In a revealing early debate in the House of Representatives, he explicitly rejected such treatment for George Washington. The Constitution might receive the unreflective veneration of the people, but a magnificent title for the president should be opposed "in principle." Such august trappings, he insisted, "diminish the true dignity and importance of a republic." As Madison summarized the peculiar excellence of self-government when seen through the lens of the social compact, "The more simple, the more republican we are in our manners, the more rational dignity we acquire."[92]

Substance over Forms

With *Federalist* 40, Madison finally reaches the details of the Federal Convention itself, having artfully prepared the way in the preceding essays. His discussion is divided into two parts, corresponding to the questions introduced but left unanswered in Number 39: "whether the Convention were authorised to frame and propose" such a Constitution and "how far considerations of duty arising out of the case itself, could have supplied any defect of regular authority."[93] The posing of the second question implies, of course, a negative answer to the first. For Madison and his contemporaries, friend and foe alike, it was no secret that the Federal Convention had exceeded its authority.[94] The controversy concerned the nature of its transgressions and their seriousness.

There were two primary charges. Substantively, that the Convention had promulgated a national rather than a federal government, in defiance of the states' wishes and the principles of the Articles of Confederation. Procedurally, that its terms for ratifying the Constitution—approval by popular conventions in nine states—openly flouted the Confederation's provisions for amendment, which assigned a formal role only to Congress and the state legislatures and, notoriously, required unanimity among the states. Madison's presentation of these complex issues is equal parts obfuscation and principle. While he tries to hide the full extent of the Convention's assumption of power, he also justifies it by invoking the social compact, modified to accommodate the prerogatives of those of outstanding prudence.

Though "in strictness" the authority of the Federal Convention was to be found in the "commissions given to the members by their respective constituents," Madison begins by quoting at length the recommendations from the Annapolis Convention and from Congress in response to which all the states appointed their delegates.[95] He is thus spared from examining the largely repetitious state commissions but also from the embarrassing fact that Delaware's instructions expressly prohibited any deviation from the Confederation's requirement that each state have precisely one vote in Congress.[96] This tack also allows him to gloss over the character of the Convention's "constituents," who were state legislatures rather than the people of the states—a matter of some importance considering the centrality of popular rights in his later arguments.

Having summarized the substantive expectations of the two authorizing documents—that the Convention was "to frame a *national government*, adequate to the *exigencies of government* and *of the Union*, and to reduce the articles of confederation into such form as to accomplish these purposes"—Madison proceeds to a "fair construction" of these directives. This turns out to be a rather legalistic exercise. Every part of a law should be assumed to have some meaning, he asserts, but if the parts are incompatible, a distinction must be made between those that are more and those that are less important. As he renders it, means must be sacrificed to ends. It was "the judgment of the Convention" that their authorizing instructions imposed such a choice, so they concluded that preserving the Articles of Confederation was secondary to establishing an adequate national government.[97]

Madison challenges "the most scrupulous expositors of delegated powers" to criticize this line of reasoning, and indeed they might. If nothing else, it is obvious that those authorizing the Convention saw no contradiction between the two parts of their instructions. Nor did they distinguish between means and ends. Acting on the conclusion that a sufficiently vigorous national government could be devised within the framework of the existing confederation, they set limits to the "judgment" of their agents. It was the one meaningful restriction, the one piece of prudential guidance, given to the members of the Convention by their constituents.[98] Madison well knew that, given the choice, many of the states might opt for the Confederation or some version of it—that is, for relatively untrammeled sovereignty—over an adequate national government. His distinction between means and ends would have to be substantiated.

Turning to procedural matters, Madison is forced to make a concession, admitting that in "one particular" the Convention had "departed from the tenor of their commission": "Instead of reporting a plan requiring the confirmation *of the Legislatures of all the States,* they have reported a plan which is to be confirmed by the *people,* and may be carried into effect by *nine States only.*"[99] Though he had described the Confederation's ratification procedures earlier in the essay, he neglects to mention that the Convention had also dispensed with the formal approval of Congress. He may not have wished to draw attention to the constitutional qualms expressed by Congress when it was asked first to endorse the proceedings of the Convention and then merely to transmit them to the states.[100] Nor would one gather from the word "tenor" that the commissions of eight of the twelve state delegations—the source "in strictness" of the Convention's powers—had explicitly confirmed the ratification procedures of the Confederation.[101] Madison dismisses these procedural objections because, "though the most plausible," they had been "least urged" by the opponents of the Constitution.[102] In point of fact, Richard Henry Lee and Luther Martin, to give two prominent examples, loudly objected to the

Convention's provisions for ratification. They expressed indignation that the fundamental law of a duly established government could be so lightly discarded.[103] No less angry were defenders of the state constitutions, who realized that the Constitution would make inroads into their charters without going through the ordinary channels for amendment. Madison was aware of this difficulty, but he passes over it in silence in Number 40.[104]

Countering with a spirited argument of his own, Madison instead recalls Rhode Island's dogged exploitation of the Confederation's unanimity principle, "an example still fresh in the memory and indignation of every citizen who has felt for the wounded honor and prosperity of his country."[105] Here he begins to give the grounds for his earlier assertion of means and ends. Citizens should take pride both in defending their particular constitution and in meeting the standards by which all constitutions are judged. If this proves impossible, however, the priority is clear: performance must take precedence over forms. Pride in a feeble or destructive government, though an understandable consequence of liberal constitution-making, is dangerously misplaced. It should—and will—yield to impending disorder.

Having conceded his "one particular," Madison can now openly discuss those "considerations" that made up for any "defect of regular authority" on the Convention's part. He first protests that the Convention's powers were "merely advisory and recommendatory." But this not only ignores the extent to which the Convention's peculiar standing gave it a certain finality; it also, more fundamentally, skirts the issue of authority. Shifting responsibility for any irregularities to those who might ratify them in the end, he does not explain why irregularities were necessary in the first place.

Madison next suggests that the real justification for the Convention's actions lay in two circumstances, both of which made the situation among the states akin to a state of nature. First, there was the national "crisis," the impetus for the country's declaring "almost with one voice" that it was prepared to undertake "so singular and solemn an experiment." For "the great body of citizens," it was a moment of "hopes and expectations" marked by "the keenest anxiety." As a result, ordinary attachments, particularly to the proud claims of the states, might be transcended. Second, there was a general dissolution of the constitutional forms responsible for the crisis. Here Madison radicalizes the view of the Convention's opponents. He points out that the record of violations long preceded the meeting in Philadelphia. The liberty "assumed" at the meeting at Annapolis, one "wholly foreign" to the commission of the delegates, had been approved by twelve of the thirteen states, who in turn "*usurped the power* of sending deputies to the Convention, a body utterly unknown to their constitutions." Congress too had connived in the appointment of the Convention, a body "equally unknown to the Confederation."[106] In brief, the Convention had simply acted on the disregard for forms implicit in its very existence.

As Madison knew, the Convention could be blamed for violating not only conventional (or constitutional) standards but natural standards as well. If "forms" were "to give way to substance," as he argued, it was necessary to consult the original rights of the people, especially the most "transcendent and precious" of them, what I have called the political right of nature. He thus turns at last to the Declaration of Independence. But his excerpt from it contains a telling omission, included here in brackets. As Madison would have it, it was the right of the people to "abolish or alter their governments [and to institute new Government, laying its Foundation on such Principles, and organizing its Powers in such Form] as to them shall seem most likely to effect their safety and happiness." His abridgement, unnoted in the text, is a subtle challenge to the prudential claims of the people. It suggests that though they were capable of recognizing the urgency of their situation, they themselves could not choose a remedy. Forms were beyond them.

To whom, then, did this assignment fall? Madison's revision of the Declaration's principles continues: "Since it is impossible for the people spontaneously and universally, to move in concert towards their object . . . it is therefore essential, that such changes be instituted by some *informal and unauthorized propositions,* made by some patriotic and respectable citizen or citizens." The people, we might surmise, were incapable of concerted action not only because of their great number and geographic distribution but also because of their various proud and interested attachments. Their lack of ability was compounded by a fickle devotion to the public good.

Madison's proffered solution, the intervention of "patriotic and respectable" sorts, is familiar by now. What is striking in its presentation in *Federalist* 40 is a small addendum. Having earlier located the superiority of the American mode of establishing governments in its reliance on an assembly, he now flatly declares what he only hinted at before: that a single "respectable citizen," the mode preferred by the ancients, might do just as well. With this admission, the Convention's "irregular and assumed privilege" is placed at a still greater distance from the claims of the many. According to Madison, however, these extremes can be reconciled. The "approbation" of the people will blot out "all antecedent errors and irregularities."[107] In his telling, the people continue to sit in judgment over forms of government, but they do so through the safe mediation of the few—or the one.

With this, Madison concludes his account of founding, having brought to the social compact a new realism and practicality—but also, it must be said, having burdened the Constitution with several dangerous precedents. First, there was his appeal to the original authority of the people, which was, he readily admitted, inconsistent with a "zeal for adhering to ordinary forms."[108] It was a useful recourse when the regime in question was the Articles of Confederation, but it would apply with no less force to the Constitution, which Madison hoped the people would come to venerate. The case against a reflexive adherence to forms was powerful, and not just in revolutionary circumstances. If the people were the ultimate arbiter of their political institutions, why should they not exercise their original rights more regularly, thereby ensuring the fidelity and effectiveness of government?

On the other side of Madison's new social compact were the few, those actually responsible for bringing about the Constitution. As we have seen, Madison did not wish to entrust the nation's welfare to this select group in any lasting way. He believed that self-government was more likely to protect the people's rights and interests and, further, that it promoted a praiseworthy kind of public character—proud, independent, vigilant. But as Hobbes might have told him, the supremely prudent, having once exercised certain prerogatives, were unlikely to yield them. If a small number of "patriotic and respectable" men were, in fact, the necessary agents of constitutional change, why in the future should their decisions wait for the ratification of the people, to whom they were superior in so many ways?

As events would shortly prove, both sets of claims—those of the many and of the few—had indeed been unleashed during the campaign to establish a new national government. In the years ahead, they would come to be embodied in the constitutional politics, respectively, of Thomas Jefferson and Alexander Hamilton, leaving Madison to seek an alternative in the Constitution itself and its authoritative ways.

Chapter Five

Confronting Jefferson and Hamilton

Giving serious attention to Madison's constitutional thought during his long career *after* the Constitution's establishment requires something of an apologia. Though widely credited with a leading role in the Federal Convention and the events surrounding it, Madison is often treated as a secondary figure in the constitutional politics of the new regime's first several decades. In most accounts, the "Father of the Constitution" fades into the partisan background after the early 1790s, adding little of originality to the bitter dispute between Federalists and Republicans. As Morton J. Frisch would have it, "Madison's thought moves between the boundaries drawn by Hamilton and Jefferson. He was between them. He was a consummate trimmer."[1] Assigning a place to Madison along this spectrum becomes the chief interpretive task. At one extreme, he can be seen as an "almost pure Hamiltonian," in the words of Richard K. Matthews, softened by "a touch of Jeffersonian humanism."[2] At the other, he appears as a practical, tough-minded version of Jefferson, an "astute politician" who, according to Adrienne Koch, restrained the "overambitiousness" of his "more speculative and more daring" partner.[3] More often, his constitutional views are simply deemed inconsistent over time, being Hamiltonian at certain points (in the 1780s and toward the end of his own presidency) and Jeffersonian at others (in the 1790s and during Jefferson's administration).[4]

In contrast to this orthodox view, I hope to demonstrate in this and the following chapter that Madison's constitutional thought was a distinct, coherent alternative to the better-known positions of his contemporaries. His recognition of the Federal Convention's rare achievement led him to resist the continued assertion of the claims that made it possible—those of the people, on the one hand, and those of aristocratically minded gentlemen, on the other. For Madison, these claims, as stated by Jefferson and Hamilton, represented a dangerous reversion to extraconstitutional principles and a serious threat to the ends of civil society. Fidelity to the Constitution itself—to the specific forms worked out in Philadelphia and ratified by the states—was far more likely, as he saw it, to secure the varied set of goods for which Americans had established a national government.

Needless to say, the relationship of Madison to Jefferson and Hamilton was complex and could be discussed from any number of angles. My treatment here is necessarily narrow, focusing on certain selected disputes. What I wish to show is that Madison's constitutional disagreements with Jefferson and Hamilton—though surely less consequential with respect to his Virginia confidant and fellow Republican—did not stem from temperament, political expediency, or conflict at the level of mere policy (the motives favored in most other accounts). Rather, his criticisms flowed from a different understanding of the social compact, one far more keenly attuned to the destructive potential of the principles implicit in the republic's founding moment.

Jefferson represented the popular side of the equation. Like Madison, he wanted the people to take a proprietary interest in their Constitution, to see the government under which they lived as a thing of their own making whose maintenance depended on their jealous vigilance. Unlike Madison, however, he believed that this sentiment could only be produced by actual participation in the act of founding. He wished to restore the part of the Declaration of Independence that Madison silently elided in *Federalist* 40. Indeed, in Jefferson's view, if government was to serve its ends, this recurrence to first principles had to take place often, within the political experience of every citizen.

Madison's response was to preserve the popular principle while avoiding its most harmful consequences. He offered a sophisticated argument for tacit consent (one that surpasses Locke's in important ways) and, more controversially, a defense of popular constitutional "prejudice." Though some students of Madison have detected a conservative quietism in these doctrines, I believe that they represent a significant refinement of liberal republicanism, limiting but still very much recognizing popular sovereignty.

If Jefferson erred on the side of the people, Hamilton was too ready to heed the claims of the few. He wished to extend the aristocratic principles that Madison had admitted into the social compact, moving beyond constitution making to the actual conduct of government. Whereas Madison viewed the Federal Convention as a unique event, a necessary but exceptional exercise of prudential prerogative, Hamilton considered it a precedent for seeking the public good and sought to exploit it through a broad interpretation of the Constitution's powers. Deeply skeptical about the capacity of popular government to serve liberal ends, he favored instead a regime on the English model, considerably more distant from the people and checked almost exclusively by the separation and balance of powers.

In answering Hamilton, Madison exposed the aristocratic premises of his one-time ally's approach to administering the Constitution. In its place, Madison offered a considered defense of the Constitution as ratified, insisting that the people themselves were vital to securing the liberal ends so central to Hamilton's thought. As with his response to Jefferson, authoritative or "true" opinion respecting the Constitution emerged as a necessary restraint on those who would undermine the political forms that regulated and gave shape to civil society.

Perpetual Refounding

The closing months of 1789 found James Madison and Thomas Jefferson at very different points in their careers. Madison had just emerged from the long and arduous effort to establish a new frame of government for the United States, a movement that had repeatedly teetered on the brink of failure. Even with the Constitution duly ratified, opposition lingered while the amendments that would eventually compose the Bill of Rights, approved by Congress the preceding summer, slowly made their way through the state legislatures. Jefferson, on the other hand, had observed these developments from afar, having served as American minister to France since 1785. His immediate experience of constitution making was rather different. A witness to the early events of the French Revolution, he had become an adviser to the Marquis de Lafayette and his liberal, reform-minded circle. It was apparently through these connections that Jefferson first encountered the English radical Richard Gem, a physician and physiocrat then in residence in Paris and the inspiration, it would seem, for his thoughts on the question, "Whether one generation of men has a right to bind another," the subject of a letter that Jefferson penned to Madison in September 1789, just weeks before his tour of duty in France came to an end.[5]

Jefferson's own answer—"that no such obligation can be so transmitted"—led him to the radical proposition that all public measures, constitutions included, naturally expired along with a majority of the generation responsible for them, a period of some nineteen years by his own actuarial calculations.[6] Given the wild impracticality of this argument, scholars have been tempted to dismiss it as a passing fancy, a product of the intellectual and political milieu of revolutionary France. Indeed, Julian Boyd, the editor of Jefferson's *Papers*, suggests that the doctrine was not intended to be generally applicable, that it was little more than "an instrument of justification for constitutional reforms then under discussion" in France. Jefferson merely wanted to share a working memorandum with his fellow Virginian, framing it as political speculation in order to protect his delicate position as a diplomat accredited to the French court.[7]

As Boyd was aware, however, Jefferson's interest in the notion that "the earth belongs in usufruct to the living" long outlasted his stay in France. Moreover, as Koch has documented, the idea was hardly idiosyncratic. It arose from impeccable liberal and republican assumptions, which perhaps explains why Thomas Paine, another member of Jefferson's Paris circle, so readily adopted it.[8] Though undoubtedly influenced by his immediate circumstances in 1789, Jefferson remained attached to the doctrine for the simple reason that it conformed to his view of the social compact, the animating core of his politics no less than of Madison's.

Jefferson begins his "proof" by asking Madison to consider what happens to an individual's land when he "ceases to be." In the ordinary course of things, the property "reverts to society," whose "rules" determine who is to take possession of it and how.

These are the conventional arrangements of civil society, a body formed expressly for the purpose of resolving such matters: "The child, the legatee, or creditor takes it, not by any natural right, but by the law of the society of which they are members, and to which they are subject." Civil society and the law regulating it replace the economic relationships among individuals that would prevail in a state of nature, where such land would belong to "the first occupants" after the deceased.[9]

But what of civil society itself, taken in its corporate sense? Can it impose obligations on a future civil society just as it does on the individuals who constitute it at a given moment? Jefferson says that it cannot.

> A material difference must be noted between the succession of an individual, and that of a whole generation. Individuals are parts only of a society, subject to the laws of the whole. These laws may appropriate the portion of land occupied by a decedent to his creditor rather than to any other, or to his child on condition he satisfies the creditor. But when a whole generation, that is, the whole society dies, as in the case we have supposed, and another generation or society succeeds, this forms a whole, and there is no superior who can give their territory to a third society, who may have lent money to their predecessor beyond their faculties of paying.

For Jefferson, this was a matter both of authority and of the fair distribution of resources across generations. A civil society can rightfully dispose of the property of its members because they have ceded their own natural right to do so. But this authority depends on the continued existence of those who created it. It lasts only as long as they do—or, as Jefferson would have it, as long as a majority of them do. Each discrete incarnation of civil society must decide for itself how best to use its own share—and only its own share—of humankind's common stock. For a civil society to regulate property beyond this limit would be to impinge on the natural rights of its descendants.

From these observations on property in its strictest sense, it was only a short step to property conceived more broadly, in the Lockean sense of "life, liberty, and estate." This brought Jefferson

to the question of "persons," the second great object of government.[10] Here his reasoning ran a parallel course, if one considerably
more far-reaching in its consequences. Just as the earth itself always belongs to the living generation, so too are its members the
"masters" of "their own persons," which they may govern as they
see fit during their appointed time. Though touching on the most
comprehensive concerns of civil society, Jefferson does not soften
his basic principle: "Every constitution then, and every law, naturally expires at the end of 19 years. If it be enforced longer, it is an
act of force, and not of right." Nor, Jefferson hastened to add, is the
hypothetical possibility of repeal or the existence of popular government an adequate substitute. However well contrived a form of
government, it inevitably creates impediments to the expression of
the true "will of the majority." The only way to ensure that constitutions and laws are not an imposition—"an act of force"—is to
require the people to start anew at some regular interval.[11]

For all of Jefferson's high-flown rhetoric, his concrete proposals in the letter to Madison were rather modest: a preamble to a
law on public debt and a measure for protecting copyrights. And
though he invoked his argument about the limits of generational
authority on several occasions in the years to come, he continued
to restrict its application to relatively narrow questions of policy.
As Charles A. Miller archly observes, Jefferson served as president
in the Constitution's nineteenth year and "breathed no hint of the
document's lapsing according to natural law."[12]

Stripped of its demographic naiveté and its mechanical crude-
ness, however, Jefferson's argument appears more reasonable. His
aim was to bring about a periodic return to first principles, to the
ideal of popular sovereignty. If the people were the true source of
all just political authority and if government was the instrument
by which they achieved their ends, there should be some regular
opportunity, Jefferson reasoned, for them to review their handiwork as a whole, free from the obstacles posed by everyday politics.
This would guard, in the first place, against corruption, since the
people themselves were the only reliable agents of the common
good: "Factions get possession of the public councils. Bribery cor-
rupts them. Personal interests lead them astray from the general
interests of their constituents."[13] Moreover, recourse to the people
would allow them to decide whether their political institutions

were still effective and appropriate. As Jefferson put it in a well-known letter during his retirement, "It is a mistake to ascribe to the men of the preceding age a wisdom more than human, and suppose what they did to be beyond amendment. . . . [L]aws and institutions must go hand in hand with the progress of the human mind. As that becomes more developed, more enlightened, as new discoveries are made, new truths disclosed, and manners and opinions change with the change of circumstances, institutions must advance also, and keep pace with the times."[14] Jefferson invited the people to deliberate often about the relationship between their political means and ends. Regular recurrence to the natural standard of the social compact would, he hoped, "keep the Spirit of 1776 perpetually alive," as Richard K. Matthews has written,[15] ensuring that the principles of the Declaration of Independence were practiced and not just revered.

In his reply, Madison seems at first to be concerned solely with the details of Jefferson's argument. Placing the acts of "political society" under three headings (in descending order of permanence), he describes the harm that would come to each from Jefferson's proposed time limit. The dissolution of the "fundamental constitution" would create general turmoil and perhaps render impossible the re-establishment of an adequate government. A prohibition on laws with a term of more than nineteen years, Madison continues, would prevent the present generation from making certain necessary exertions "for the benefit of posterity," provision for the revolutionary war debt being an outstanding example. Finally, if ordinary laws lapsed at stated times, "violent struggles" would ensue over the fundamentals of property relations, leading at best to an arbitrariness incompatible with "every effort of steady industry" and at worst, considering the "checks and difficulties" that always stood in the way of new laws, to anarchy.[16]

For many students of the relationship between the two great Virginians, this part of Madison's response neatly summarizes their relative standing as thinkers. Matthews offers a typical, if somewhat overstated, reading: "Where Jefferson wants to initiate a theoretical dialogue concerning the optimum method to ensure the possibility for the happiness, harmony, and autonomy of succeeding generations, Madison only wants to be practical. And so, rather than even enter into speculative discourse, he elects to quibble."[17] Madison does, in fact, repeatedly appeal to practice in telling Jefferson that his doctrine is "not *in all respects,* compatible with the course of human affairs."[18] But to oppose theory to practice in this context is misleading. Madison tended to associate "practice" with the *ends* of liberalism and "theory" with its account of *origins.* Late in his career, while presiding as elder statesman at a convention to revise (at last) the Virginia constitution, he described this relationship in a speech about the possible extent of equal citizenship: "It would be happy if a State of Society could be found or framed, in which an equal voice in making the laws might be allowed to every individual bound to obey them. But this is a Theory, which like most Theories, confessedly requires limitations and modifications, and the only question to be decided in this as in other cases, turns on the particular degree of departure, in practice, required by the essence and object of the Theory itself."[19] Here Madison asserted the theoretical respectability of his practical concerns, alluding to such matters as stability, security, and public peace and putting them on par with popular authority over governments. His objections in this instance, as in the letter to Jefferson, suggest the particular limits that must be placed on liberal first principles if liberal ends are to be served.

In the second half of Madison's reply, however, it becomes clear that he doubted the soundness of the general principle itself, at least as Jefferson described it. Madison opposed not just the expiration of all laws and constitutions with each new generation but the very idea that the people must be encouraged periodically to reconsider their basic political arrangements. After reviewing the likely consequences of Jefferson's proposal, he thus appeals to "the received doctrine that a *tacit* assent may be given to established Governments and laws, and that this assent is to be inferred from the omission of an express revocation. . . . Is it not doubtful whether it be possible to exclude wholly the idea of an implied or tacit assent, without subverting the very foundation of Civil Society?"[20] The best-known doctrine of tacit consent, and surely the "received" one to which Madison refers, is Locke's. For Locke, one's consent to an established government can be inferred from a range of actions that fall well short of personal participation in the making or ratification of a constitution. An obligation of obedience can arise from accepting property within a certain dominion, sojourning there for a time, or even setting foot on its highways.[21]

The problems with this view are obvious. As Hanna Pitkin argues, not only does it make consent so attenuated as to be almost meaningless, but it seemingly imposes an obligation of obedience on the subjects of even the most tyrannical regimes. Her solution (and Madison's as well) is to stress the substantive rather than the procedural aspects of Locke's political thought—that is, she understands Locke to be worried less about consent than about a given government's performance in protecting its citizens and their basic liberties: "If it is a good, just government doing what a government should, you must obey it; if it is a tyrannical, unjust government trying to do what no government may, then you have no such obligation."[22] This interpretation allows the more "practical" of Madison's theoretical concerns to emerge. Consent ceases to be the basis for constitutional legitimacy and becomes an issue only when a government proves itself either unable to secure the ends of the social compact or actively hostile to them.

Still, Madison was not wholly content with this approach. Having endorsed the doctrine of tacit consent in his reply to Jefferson, he quickly adds that it is necessary to find some remedy for its "pestilent operation . . . in the unlimited sense in which it is at present rec[eive]d."[23] Consent should not be confined to those few revolutionary moments when the people, compelled by circumstance, accepted a new form of government. For Madison, Locke's political philosophy failed to give the people their due: it did not sufficiently accommodate either their rights as persons (as opposed to holders of real property) or their proud political claims. Though in this exchange Madison scrupulously avoids any reference to the political right of nature, which Jefferson invokes at every turn, he does suggest that the impulse it represents can find a place within the forms of a constitution. If consent is unruly and dangerous as it appears in the state of nature, he nonetheless thinks it possible to tame it in "well constituted Governments,"[24] relying on the gentle instruction of convention. For Madison, governments need not be sacrificed in order to vindicate the rightful sovereignty of the people.

One remedy would be an arrangement like the Constitution's own provisions for amendment. While Jefferson grants the authority to revise constitutions to a mere social majority, Madison insists in his reply that a society bound together by a "compact founded on utility" could also change the very terms of its own rule: "A greater proportion [than a majority] might be required by the fundamental Constitution of Society, if under any particular circumstances it were judged eligible."[25] Madison's own experience of such a "circumstance" was quite recent. Only months before he had shepherded what would become the Bill of Rights through Congress, winning the required two-thirds majority. As he was writing to Jefferson, the long process of ratification by three-fourths of the states—a still more formidable supermajority—had just begun. Under the provisions of Article V, the Constitution remained an instrument of the people, but its revision could not be undertaken lightly, for reasons that fell short of a far-reaching social consensus. The "constitutional road to the decision of the people" was reserved "for certain great and extraordinary occasions."[26] As Madison suggested in proposing his list of amendments to the House, the "concurrence" required by the Constitution militated against a reconsideration of the government as a whole. It presupposed the essential goodness of the regime, thwarting the "respectable characters" (that is, the Anti-Federalist leaders) who would recast its fundamentals but allowing the more moderate demands of the "great mass of the people" to be satisfied. Accordingly, he could confine his amendments to establishing safeguards for "particular rights" without having to take up "the principles and the substance" of the Constitution's powers.[27]

For Madison, it was only under such reasonable restrictions that it became possible to proclaim popular sovereignty as a public principle. The first of his recommended amendments to the Constitution is instructive in this regard: carefully modifying the language of the Declaration of Independence, he affirmed the people's "indubitable, unalienable, and indefeasible right to *reform* or *change* their Government, whenever it be found adverse or inadequate to the purposes of its institution."[28] Absent is any suggestion of the more radical right to "abolish" a government or "institute" a new one. As Robert A. Goldwin writes of this "much modified" version of the Declaration's principles, Madison had apparently concluded that the Constitution was "no place for a permanent and emphatic reminder of the ultimate consequence of the natural right to resist tyranny."[29] In the "compact founded on utility" that he envisioned, the people would continue to be sovereign, but they would be encouraged to show proper respect for that rarest of events—the creation of a sound constitution.

Madison's endorsement of tacit consent was also qualified by

his republicanism, perhaps the primary way in which a "well constituted" government could avert the "pestilent operation" of the
doctrine. He did not subscribe to Jefferson's dire pronouncements
about the inevitable corruption of the public councils and the impossibility of designing a form of government that would reliably
reflect the will of the majority. In fact, Jefferson can be compared in
this regard to Madison's Anti-Federalist opponents. One detects
his general agreement with the likes of Samuel Bryan, who found
the Constitution "devoid of all responsibility or accountability to
the great body of the people," or with Robert Yates, who predicted
that "the great officers" of the national government "would soon
become above the controul of the people, and abuse their power to
the purpose of aggrandizing themselves and oppressing them."[30]
While Jefferson, unlike these Anti-Federalists, supported ratification of the Constitution, his argument for perpetual refoundings
(like his insistence on a bill of rights[31]) betrays a similar distrust of
distant, representative government.

Madison was clearly not inclined to enter into a *Federalist*-style
polemic with his friend, but his restrained reply was certainly Pub-
lian in spirit. A "well constituted" government, like the Constitution, could indeed provide for a proper institutional dependence of
its officers on the people—and continue to do so indefinitely. Moreover, given such formal arrangements, a spirited people, taught to
regard government as their own creation, would be vigilant enough
to see that their rights and interests were attended to. As an exas-
perated Madison declared to his Anti-Federalist critics, "What are
we to say to the men who profess the most flaming zeal for Republican Government yet boldly impeach the fundamental principle of
it; who pretend to be champions of the right and the capacity of
the people to chuse their own rulers, yet maintain that they will
prefer those only who will immediately and infallibly betray the
trust committed to them?"[32] This was the paradox at the heart of
Anti-Federalist thought, and it applied with special force to Jefferson's proposal. If the people lacked the character and intellect necessary for maintaining a republic, as he suggested, how could they
be expected to model their constitution anew in every generation?
Madison's combination of tacit consent, formal amendment, and
popular, representative government may have lacked the grandeur
of the political right of nature, defended by Jefferson in all its

breadth, but it had the considerable merits of consistency and "practicality."

Madison's reliance on republicanism as a relatively safe expression of consent was problematic in one important respect, however. It depended on the people's willingness to abide by the forms of the Constitution. Without such self-control, the present generation might rule with the same absolute sway promised to it under Jefferson's scheme. If republicanism was not to be capricious or oppressive, temporary *governing* majorities had to be prevented from mistaking themselves for the *sovereign* majority of the social compact. But how could this be accomplished?

Madison's solution was a kind of constitutional passion, an unthinking attachment to the Constitution as an end in itself. He briefly mentioned this idea in one of his queries to Jefferson: "Would not a Government so often revised become too mutable & novel to retain that share of prejudice in its favor which is a salutary aid to the most rational Government?"[33] But a fuller statement had come earlier, in *Federalist* 49, where he had aired another notable disagreement with Jefferson. In Number 49 Madison replied to a more limited application of Jefferson's concept of popular sovereignty: a proposal to resolve disputes over constitutional matters—particularly the separation of powers—by referring them to the people as a whole, acting through conventions. Even in this diluted form, Jefferson's resort to the people posed a threat to the political sentiments that Madison wished to cultivate.

> As every appeal to the people would carry an implication of some defect in the government, frequent appeals would in great measure deprive the government of that veneration, which time bestows on everything, and without which perhaps the wisest and freest governments would not possess the requisite stability. If it be true that all governments rest on opinion, it is no less true that the strength of opinion in each individual, and its practical influence on his conduct, depend much on the number which he supposes to have entertained the same opinion. The reason of man, like man himself is timid and cautious, when left alone; and acquires firmness and confidence, in proportion to the number with which it is associated. When the examples, which fortify opinion, are *antient*

as well as *numerous*, they are known to have a double effect. In a nation of philosophers, this consideration ought to be disregarded. A reverence for the laws, would be sufficiently inculcated by the voice of an enlightened reason. But a nation of philosophers is as little to be expected as the philosophical race of kings wished for by Plato. And in every other nation, the most rational government will not find it a superfluous advantage, to have the prejudices of the community on its side.[34]

Madison's language in these two passages—"prejudice," "veneration," "reverence"—seems to recommend an attitude of quiet respect, if not outright submission, on the part of the people. His tone is that of a traditionalist, of someone anxious to preserve established institutions. By commending the old, the customary, and the familiar, he evokes a set of claims seldom heard in American political thought. It is little wonder that these brief statements, uncharacteristic though they are, have led so many commentators to describe Madison as a conservative of a Humean or even a Burkean stripe.[35]

Is such a view tenable? Did Madison in fact concur with Hume in believing that "antiquity always begets the opinion of right"?[36] Or with Burke, that society is "a partnership not only between those who are living, but between those who are living, those who are dead, and those who are to be born"?[37] The difficulty with the comparison is that Madison's "conservatism" was conditional: it was not deference to the past as such, taken as a principle of social change and political action, but rather deference to a particular historical act, to *this* Constitution. The premise of his argument was that the regime in question could be classed among the "wisest," the "freest," and the "most rational" of governments. Such a regime would be endangered by a frequent return to first principles not because, in its respect for the past, it ignored the public good—this being the most serious charge against traditionalism per se—but because the people would not be able to see the extent to which the regime itself was the *source* of the public good. Only "a nation of philosophers" could learn reverence for the laws by observing this relationship directly.

More common sorts had to rely on mere "opinion" of a constitution's soundness—and not just the opinion of their contemporaries. In a regime based explicitly on the people's transhistorical right to alter or abolish constitutions, the fact that previous generations had not felt the need to avail themselves of this right had to carry some weight. The past became an extended referendum on constitutional arrangements. "Antient" examples fortified opinion not because they represented the superior wisdom or inspiration of founders but because they multiplied the number who had held that opinion. For Madison, veneration was to be a consequence of constitutional success over time, insulating a regime from precipitous change but not from all critical scrutiny. Thus, it was only a "salutary aid." The performance of a regime, its "rationality" in terms of its declared ends, was what ultimately decided its fate under the social compact. As Thomas L. Pangle aptly summarizes the relationship between reason and opinion in this passage, "One must not miss the forest for the trees."[38]

Madison does not explore the precise character of the veneration that he describes, but it is plainly a kind of prejudice or unconsidered opinion. It seems akin to republican virtue in Montesquieu's sense: "love of one's country, that is, the love of equality."[39] Yet Montesquieu's patriotic devotion is too vehement to be equated with Madisonian veneration.[40] Moreover, its operation is confined to a small republic where citizens constantly experience their equality in political activity.[41] Closer to the mark, as I have suggested, is what Aristotle calls "true opinion" *(doxa alēthēs)*. This virtue allows those who are ruled to make correct decisions, despite their lack of "political" prudence, which remains the ruler's peculiar virtue. Just as a flute player, with his broader understanding of the purposes of a flute, instructs the flute maker, so too do men of outstanding prudence instruct those who must participate in and perpetuate a regime.[42] In the American case, Madison apparently saw veneration as a way for the people to share the advantages of the Federal Convention's prudence without actually possessing that capacity themselves.

As compared to the political right of nature, Madison's version of "true opinion" may seem to describe "an almost abject trust" in "governmental power," as Garry Wills suggests.[43] Inasmuch as such opinion merely reflects the views of a given ruler, this is perhaps the case. For Madison, however, true opinion was to be attached not to the officers of the American regime but to its offices, not to its laws but to its Law. Instead of promoting popular resignation in the face of authority, this most rational of prejudices provided a standard against which the people could judge the actions and intentions of their representatives. It allowed them to preserve the constitutional forms that had served them well.

It is useful in this regard to contrast the responses of Madison and Jefferson to a patent violation of those forms—the Alien and Sedition Acts of 1798, a clumsy attempt by opportunistic Federalists to root out French agents and to suppress their Republican sympathizers. While the two Virginians agreed that the Federalist administration had acted far beyond the warrant of the Constitution and that opposition should come from the states, they framed the issue in very different terms. In his original draft of the Kentucky Resolutions, Jefferson proclaimed the unilateral authority of a state to act upon its view of a federal law's constitutionality: "Every state has a natural right in cases not within the compact . . . to nullify of their own authority all assumptions of power by others within their limits."[44] Though the state legislature softened this extraconstitutional language, the final version of the Kentucky Resolutions still showed a remarkable readiness to resort to first principles: "each party" to the dispute had "an equal right to judge for itself" both "the mode and measure of redress." The states possessed a "natural right" to declare the acts of the federal government "void and of no force." That this stance was to be taken in all seriousness was underscored in a second set of resolutions, passed a year later, in which Kentucky returned to Jefferson's original formulation, calling "nullification" the "rightful remedy" for "all unauthorized acts done under color" of the Constitution.[45]

Madison's Virginia Resolutions, while no less indignant, carefully avoided any appeal to a natural standard. He wrote as a defender of the Constitution itself rather than of the rights that made the creation of the Constitution possible. Though he exhorted the states "to interpose for arresting the progress of the evil," his purpose was clearly political—to encourage resistance to the Alien and Sedition Acts through the ordinary channels of republican government.[46] There was no suggestion of interfering with enforcement of the offending laws. As he explained, the Virginia Resolutions were meant to have no "other effect than what they may produce on *opinion*." Madison believed that recurring to the plain meaning of the

Constitution would rouse the people from their indifference, reminding them of the limits imposed in their name. In this way, the federal government's usurpations could be opposed through "the *legislative* expression of the general will."[47] The *sovereign* expression of that will—Jefferson's solution—was not required to restore constitutional government and would, just by being called forth, undermine its very foundations.

Late in his career, Madison was forcefully reminded of the problem posed by Jefferson's precedent. Confronted with the nullification doctrine of South Carolina, he could credibly claim that his own Virginia Resolutions provided no support for such state action.[48] But Jefferson's legacy was far more ambiguous, and Madison could protect his friend from posthumous appropriation by the nullifiers only by exposing the radicalism of his doctrine. What John C. Calhoun and his followers failed to see was the "essential distinction between a constitutional right and the natural and universal right of resisting intolerable oppression." Jefferson invoked the latter, not the former, in speaking of nullification; he did not suggest that "a single state could constitutionally resist a law of the Union while remaining within it." Jefferson, in short, was an advocate of secession.[49] As Madison well knew, this interpretation was useful for the case at hand: South Carolina was not prepared to assume sovereignty in the fullest sense. Its implications were more troubling for the events of 1798–99, however, and here Madison was notably silent. Far from returning the Constitution to its original aims, the Kentucky Resolutions, had they been acted on, would have brought the new American regime to an end. What Madison intended to venerate, Jefferson would have destroyed.

Government As It "Ought to Be"

In the spring of 1792, Alexander Hamilton was at the height of his success as the first secretary of the Treasury and as the de facto prime minister of George Washington's cabinet. Having convinced both Congress and the president that such measures as funding the national debt, nondiscrimination between its present and original holders, assumption of the states' debts, and the establishment of a national bank were all desirable and, in the case of the bank, constitutional, the major elements of his ambitious economic program were in place. Yet Hamilton was troubled. His efforts had generated strenuous opposition from a most unexpected source. "When I accepted the Office, I now hold," he confided to a correspondent, "it was under a full persuasion, that from similarity of thinking, conspiring with personal goodwill, I should have the firm support of Mr. Madison, in the *general course* of my administration. Aware of the intrinsic difficulties of the situation and of the powers of Mr. Madison, I do not believe I should have accepted under a different supposition."[50] At every turn, Hamilton had seen his collaborator at the Federal Convention and on *The Federalist* resist policies intended to secure the sort of national government that both men, it seemed, had so ardently sought: "This kind of conduct has appeared to me the more extraordinary on the part of Mr. Madison as I know for a certainty it was a primary article in his Creed that the real danger in our system was the subversion of the National authority by the preponderancy of the State Governments. All his measures have proceeded on an opposite supposition."[51] As Hamilton saw it, Madison was guilty of betrayal, both personal and political. Watching him assume the leadership of those "disposed to narrow the Federal authority," Hamilton could only conclude that his erstwhile ally had been so "seduced by the expectation of popularity and possibly by the calculation of advantage to the state of Virginia" that he had come to believe in the existence of "some dreadful combination against State Government and republicanism."[52]

Historians of the period have tended to echo Hamilton's assessment. According to the standard accounts, Madison underwent a dramatic political conversion between 1787 and the early 1790s, repudiating the nationalism that had guided him as a member of the Continental Congress and the Federal Convention and adopting in its stead the twin doctrines of states' rights and strict constitutional construction. The turning point, all agree, was his opposition in early 1791 to the chartering of a national bank, a move that he himself justified primarily on constitutional grounds. Students of these events, from Forrest McDonald to Irving Brant and Ralph Ketcham, have preferred to explain this supposed reversal on grounds of self-interest and ideological confusion—the motives identified by Hamilton—apportioning the two in conformity with their general attitude toward Madison.[53] Historians occasionally find a more principled reason for Madison's opposition—the knowledge, as Gaillard Hunt puts it, that "Hamilton's system was repugnant to a great majority of the people of America, whose attachments were local or sectional," or a recognition of what Brant calls "the need to impose general checks against a mounting federal imperialism."[54] Yet even they suggest that his appeal to fundamental law in opposing the bank was instrumental, even cynical.

This interpretation seems further confirmed by Madison's actions during his presidency, when he appeared to revert in part to Hamiltonian principles. Two key decisions combine to give the impression of inconsistency: his signing into law the charter of the second Bank of the United States and his nearly simultaneous veto of the bonus bill, a comprehensive plan for internal improvements, for reasons similar to those he cited in his original opposition to a national bank. Strict construction had apparently been left behind, or at least modified, as George W. Carey argues, but his new standard was difficult to discern.[55] In this view, Madison's career as a whole defies justification not only at the level of constitutional principle but also in terms of any wider theory.

The chief drawback of all these analyses is that they collide with a single, indisputable historical fact: Madison's repeated assertions of his own consistency. As he wrote toward the end of his life, "There were few, if any, of my contemporaries, through the long period and varied scenes of my political life, to whom a mutability of opinion was less applicable, on the great constitutional questions which have agitated the public mind."[56] To be sure, such a claim might be self-serving, a mere rationale for past mistakes. But it cannot be dismissed out of hand. I believe that Madison's claim can, in fact, be substantiated, that his seeming reversals point to a profound appreciation for the peculiar character of the Constitution and its origins in the social compact. "True opinion," so important in interpreting his dispute with Jefferson, also illuminates his break with Hamilton and (as discussed in the next chapter) the vexing constitutional issues of his own presidency. Madison's abiding constitutional principles are to be discovered in his efforts to restrain the overreaching of the few no less than of the many.

Because Alexander Hamilton is closely identified with the

movement in the 1780s for constitutional reform and with Washington's first administration, it is sometimes forgotten that he had deep reservations about the Constitution devised by the Federal Convention. As he confessed early in the proceedings at Philadelphia, he did "not . . . think favorably of Republican Government." He was of the opinion that the "British Government was the best in the world," that it was unique among known regimes in uniting "public strength with individual security." Recognizing that his was a minority view, he encouraged his republican-minded colleagues at least "to tone their Government as high as possible."[57]

This was the apparent intent of his own plan of government, presented in what is perhaps the Convention's single best-known speech. Hamilton proposed a national government with plenary powers of legislation, vested in an assembly that would be elected by the people every three years and in a senate and president who would be chosen by electors for terms limited only by good behavior. State governors, appointed by the national government, would have an unconditional veto over state laws. As Hamilton saw it, this was going "as far . . . as republican principles [would] admit" in order to achieve the "stability and permanency" required by good government.[58] Though the plan was indeed republican in the strictest sense, Hamilton's obvious distrust of the people, his designs on the state governments, and his great affection for monarchy did not sit well with the rest of the Convention. It was especially upsetting to Madison and his allies, who had carefully avoided any suggestion of monarchy or consolidation. However much they might have shared some of Hamilton's aims and concerns, they were astonished at his impolitic candor.[59]

By working assiduously for ratification of the Constitution, Hamilton helped to allay lingering doubts about his loyalty to so popular a regime. For his part, Madison welcomed the participation of Hamilton in the new administration, showing appreciation for the secretary of the Treasury's talents even while disagreeing with many of his early financial measures.[60] It is significant that Madison's tone was fairly amicable in resisting the purely economic part of Hamilton's program. Though Madison thought Hamilton wrong in, say, failing to compensate the deserving original holders of the national debt, he did not consider this a breach of fundamentals. Only with the bank bill—and what it revealed about

Hamilton's understanding of the Constitution—did Madison's opposition start to turn partisan.[61] As Jack N. Rakove puts it, "Manageable differences over policy began to develop into more volatile disagreements over principle."[62]

Madison would conclude over the course of the next year that it was Hamilton's intention to continue exercising the latitude assumed by the Federal Convention, to make founding an ongoing part of the regime by attempting to "administer the Government . . . into what he thought it ought to be."[63] Whereas Madison wished to suppress the distinction between the many and the few, thinking it incompatible in the end with the purposes of the social compact, Hamilton was set on perpetuating it by way of administration. He aimed to bring about a more adequate Constitution, even if it was not the one ratified by the people.[64] Since Madison himself had granted a measure of legitimacy to such prudential claims, it became his burden to make the case for fidelity to the limited, federal regime that had emerged from the one founding moment he was willing to recognize.

The dispute between Hamilton and Madison is usually thought to hinge on their interpretations of the Constitution's enumerated powers, with Hamilton seeking to exploit every possible implication and Madison insisting on a narrower, more literal view. Yet the issue is better understood if framed more broadly. Ultimately, it concerns not the *degree* to which enumerated powers ought to limit discretion but *whether* they should. In other words, the disagreement between Hamilton and Madison goes beyond this particular constitution and considers the nature of modern constitutionalism itself.

A progression can be detected in Hamilton's thought on these matters, or at least in his exposition of it. In defending the bank bill, he did not pretend that the power of incorporation was among those listed in the Constitution. Instead he classed it among "implied" as opposed to "express" powers. It was simply an *"instrument"* or *"mean"* for carrying into effect powers that were indisputably granted to the national government (in this case, borrowing money and laying and collecting taxes). To the objection that such a measure could not be described as "necessary and proper" (in the sense of Article I, section 8), Hamilton replied that "necessary" in this instance was not to be taken in a restrictive sense, "as if the word *absolutely* or *indispensably* had been prefixed to it," but rather in its more common usage, as meaning "*needful, requisite, incidental, useful,* or *conducive to.*" As Hamilton acknowledged, this amounted to a grant of "plenary and sovereign authority" to the national government, but only with respect to its "*specified powers* and *objects.*" He justified this interpretation of the Constitution on grounds familiar to any reader of *The Federalist:* "The means by which national exigencies are to be provided for, national inconveniencies obviated, national prosperity promoted, are of such infinite variety, extent and complexity, that there must, of necessity, be great latitude of discretion in the selection & application of those means. Hence consequently, the necessity & propriety of exercising the authorities intrusted to a government on principles of liberal construction."[65] The urgent needs of the nation could be addressed within the scope of the Constitution, provided that its powers were understood to include a wide array of means.

A secondary theme of Hamilton's defense of the bank bill was more troubling, however. At points he suggested that the power in question belonged to the national government not because of its relationship to a specific constitutional provision but because it was necessary to accomplish the broad ends of civil society. Thus a liberal construction of the Constitution was not just intended to give operational energy to enumerated powers; it also provided a license for the "general administration of the affairs of the country"—"its finances, trade, defence, etc."—to be conducted in such a way as to achieve the "advancement of the public good." As Hamilton said in a telling passage, "This rule does not depend on the particular form of government or on the particular demarkation of the boundaries of its powers, but on the nature and objects of government itself." Needless to say, public authority could not be arbitrary in the pursuit of these goals: "No government has a right to do *merely what it pleases.*" Rather, government was limited in both a negative and a positive sense: by "restrictions and exceptions specified in the constitution," on the one hand, and by "the essential ends of political society," on the other. Hamilton said nothing here about the restrictive meaning of granted constitutional powers.[66]

As Hamilton tried to expand his program, he was compelled to rely more heavily on this second argument. The liberal construction of specified powers would no longer do. He had to state more forthrightly what he had only implied in his defense of the bank bill: that the public good was the sole general constraint on the powers of the national government. This principle first emerged in his famous "Report on Manufactures." The power in question on this occasion was the establishment of bounties to encourage particular industries—again, a power not specified in the Constitution. Hamilton asserted that the objects for which public monies could be appropriated were "no less comprehensive . . . than the payment of the public debts and the providing for the common defence and *'general Welfare.'*" Whereas before he had relied on the "necessary and proper" clause for an expansive reading of the national government's *powers*, he now turned to the "general welfare" clause to go still further, to give the government a wide authority to determine its own *objects*.

> The terms *"general Welfare"* were doubtless intended to signify more than was expressed or imported in those which Preceded; otherwise numerous exigencies incident to the affairs of a Nation would have been left without a provision. The phrase is as comprehensive as any that could have been used; because it was not fit that the constitutional authority of the Union, to appropriate its revenues shou'd have been restricted within narrower limits than the "General Welfare" and because this necessarily embraces a vast variety of particulars, which are susceptible neither of specification nor of definition. . . . It is therefore of necessity left to the discretion of the National Legislature, to pronounce, upon the objects, which concern the general Welfare, and for which under that description, an appropriation of money is requisite and proper.[67]

With this formulation, Hamilton could finally leave behind the constitutional shackles that interfered with a vigorous prosecution of the public good. So ample a "discretion" for the national legislature meant latitude for the government as a whole, and not least for an administration prepared to endow it with energy, purpose, and a general bearing rather different from what was intended by its architects and ratifiers.

Such an elevation of the public good was hardly unique to

Hamilton. Indeed, it is integral to the social-compact tradition, though not to that part of it most important to his political opponents. Hamilton seemed to be of two minds with respect to the relationship between the people and their government. He often joined Madison in presenting the social compact as a trusteeship, a limited commission that might be modified or revoked as the people saw fit. Yet he also maintained at times that an established government was as much a party to the social compact as those who created it. As he argued in one of his earliest writings, "The origin of all civil government, justly established, must be a voluntary compact, *between* the rulers and the ruled."[68]

If trusteeship showed the influence of Locke, the idea of reciprocity was derived from William Blackstone, a writer who exerted a strong influence on the young Hamilton.[69] This latter view, it should be noted, was also based on the modern doctrine of natural equality. As Hamilton observed, Blackstone's law of nature embraced "the natural rights of mankind," which included "the means of preserving and beatifying [their] existence."[70] Where this teaching on the law of nature departed from its Lockean counterpart was in bestowing on government a presumptive right to determine the means necessary for giving effect to that law. Because the government, no less than the people, had something of an independent standing, it could decide on its own what was necessary to fulfill its obligations. Civil authority was not limited by the people's notion of what would conduce to the preservation of society; it acted in the belief that, ultimately, its performance would win popular confidence and support.

Such willingness to give a free hand to government in upholding its end of the social compact was also not completely foreign to Locke, whom Hamilton mentioned as an advocate of the natural rights of mankind in almost the same breath with Blackstone.[71] This was not to deny the centrality of the popular right of revolution in Locke's political thought, where the people alone finally judge a government's fidelity to its trust. But Locke clearly held that a just government is limited much more by its objects than by the particular means available to achieve them. Thus, the legislative power is "absolute" so long as it pursues the ends of civil society; enumerated powers do not enter into the picture.[72] At the same time, government must not be "arbitrary." Its authority, though absolute in its sphere, must be exercised moderately and without making invidious distinctions among persons. To achieve these ends, Locke defined constitutionalism in terms of the various formal limits—separation and balance of powers, the rule of law, consent to taxation—that all governments had to respect.[73]

Hamilton understood constitutionalism in much the same way. As we have seen, the plan that he presented to the Federal Convention, while giving the national government plenary powers of legislation, also attempted to ensure the safe exercise of those powers: the people would possess a real (if circumscribed) voice, and the departments of government would be placed on a footing that encouraged their independence and the vigorous defense of their own prerogatives. Such a government—soundly partitioned and operating through the rule of law—was "free" according to Hamilton. In this account, the primary purpose of a constitution is not to decide what powers are necessary for the security and prosperity of the people but to see that necessary powers are not used arbitrarily.[74] The choice of means and of objects (in all but the very broadest sense) belongs to government—which is to say, to the governors.

Whatever his final opinion of Hamilton's motives, Madison initially treated the constitutional doctrines of the secretary of the Treasury and his supporters as mistaken rather than sinister. In opposing the bank bill on the floor of the House, he did not even begin with the question of authority and instead briefly cited his objections on policy grounds. But his main concerns were constitutional, and he matched the emphases in Hamilton's own argument. On the matter of how to interpret the Constitution's enumerated powers, Madison agreed that a narrow literalism would render the government inoperable. The "necessary and proper" clause *was* intended to give Congress a certain latitude—but only in the execution of its specified powers. In place of the "diffuse and ductile" terms favored by friends of the bill as synonyms for "necessary," he suggested that only "direct and incidental" means were available under the Constitution. Without such a rule of construction, the "essential characteristic of the government, as composed of limited and enumerated powers, would be destroyed." "Mark the reasoning on which the validity of the bill depends," he warned. "To borrow money is made the *end* and the accumulation of capitals, *implied* as the *means*. The accumulation of capitals is then the *end*, and a bank *implied* as the *means*. The bank is then the *end*, and a charter of incorporation, a monopoly, capital punishments, &c. *implied* as the *means*. . . . If implications, thus remote and multiplied, can be linked together, a chain may be formed that will reach every object of legislation, every object within the whole compass of political economy." The danger of such reasoning was forcefully illustrated by the very power in question. Not only was a right to grant charters of incorporation not included in the Constitution but, Madison declared, it had been explicitly proposed and rejected at the Federal Convention—a point that he must have recalled with some irony, since he had been the chief proponent of the power in Philadelphia.[75]

Madison did not devote much time to rebutting Hamilton's more ambitious (but less prominent) argument—that this kind of power belonged to government as such and was inseparable from its capacity to secure the public good. He did show an awareness, however, of this proposition's great potential for mischief. While certain lesser, instrumental powers could be deduced from those enumerated in the Constitution, he argued, no additional powers "could be inferred from the general nature of government." It was the "peculiar nature" of the national government that its authority was expressly described, no matter how crucial certain absent powers might appear to be. Thus, if "the power of making treaties, for example, [had] been omitted . . . the defect could only have been lamented, or supplied by an amendment of the constitution."[76] He was willing to accept the view that "government necessarily possesses every power." But it was true only "in theory" and did not apply to the government of the United States.[77]

As these statements suggest, Madison also followed Locke in considering government absolute in its proper sphere. He differed from Hamilton, though, in seeing the Constitution as an unprecedented but necessary attempt to divide that sphere. Writing as Publius just a few years earlier, he had urged that the new regime not be compared to the "idea of a national Government," which "involves in it . . . an indefinite supremacy over all persons and things, so far as they are objects of lawful Government."[78] Only the state governments, in the wide sphere left to them by the Constitution, possessed such unbounded jurisdiction.[79] Though the most obvious reason for confining the national government in this way was to accommodate the pretensions of the states, it had other grounds as well. As we shall see, Madison believed that so distant an authority could be superintended by the people only if its powers were both strictly enumerated and popularly held to be such.

Whatever the rationale for the breadth of interpretation assumed by the sponsors of the bank bill, Madison insisted that it would confirm the worst fears of the Constitution's detractors. Advocates of the Constitution had initially opposed a bill of rights because, they claimed, "powers not given were retained" and "those given were not to be extended by remote implications." This was certainly the belief that had prevailed in the state ratifying conventions, and it had been reiterated in the "explanatory amendments"—what would become the Ninth and Tenth Amendments to the Constitution—proposed by Congress itself. Now, Madison argued, Congress was giving serious thought to overthrowing these common understandings. Drawing a parallel to the Federal Convention, he suggested that the bank bill was an attempt to extend the process of constitution making beyond its legitimate term: "With all this evidence of the sense in which the constitution was understood and adopted, will it not be said, if the bill should pass, that its adoption was brought by one set of arguments, and that it is now administered under the influence of another set; and this reproach will have the keener sting, because it is applicable to so many individuals concerned in both the adoption and the administration." At this point, Madison was not prepared to say that such principles of administration represented an actual conspiracy against the Constitution. But he did emphasize that they would be seen in this light by those distrustful of the few. Out of "respect for ourselves," he told his colleagues, "the appearance of precipitancy and ambition should be shunned."[80] If they failed to do so, they would threaten "the principles on which . . . this government ought to be administered": "the enlightened opinion and affection of the people."[81]

These themes assumed special prominence as Madison's struggle against Hamilton intensified, leading him to conclude finally that the secretary of the Treasury was, in fact, the head of an aristocratic plot to undo the Constitution ratified by the people. The precipitating event for Madison was Hamilton's outright endorsement, in his "Report on Manufactures," of the view that the "general welfare" was the only meaningful constraint on national power. As Madison observed, "The federal Gov[ernmen]t has been hitherto limited to the Specified powers, by the greatest Champions for Latitude in expounding those powers. If not only the *means*, but the *objects* are unlimited, the parchment had better be thrown into the fire at once."[82] Should such a "usurpation" succeed, "the fundamental and characteristic principle of the Gov[ernmen]t" would be "subverted."[83] With this, Madison's opposition, which had previously centered on the particular measures of Hamilton's program, turned to the administration itself. The republican cause was transformed into the Republican Party, with the political demise of Hamilton and his principles as its end.[84]

The clearest sign of this change can be found in a series of anonymous essays that Madison wrote soon after for the *National Gazette*. In these short, polemical pieces, Madison located the origin of the "anti-republican" party in the movement for the Constitution or, more precisely, in a few individuals "who were openly or secretly attached to monarchy and aristocracy" and "hoped to make the Constitution a cradle for these hereditary establishments." Even in the heat of partisan rhetoric, however, Madison recognized that this minority was not merely self-seeking, that it acted on a public principle. It was persuaded that "mankind are incapable of governing themselves" and had, accordingly, adopted a plan of administration under which the government "may by degrees be narrowed into fewer hands, and approximated to an hereditary form." The "Republican party"—as Madison calls it in his first recorded use of the term—sought to disprove these views. It regarded them as "an insult to the reason and an outrage to the rights of man," maintaining that public measures ought to appeal "both to the understanding and to the general interest of the community." Nor was this simply a matter of republican pride. However convinced the enemies of republicanism might be that the people did not know how to serve their own broad interests, they themselves had proved to be imperfectly attentive to the public good. In their efforts to bring about a more oligarchical regime, they had found it necessary to "strengthen themselves with the men of influence, particularly of moneyed, which is the most active and insinuating influence." In practice, this had meant not a government more capable of pursuing the general welfare but one whose measures were pointed "less to the interest of the many than of the few."[85]

Money-fed political corruption was the bête noire of the eighteenth-century "country" ideology that Madison is sometimes said to represent. According to the adherents of the "ideological" school, this strain of Anglo-American republicanism stood in explicit opposition to liberalism and its selfish material concerns. As Michael P. Zuckert has shown, however, country ideology, properly understood, often employed the rhetoric and practice of republicanism to achieve liberal ends.[86] Indeed, Madison's attack on "influence" fits neatly with his long-standing determination to see a balance struck between the rights of property and the rights of persons. For him, corruption was a deliberate challenge to constitutional government on the part of "interested partisans" who sought to establish "a real domination of the few" in the midst of "an apparent liberty of the many."[87] The danger was not just that administration and policy might become one-sided. It was that the national government, drawing an ever greater number of public responsibilities to itself, might soon overwhelm the people's capacity for informed "control" of the legislature, which was "essential to a faithful discharge of its trust." Under such "universal silence and insensibility," the government would soon be left to a *self directed course.*[88]

And how was this counterrevolutionary movement to be resisted? In the most hortatory of his essays for the *National Gazette,* Madison invokes the logic of the social compact, trumpeting its proud claims of popular self-sufficiency in the hope of creating a fuller—and more active—attachment to the Constitution's forms and limits. The people, he insists, had to think of their regime much as they did their property, as a personal possession that required jealous and energetic protection:

> In bestowing the eulogies due to the partitions and internal checks of power, it ought not the less to be remembered, that they are neither the sole nor the chief palladium of constitutional liberty. The people who are the authors of this blessing, must also be its guardians. Their eyes must be ever ready to mark, their voice to pronounce, and their arm to repel or repair

aggressions on the authority of their constitutions; the highest authority next to their own, because the immediate work of their own, and the most sacred part of their property, as recognising and recording the title of every other.[89]

In another essay, this one reminiscent of *Federalist* 49 and his exchange with Jefferson, Madison wrote of the need for "a more than common reverence for the authority which is to preserve order thro' the whole." This species of opinion was peculiar to a regime of the American type and crucial to its ultimate success: "How devoutly is it to be wished . . . that the public opinion of the United States should be enlightened; that it should attach itself to their governments as delineated in the *great charters*, derived not from the usurped power of kings, but from the legitimate authority of the people; and that it should guarantee, with a holy zeal, these political scriptures from every attempt to add to or to diminish from them."[90]

Though Madison speaks metaphorically in these passages, his tropes were not accidental. Expressions like "blessing," "sacred," "reverence," "devoutly," "holy zeal," and "political scriptures" point to the very heart of his intention. It is no exaggeration to say that his answer to Hamilton was to propose a kind of godless civil religion, with the Constitution serving as an altar on which the people could proudly declare the sanctity of the political right of nature. The most immediate purpose of this faith was to rebuke the aristocratic pretensions of Hamilton and his followers. The people, for all of their faults, remained the surest guardians of their own legitimate rights and interests. Whatever the requirements of founding, with its necessary distance from popular views, it was unsafe for government to ask "nothing but obedience" from the people while "leaving the care of their liberties to their wiser rulers."[91] Instead, the people owed obedience to the Constitution and thus, indirectly, to themselves.

Even as he battled Hamilton in the name of the people, however, Madison did not lose sight of the possibility of popular wrongdoing. For all the energy that he devoted to resisting a minority faction—no small irony in light of his analysis in *Federalist* 10—he understood that the majority was the abiding threat. Here too he expected veneration to act as a constraint on popular passions and interests. By "establishing permanent and constitutional maxims of conduct," he wrote, "the will of the society" could be subjected to "the reason of the society." In this way, the Constitution could prevail over the people's "occasional impressions" and "inconsiderate pursuits."[92]

Madison realized that his version of strict constitutional construction, even when given practical effect by public opinion, was not sufficient for dealing with all the questions of authority that might arise under the Constitution. In the first place, Hamilton had largely succeeded. Though his principles were ultimately repudiated by the electorate, his achievements remained: whether or not it was warranted by the Constitution, the Bank of the United States had been established, complete with national charter, and had quickly become a key instrument of national economic policy. Moreover, Hamilton had set certain precedents for interpreting the Constitution. If his political failure meant that these views could no longer be put in the service of the few, the same was not true of the many. Liberal construction, based on a broad view of the "general welfare," was not peculiar to crypto-aristocrats. The people could employ it too, furthering their notions of the public good while ignoring the dangers inherent in such discretion. For Madison, American constitutionalism would be successful only if it could continue to inculcate "true" opinion while accommodating the inevitable excesses of both the many and the few. Past usurpations would have to be constitutionalized—that is, accepted as being consistent with the Constitution—but in such a way as to discourage their repetition.

Chapter Six

The Legitimate Meaning
of the Constitution

Considering the heated disputes over constitutional interpretation that erupted almost immediately after the new government's inauguration, it is surprising to discover how little discussion of the subject there is in the proceedings of the Federal Convention and in the debate over ratification that followed. This can be explained in part by the self-defining character of much of the Constitution. The text speaks with great clarity on such structural questions as the division of the legislative branch into the House and Senate and the qualifications and tenure of the president. But the Constitution was necessarily vaguer with respect to its powers. All conceded that it would have been impractical to describe every lesser power needed to implement the enumerated grants of authority. It would have demanded, as Madison wrote, "a complete digest of the laws on every subject to which the Constitution relates."[1] Such particulars were too various and minute to be included in a fundamental law and, moreover, would have to change with circumstances. Looking ahead to the new regime, Madison assumed that the extent of national authority would simply emerge with constitutional practice over time, its precise contours "liquidated and ascertained by a series of particular discussions and adjudications."[2]

As Madison quickly learned, however, it was essential to have a more definitive answer to this question of national authority. Hamilton had one, to be sure. His insight, as we have seen, was to recast the problem, viewing it in terms not of the government's powers but of its objects. These he understood expansively, taking his guidance less from the specific provisions of the Constitution than from the widest aims of the social compact—peace, prosperity, and the national greatness that might secure them. If the government's powers were not commensurate to these ends, then civil society had no purpose; it was a cruel ruse, pretending to overcome the state of nature while inviting its return. For Hamilton, then, the Constitution *was* limited, but only by its division and balance of power and by the rights that it explicitly protected. With this plausible and forceful reading of the social compact, he offered what Madison lacked, or at least what he had thus far failed to articulate: a theory of constitutional interpretation.

In coming to terms with this defect in his own thought, Madison gave practical effect to his criticisms of both Hamilton and Jefferson. His aim was to transcend the constitutive claims of the social compact, to prevent both the few and the many from exercising an arbitrary authority. This called for an emphasis on the *legitimacy* of the founding, on the right of the people, acting in their sovereign capacity, to establish a binding fundamental law. Madison advocated a species of what is now known as constitutional originalism, stressing the plain meaning of the text itself and the sense in which it was understood when ratified. Legitimacy, in this view, was the counterpoint to prudence—that is, to the ongoing authority of the Federal Convention and those who considered themselves its successors. Like many present-day advocates of originalism (but with key differences), Madison wished to deprive the few of any special privilege in deciding the meaning of the Constitution. In this way, he at once answered Hamilton and suppressed the most controversial claims in his own distinctive account of the social compact.

If originalism bears an obvious relation to the constitutional veneration so central to Madison's political thought, the same cannot be said of his second important rule of interpretation: that long-established legislative precedents, when widely accepted, attain constitutional standing, even if unauthorized by the Constitution. Here we enter into the much-disputed decisions of Madison's presidency—his signing into law the second Bank of the United States and his veto of the bonus bill, a comprehensive measure for internal improvements. These decisions, I will argue, represent a principled attempt to maintain a distinction between the governing majority and the sovereign majority of the social compact. For Madison, the abiding danger posed by Hamilton's example was that it might prompt the people to overleap the bounds of the Constitution, especially in pursuit of some ostensible public good. By allowing for the possibility of a "prescriptive" Constitution,[3] he hoped to control the construction placed on such inevitable usurpations and to turn them into narrow constitutional amendments of a sort, thereby resisting any effort to draw wider principles from them.

Text and Context

For many students of Madison's political thought, his activities in the 1790s are virtually irreconcilable with those of the previous decade, especially on the question of constitutional interpretation. Irving Brant, in his great biography, set the tone for these accounts. On the bank issue, he wrote, Madison broke "sharply with his generally broad concept of federal power." Fearing the rise of a financial oligarchy, he was "propelled ... into a lifelong argument against some of the most important principles he had helped to plant in the Constitution."[4] Other scholars have seen in these events a similar repudiation of earlier positions. Instead of joining in "seemingly natural alliance with the forces of an energetic national government," observes Paul C. Peterson, Madison in the 1790s emerged as the co-leader of "the forces of a restricted and decidedly non-energetic government." The realignment was "enigmatic."[5] Less charitably, it was, in the words of George W. Carey, "schizophrenic."[6]

These indictments of Madison are based on a false premise. They assume that his "nationalism" necessarily implied the broad construction of national powers, that the Constitution was a meaningful reform only if animated by Hamiltonian principles of administration. From this perspective, it is not enough that both Madison and Hamilton sought a more energetic national government as the Articles of Confederation crumbled; it must be supposed as well that they were of a single mind as to the extent of the government's powers, its relation to the states, and the substantive ends of its economic policies. As Lance Banning has so ably demonstrated, this line of reasoning is insupportable. It turns the real but limited consensus among the Constitution's supporters into a monolith of thought and action.[7]

Madison's distinctiveness is nowhere more evident than with respect to constitutional interpretation. From the moment he entered national politics, he was a vocal and consistent advocate of strict construction. Though the defects of the Articles of Confederation were apparent to him from the start, he repeatedly urged restraint on the Continental Congress in the face of its enumerated powers. The most interesting of these cases for the present discussion concerned the chartering of a national bank—the Articles of Confederation, like the Constitution, were silent on the power of incorporation—but Madison expressed his constitutional scruples across a full range of policies that he both favored and opposed on their merits. He raised doubts about congressional action on such matters as coercing states that failed to comply with national measures, resolving territorial disputes among the states, regulating illicit trade, maintaining a peacetime army, establishing the jurisdiction of Congress over its permanent seat, and managing relations with the Indians.[8] In language soon to be heard again in the partisan disputes of the 1790s, he asserted that "the spirit of a free constitution" required that "all exercise of power be explicitly and precisely warranted" and warned of "the poisonous tendency of precedents of usurpation."[9] Despite his concerns in this period about the feebleness of the national government, Madison never suggested that the solution lay in giving it a general and unrestricted authority to seek the public good.[10]

At the same time, Madison did not insist upon a crabbed and crippling literalism in arriving at the meaning of a constitution's provisions. As we have already seen, he was no enemy of implied powers, so long as such powers bore some immediate relationship to those that were enumerated. Under the Articles of Confederation, for instance, he showed little patience for the jealous advocates of states' rights who wished to deny Congress the right to grant flags of truce, a privilege unmentioned in the articles. "It is a lesser power evidently involved in the major one of making peace," Madison wrote. "A flag is a partial truce as a truce is a temporary peace."[11] Likewise, under the Constitution, he was fully prepared to see its terms read with a reasonable breadth. In an early controversy over whether or not the president could remove an appointee unilaterally (that is, without the concurrence of two-thirds of the Senate), Madison found ample room for the prerogative in the very nature of executive authority as described by the Constitution. Otherwise, the power of the president would be a "mere vapor," his "responsibility . . . annihilated," thus depriving the executive branch of its special character in relation to the other departments and the people. This was manifestly not the Constitution's intent.[12]

These examples clarify Madison's more general statements that supposedly reveal a Hamiltonian readiness to empower the federal government. Accordingly, whatever hairsplitting one might do with the peculiar locutions of *Federalist* 44,[13] Madison plainly asserts that only those "particular powers, requisite as means of executing general powers," belong to the general government "by unavoidable implication."[14] This principle removes any sinister inference that might be drawn from his reluctance to see the national government confined to "express" powers in the wording of what would become the Tenth Amendment.[15] He had long maintained that it was impossible for any government to be so delimited and, unlike latter-day analysts of his thought,[16] did not see this relatively permissive language as incompatible with strict construction.[17]

Until the appearance of the bank bill and the arguments that were put forward to justify it, Madison said little about the grounds for this approach to constitutional interpretation. He may simply have considered it the obvious method for applying a government charter, deriving from the known "rules of construction" and "legal axioms" to which he referred on occasion and which modern scholars have associated with the techniques of the common law.[18] But Hamilton's theory had to be met by a theory, and Madison was compelled to elaborate. If Hamilton and his allies stressed the open-endedness of constitution making, implicitly appealing to the prudential claims of the Federal Convention, Madison would have to rely on the more conventional aspect of the founding—the indubitable authority of the people. What mattered, he would insist, was not the *intentions* of the framers but rather the *common understandings* of the ratifiers.

The need for an argument that distinguished between the

making of the Constitution and its establishment apparently occurred to Madison during the controversy over the bank bill. In the debate on the measure, as we have seen, he himself turned to the authority of the Federal Convention, recalling that the power of incorporation had been considered and rejected in Philadelphia. It was the first and last time that he would use such an argument in public. His position was untenable, he realized, since almost half of the members of the Senate, which gave its unanimous approval to the bill, had been delegates to the Federal Convention, as had five of the bank's supporters in the House.[19] This discord pointed to the difficulty of determining the framers' intent, whether with respect to specific powers or general rules of constitutional construction. More importantly, the very nature of the argument gave the framers a privileged position in interpreting the Constitution, allowing their intentions to be invoked against, as Madison saw it, both the plain meaning of the text and the sense in which it was accepted by the people. In a few short years, he would offer an alternative theory of constitutional interpretation, one that would greatly circumscribe these claims:

> Whatever veneration might be entertained for the body of men who formed our Constitution, the sense of that body could never be regarded as the oracular guide in expounding the Constitution. As the instrument came from them it was nothing more than the draft of a plan, nothing but a dead letter, until life and validity were breathed into it by the voice of the people, speaking through the several State Conventions. If we were to look, therefore, for the meaning of the instrument beyond the face of the instrument, we must look for it, not in the General Convention, which proposed, but in the State Conventions, which accepted and ratified the Constitution.[20]

To preserve veneration for the Constitution, veneration for its architects would have to be kept in check.

This helps to explain Madison's stubborn refusal to publish during his lifetime his notes from the Federal Convention—easily the most careful and comprehensive ones taken during the summer of 1787. As he wrote in his retirement, he had thought it best to delay publication "until the Constitution should be well settled by practice," when the Convention's more controversial discussions "could be turned to no improper account." The record of the debates possessed, after all, "no authoritative character" as a "guide in expounding and applying the provisions of the Constitution," the "origin" of the instrument being a separate matter from its "legitimate meaning."[21] His determination to exclude the Convention from constitutional disputes was tested on several occasions, but even when confronted after 1828 by the movement for nullification, he refrained, as Donald O. Dewey points out, from direct appeal to sources that he alone possessed.[22]

For Madison, the argument of original intent, as applied to the framers, was powerfully associated with Hamiltonian rules of construction. It depended on "the opinions entertained in *forming* the Constitution" as opposed to "its true meaning as understood *by the nation* at the time of its ratification"—the meaning that all were duty-bound to support. Original intent could thus serve as a rationale for "political tenets . . . which were capable of transforming [the Constitution] into something very different from its legitimate character as the offspring of the National Will."[23] If the Convention's understanding of the scope of national authority ranked above that of the people, it perhaps followed that the government's view of the matter did as well.

Predictably, Madison's position on these issues has been of interest in the modern debate over a jurisprudence of original intent. Though his own constitutional concerns focused mainly on the legislative branch (a telling difference between eras in itself), his views can indeed be transposed, with due care, to judicial questions. That said, it would be fair to cast him as a critic of the cruder expressions of original-intent jurisprudence, which elevate the meaning attached to the Constitution by the members of the Federal Convention.[24] For Madison, such reliance on the framers was both inconclusive and dangerous. Nevertheless, his ideas are rightly seen as a variety of originalism. He is the inspiration for those present-day versions of the doctrine that depend on the popular or general understanding of constitutional provisions at the time of their ratification (though, as we shall see, Madison applied this test with far greater consistency than do many of his intellectual heirs).

What Madison shares with contemporary advocates of judicial

restraint is a profound fear of oligarchy disguised as republican constitutionalism, of rule by the few under the forms but not the substance of limited, popular government. The epithets that conservatives direct at the modern Supreme Court—charging, for example, that its decisions often represent little more than "the unfettered and inevitably arbitrary wills of an elite few"[25]—bear a striking and not coincidental resemblance to Madison's denunciations of Hamilton and his allies. Like Justice Hugo Black, dissenting in *Griswold* v. *Connecticut*, Madison was wary of any principle of construction that would turn a branch of the national government into a "day to day constitutional convention."[26] In fact, his primary political aim in the 1790s was to overcome the example of the Federal Convention and to tame the notions of prudential prerogative that it imparted to the politics of the early republic.[27]

Madison was not unaware of his theory's difficulties. After all, how was one to determine the popular understanding of a given constitutional provision at the time of ratification? Who counted as a ratifier? What was one to make of disagreement among the ratifiers or of their silence respecting some controversial point? As with the attempt to determine the intention of the framers, serious questions of authority remained.

Madison did not pretend that it was possible to establish the definitive views of the popular sovereign, of the people themselves as ultimate ratifiers. The ratifying conventions were a close enough approximation, but even then his standards were not especially exacting. Records of the debates were available from only a few states in his day, and most of these were far from complete. Thus, in defending the power of the national government to impose a protective tariff, Madison could cite relevant speeches from the Massachusetts convention but had to concede that it was "the only one in New England" whose debates had been preserved. He was content to infer that the sentiments expressed there were akin to those of similarly situated states like Rhode Island and Connecticut. From the "partial account" then available of the debate in Pennsylvania, nothing could be concluded, since there was no mention of the tariff question. And in Virginia and North Carolina, the only two southern states whose proceedings had been preserved, he could only say that "no adverse inferences" could be drawn on the subject.[28] This appeal to the actual records of the Constitution's ratification is unique in Madison's writings: nowhere else does he explicitly refer to the deliberations of the various state conventions. His usual practice was to recall, in the most general terms, the discussion in the Virginia convention of which he was a member. Evidently, exhaustive historical research was not what he had in mind when he suggested that the true meaning of the Constitution was to be found in the ratifying conventions.[29]

Nor was Madison under the illusion that fidelity to the Constitution's ratifiers would somehow put an end to all constitutional controversy. On the question of a protective tariff, there was at least some evidence of how the power over trade was generally understood by the state conventions. Other parts of the Constitution had been passed over in silence or discussed in only slight detail. Madison never suggested, for example, that the dispute over the executive's removal power might be resolved by delving into the ratification debates. Nor did he attempt to use them in ascertaining whether the House might constitutionally refuse to fund a treaty that had been duly approved by the Senate and the president—a question on which he thought the provisions of the Constitution "literally at variance with each other."[30]

For Madison, there was an irreducible degree of ambiguity and indeterminacy in the fundamental law, and no amount of attention to text or context could eliminate it. The past was simply opaque on some points of obvious practical importance. Constitutional orthodoxy would have to be decided, at least in part, in the future. As he explained late in life, echoing the view expressed years before in *Federalist* 37: "It could not but happen, and was foreseen at the birth of the Constitution, that difficulties and differences of opinion might occasionally arise in expounding terms & phrases necessarily used in such a charter . . . and that it might require a regular course of practice to liquidate & settle the meaning of some of them."[31] Respect for the ratifiers of the Constitution meant, among other things, finishing the task that they had left undone.

Having conceded the limitations of seeking guidance from the historical record, Madison cannot be charged with an unrealistic reliance on "specific intent," one of the more common criticisms leveled from both the bench and the academy at today's proponents of constitutional originalism.[32] He did not expect that deference to the state ratifying conventions would produce infallible rules of construction or settle every case. On those few occasions when he referred to the people's "intentions,"[33] he clearly construed them in a broad fashion. Over the years he preferred to speak instead of their "sense" of the ratified Constitution.[34] By this he meant their general understanding of its purposes, powers, and design. For Madison, this was the true voice of the popular sovereign, the legitimate arbiter of the Constitution's meaning. And while it was unlikely to be dispositive in a given constitutional dispute, it did set the boundaries within which such disputes could take place.

Maintaining the "sense" of the Constitution required, in the first place, that the meaning of the instrument not be transformed by changes in the meaning of words and expressions. Ever aware of the inexactitude of "the medium through which the conceptions of men are conveyed to each other,"[35] Madison feared that linguistic innovation might take its toll on the Constitution. "If the meaning of the text is to be sought in the changeable meaning of the words composing it," he wrote, "it is evident that the shape and attributes of the government must partake of the changes to which the words and phrases of all living languages are constantly subject. What a metamorphosis would be produced in the code of law if all its ancient phraseology were to be taken in its modern sense!"[36] For this reason, constitutional terms had to be defined as they were at the time of ratification, in accord with "the original and authentic meaning attached to them."[37]

Unfortunately, it is hard to know exactly which terms Madison thought most in jeopardy. He offered only one illustration of a spurious redefinition, and it was not even strictly constitutional: he repeatedly insisted that the word "national," as used in the Virginia Plan at the Federal Convention, was not to be equated with "consolidated," though some considered them synonymous by the 1830s.[38] On the evidence of his more general view, however, one can safely assume that he would have objected to methods of construction that favor contemporary or "evolving" standards for the definition of key constitutional terms. For Madison, if "the ultimate question" was "what do the words of the text mean in our time," as Justice William Brennan proclaimed,[39] the Constitution ceased to be fundamental law in any meaningful sense.

Madison also thought it possible to judge proposed readings

of the Constitution by how they would have been received during the ratification debate, in relation to the known concerns of that day. As we have seen, he considered the national government's right to impose a protective tariff as firmly established by the fact that the Constitution's broad grant of authority over trade was uncontroversial in the state conventions. It prompted neither protests nor urgent demands for clarification. Even the fragmentary record of the ratification debates confirmed as much. But the tariff was an unusual issue for Madison, in that he was defending a disputed power. More often he stood in opposition, and in such instances his approach is surely more vulnerable to criticism.

How could one know if the ratifying conventions would have rejected this or that specific power, if they meant to refuse Congress the authority, say, to incorporate a national bank or to fund roads and canals? Since such disputed powers were, by definition, unlikely to have been discussed, how were the authoritative views of the ratifiers to be discovered? Madison did not make the mistake of claiming that particular powers had been considered and dismissed in the proceedings of the states. This would have implied that powers not expressly prohibited had been granted. Rather, in appealing to the ratifiers, Madison stressed the rule of construction by which the government justified its assumption of new authority. In this, he could speak more confidently of the "sense" of the popular sovereign: "It was anticipated I believe by few if any friends of the Constitution, that a rule of construction would be introduced as broad & pliant as what has occurred. And those who recollect, and still more those who shared in what passed in the State Conventions, thro' which the people ratified the Constitution, with respect to the extent of the powers vested in Congress, cannot easily be persuaded that the avowal of such a rule would not have prevented its ratification."[40] However modest or plausible a given power, it was inseparable from the method of interpretation that produced it. If the method could claim no authority from the people, neither could the power.

In a similar vein, only a rule of construction that served the Constitution's basic structure and division of responsibilities could be legitimate. In some instances, this provided a rationale for additional powers, as with executive authority to remove appointees. But Madison's most urgent political concerns were of an opposite nature. The Constitution described a "limited Government," he averred. This was its "essential character," and it had been so approved by "those who alone had a right to make the distribution."[41] Accordingly, as he argued in the debate over the bank bill, constitutional terms like "common defense" and "general welfare" were merely declaratory and granted no authority apart from "the particular enumeration subjoined." To conclude otherwise "would give Congress an unlimited power; would render nugatory the enumeration of particular powers; [and] would supercede all the powers reserved to the state governments."[42]

The same objection applied to other interpretive maneuvers that would undo this fundamental element of the constitutional design. When the Federalists justified the Sedition Act of 1798 by referring to the regulation of free speech under the common law, with its "vast and multifarious jurisdiction," they invited the overthrow of the whole regime. Their strategem would "sap the foundation of the Constitution as a system of limited and specified powers."[43] For Madison, this system expressed the authentic sense of the people. The popular sovereign had not given the government a mandate to seek the "general welfare" or to pursue the broad aims of the common law. It had instead exercised its basic prerogative under the social compact, consenting to a complex and even unprecedented instrument that it thought would best secure its rights and interests. The instrument might be imperfect, but fidelity to it affirmed the deeper principle that the people, in the end, were the most reliable agents of natural justice.

As noted earlier, Madison's originalism has found advocates in recent years. The most vocal of them is Robert H. Bork, who describes his own jurisprudence of "original understanding" in explicitly Madisonian terms. Like the founder, Bork rejects the search for the "subjective intention" of either the framers or the members of the ratifying conventions as a strategy for reading the Constitution. He instead looks to "public understanding," what "the public of that time would have understood the words to mean."[44] Though he recognizes the difficulty of the task, he argues that "permissible and impermissible ranges of meaning can be ascertained."[45] These concern, above all, the limits and the locus of authority within the American constitutional system. Like Madison, Bork recommends conscientious adherence to the boundaries laid down by the popular sovereign, insisting on the inevitable arbitrariness of any other theory of interpretation. He especially admonishes the courts in this regard: "It is as important to freedom to confine the judiciary's power to its proper scope as it is to confine that of the President, Congress, or state and local governments."[46] Despite the considerable ingenuity of contemporary legal theory, he maintains, the courts have no more of a license than any other part of the government to depart from the original understanding of the Constitution. Bork thus presents himself as a disciple of Madison, a sophisticated defender of originalism at a time when the most serious threats to the fundamental law come not from the elective branches, as in the days of the Federalists, but from the bench.

This invocation of Madison is persuasive up to a point. There *is* a recognizable lineage between Bork's denunciation of the imposed "values of an elite"[47] and Madison's warnings about aristocracy and rule by the few. Both share a concern for popular sovereignty and constitutional legitimacy, and both accept the basic postulate of the social compact—that the ends of government are inseparable from its origin in the authority of the people.

Where Bork departs from Madison is on the question of limited government or, to put a finer point on it, on the *original understanding* of limited government. For him, it is the judiciary that is uniquely bound by strict rules of construction. The elective branches, by virtue of being more democratic, are allowed far greater latitude. Consequently, Bork counsels self-restraint for judges as they apply the Bill of Rights but at the same time declares his approval of *McCulloch* v. *Maryland* (1819), the Supreme Court's endorsement of Hamilton's position in the party disputes of the 1790s.[48] The practical result, as Stephen Macedo has written, is a "jurisprudence of *selective* intent." The original understanding is consulted with respect to rights but not powers.[49] That is, Bork combines the ratifiers' view of the Constitution's enumerated freedoms—effectively narrowing them—with the expansive Federalist view of the "necessary and proper" clause. The "dilemma" to which this gives rise in Bork's account—that of securing a selected range of minority rights in the face of otherwise unrestricted government power—is hardly "Madisonian," as he would have it.[50] To the contrary, it is more fittingly described as a Hamiltonian dilemma, with the popular majority replacing the few in exercising a virtually limitless discretion.[51]

For Madison, rights and powers could not be considered in isolation from each other. Though power certainly secured rights— on this he and Hamilton agreed—it could also endanger them. This was the idea behind a limited national government, and if it prompted Madison to mount a campaign of resistance against usurpation by the few at one point in time, it did not mean that he saw the exercise of federal power by the people as benign. Despite his efforts against the Federalists, he continued to view the arbitrary sway of majorities as the preeminent threat to American constitutional government.

Principle and Precedent

If the 1790s pose certain difficulties for the defender of Madison's consistency, the last year of his presidency would seem to raise insurmountable obstacles. It is easy enough to show the continuity between the Madison who stopped short before the limits laid down by the Articles of Confederation and the one who opposed the first Bank of the United States and Hamilton's "Report on Manufactures." Strict construction united the two periods. But this principle cannot explain the most controversial constitutional decisions of his term as chief executive. In these cases, Madison relied, he said, on a new doctrine: precedent.

The first of the controversies involved the Bank of the United States. Madison had once denounced the bank as a leading example of "forced constructions" of the Constitution,[52] but by April 1816, when he renewed its charter, it had achieved constitutional respectability in his eyes. In the course of the institution's career, stretching back a quarter century, he argued, it had won legislative approval under sufficient "solemnities and repetitions" to show that the people—those with "the ultimate right to explain the grant" of constitutional power—considered it legitimate.[53] Less than a year later, in a second unexpected constitutional decision, Madison seemed to reverse course yet again. In his last official act as president, he vetoed the bonus bill, a plan for the federal funding of such internal improvements as roads and canals. In this case his reasoning was almost indistinguishable from that which he had used in opposing the original Bank of the United States. But this too was a power widely supported by the people, and it also had precedents, ones in which he had cooperated both as secretary of state and as president. How was the bonus bill different? Madison conceded that on the bank issue, there was reason for "the charge of mutability on a Constitutional question," but he strongly maintained that the inconsistency was only "apparent, not real."[54] In what lay the consistency? How could the principle of strict construction be reconciled with so seemingly arbitrary a regard for precedent?

To understand Madison's resort to precedent, it is necessary to recall the political circumstances surrounding it. By the end of his presidency, the Federalist threat had long since passed. As if to vindicate Madison's claim in *Federalist* 10 about the ultimate fate of minority factions in a republic,[55] Hamilton and his allies had met their end at the ballot box. In fact, the Republican Party had perhaps succeeded too well. It had mobilized a national majority in the name of the Constitution but, in the process, had created a general government that was acutely sensitive to the will of the people, thus producing a new sort of threat to the regime.[56]

Madison did not believe that the popular movement he had helped to found was likely to become an engine of factional oppression—at least not immediately. Rather, he feared its benign intent, its willingness to compromise the Constitution in the service of what it considered the public good. In the long run, such indifference to constitutional limits might prove every bit as destructive as Federalist usurpation, but the remedy for it, because of its source, would have to be different. Against Hamilton and his allies, it had only been necessary "to rouse the attention of the people," who could then act "thro' the forms of the Constitution." When the people themselves, acting "through the Government as the Organ of [their] will," were the culprits, however, only the corrective of persuasion was available. An appeal had to be made to "the recollections, the reason, and the conciliatory spirit of the people against their own errors."[57]

Constitutional veneration was the first line of defense in this effort. The people could be stirred to respect their own sovereign act, applying its logic to themselves just as they had to their aristocratic foes. But such spirited attachment would require a fine distinction, one that the people were unlikely to make, particularly when convinced of their own good intentions. They would have to recognize their own subordination as the *governing* majority to the *sovereign* majority that had given the Constitution its legitimacy. Failing this, the best that could be done, Madison knew, was to limit the damage done by these "errors." They would have to be constitutionalized—that is, they would have to be accepted and understood in such a way as to prevent the people from concluding that their own will was the only measure of constitutional propriety. This was the purpose of Madison's teaching on the subject of precedent.

When the Bank of the United States expired in 1811, the institution's future was uncertain. A Hamiltonian project whose twenty-year charter had allowed it to survive the decline of the Hamiltonians, it met with a decidedly cool reception in Congress, where Republicans questioned both its policy and its constitutionality. After languishing for three years, a bill for a second charter finally passed in 1814. In vetoing it, Madison made clear that his objections were to the particulars of the legislation and not to the bank itself. As he wrote in his veto message, he was waiving "the question of the Constitutional authority of the Legislature to establish an incorporated bank as being precluded . . . by repeated recognitions under varied circumstances of the validity of such an institution in acts of the legislative, executive, and judicial branches of the Government, accompanied by indications, in different modes, of a concurrence of the general will of the nation." In his annual address of 1815 he declared that a national bank might still "merit consideration." Congress thought so as well, and the following year Madison signed the second Bank of the United States into law.[58]

Though not pressed at the time to explain his position on the bank, Madison found himself increasingly criticized for the decision in the years to come, not least by those anxious to discredit him as an authority in constitutional matters. He was forced to elaborate on his 1814 veto message. Defending his apparent turnabout, he maintained that some legislative precedents achieved constitutional standing even if they did not conform to the original "sense" of the Constitution. To qualify, precedents had to be of a certain character. They had to be "deliberate and reiterated"; "deliberate, uniform, and settled"; "authoritative, deliberate, and continued."[59] "Midnight" precedents, established "under transitory impressions, or without full examination & deliberation,"[60] did not meet the test, nor did those that failed to win widespread public support. In the case of the bank, Madison held, the 1791 act under which it was originally created "had undergone ample discussions in its passage through the several branches of the Government. It had been carried into execution throughout a period of twenty years with annual legislative recognition . . . and with the entire acquiescence of all the local authorities, as well as of the nation at large; to all of which may be added, a decreasing prospect of any change in the public opinion adverse to the constitutionality of such an institution."[61]

Madison's apologetics point to a process similar in many respects to formal amendment of the Constitution, which he may well have had in mind. Here the federal and state supermajorities of Article V are replaced by sufficient signs of public and institutional support over time. The common factor, it would seem, is the deliberateness of the change and its capacity to sustain a "public opinion" of "constitutionality" (and thus the distinction between constitutional and unconstitutional). The alternative, Madison suggested, would be to resist such mistaken but well-intended and long-standing opinions, a tactic that could result in the type of heated public controversy over constitutional principles that he always tried to eschew. Constitutional veneration was more likely to be promoted by granting a degree of legitimacy to the occasional legislative excess.

As Madison understood it, this concession to precedent was just a slight modification of strict construction. This is most evident in his reaction to *McCulloch* v. *Maryland.* Though he agreed with the Court's ruling on the constitutionality of the bank, he condemned the scope of Chief Justice John Marshall's famous opinion. In resurrecting Hamilton's reading of the "necessary and proper" clause, Marshall had needlessly introduced a "general and abstract doctrine" into the case. It might well have been decided on narrower grounds, by appeal to "a regular course of practice" rather than to a broad principle of interpretation.[62]

A legislative precedent like the bank was not exactly constitutional—that is, it could not be justified according to sound rules of construction—but it did provide, in Madison's curious formulation, "a constitutional rule of interpreting a Constitution."[63] It could "expound" the Constitution but not "alter" it,[64] by which he meant that it could determine a particular case but not change the fundamental meaning of the charter. The fact that the bank passed constitutional muster did not open the door to a more general power of incorporation or an expansive interpretation of the "necessary and proper" clause. It was only a single case, with no wider implication. Just as its constitutionality did not arise from principle, so too was it impervious to claims of principle that might oppose it. Its character as precedent was the controlling factor even though Madison himself had held the bank to be unconstitutional "on the original question." Such "abstract and individual opinions" had to give way, he insisted. They could only serve "to disturb the established course of practice in the business of the community," with no prospect of a "change of construction by the public or its agents." A responsible legislator or judge would keep his "solitary opinions" to himself, allowing the constitutional question to disappear from partisan dispute and become a settled point of law.[65]

For Madison, this policy was an acceptable compromise between an impolitic originalism and, to borrow a term from our own day, an unprincipled "living" Constitution.[66] Few legislative actions could meet his high standards for a binding precedent, and those that did would be applied narrowly enough to remove any pretext for further usurpations. He had no desire to encourage informal amendment through what Bruce Ackerman has called "constitutional politics"—that is, through the "mobilized deliberation" of the people outside the provisions of Article V.[67] The Constitution itself provided the one legitimate avenue available to the popular sovereign (at least within the terms of the established regime).[68] History might ratify the overreaching of a past generation, but it was not a resource for a governing majority looking to expand its authority in the present. The same could not be said for the ruling in *McCulloch* v. *Maryland*. Far from restraining the present majority, it essentially removed "all controul on the Legislative exercise of unconstitutional powers." Its practical effect was to turn "expediency & constitutionality" into "convertible terms."[69] As dangerous as this doctrine was in Hamilton's day, it was even more so once popular rule had emerged triumphant. It promoted the legislative dominance that Madison had always considered the characteristic vice of America's republican governments.[70]

The controversy over the bonus bill illustrates the seriousness with which Madison took both his own criteria for precedent and the threat of constitutional arguments based on expedience or "utility." His veto of the bill was a surprise, given his approval of a second charter for the Bank of the United States. He had long favored the idea of federal support for the construction of canals and roads and had included it in his earliest thoughts on the Constitution and in his proposals at the Federal Convention.[71] He had not objected to Jefferson's decision to have the national government fund the Cumberland Road, connecting the Potomac and Ohio Rivers, and as president had repeatedly signed bills continuing work on the project.[72] And as recently as his annual message of 1815, in which he had made known his willingness to reconsider the bank, he had proclaimed "the great importance of establishing throughout our country the roads and canals which can best be executed under the national authority."[73] For Madison, internal improvements were a way to cement the Union, bringing its far-flung parts into closer communication and commerce with one another. More importantly perhaps, they would provide the infrastructure necessary to sustain the settlement of the frontier and the agrarian political economy that were so central to the Republican creed.[74] Having relented on the bank, the very symbol of policies he had spent the better part of his career resisting, how could he now claim to have constitutional scruples over roads and canals?

Madison's veto message may have been calculated to produce just such astonishment, especially among those who now thought him ready to read the Constitution more generously in the pursuit of wholesome republican ends. His arguments were familiar, though, and might easily have been culled from the controversies of the 1790s. The power in question could not be found among those enumerated in the Constitution, nor did it appear "by any just interpretation" to be "necessary and proper" for executing them. It could not plausibly be called a measure to regulate commerce among the states, and it surely drew no authority from Article I's reference to "the common defense and general welfare," since such a view of the Constitution would render its "special and careful enumeration of powers . . . nugatory and improper." In sum, the bill reflected both "an inadmissible latitude of construction" and—here acknowledging the expectations created by his earlier decision—"a reliance on insufficient precedents."[75]

As Madison explained to James Monroe, his successor in the executive office, there was no parallel to the bank. Though he admitted that Jefferson had not fully explored the constitutionality of the Cumberland Road and that he himself had failed to conduct "the critical investigation . . . due to the case," it still provided no precedent for the bonus bill. The road was built for the territories and fell within Congress's "general power" over that portion of the country. Like post and military roads, it had a warrant in an enumerated constitutional power. Even if such authority had been lacking, the decision to build the Cumberland Road did not possess the attributes of a binding precedent. It had not been "the subject of solemn discussion in Congress" or of the public's "critical attention," nor had it received the "reiterated and elaborate sanctions of *every* branch of Government."[76] Precedent was a serious matter, Madison was at pains to emphasize, not the last resort of those scrambling to discover some rationale for schemes unauthorized by the Constitution.

The real danger, as Madison saw it, was not that precedent would be abused but that it would be discarded along with all constitutional deliberation. The bonus bill was a disturbing sign of "the influence which the usefulness and popularity of measures may have on questions of their constitutionality."[77] In this respect, the basic thrust of the Marshall Court's rulings and the ambitions of nationalistic Republicans came together. Though the latter rejected "the general heresies of Federalism," they were all too ready to "squeeze" authority for desired projects out of the enumerated powers. "In truth," Madison wrote to Jefferson, "the great temptation of 'utility,' brought home to local feelings, is the most dangerous snare for Constitutional orthodoxy." This made the judiciary, for all its recent mischief, "a safer expositor" of the power of Congress than Congress itself. Opposing the Court's authority, as Jefferson and others advised, would only further erode the notion of fundamental law and expose the nation still more to the "omnipotent" will of the present majority.[78] What, then, was to "controul Congress when backed & even pushed on by a majority of their Constituents"? "Nothing within the pale of the Constitution," Madison suggested, "but sound arguments & conciliatory expostulations."[79]

Chief among these, it would seem, was reminding the people and their representatives of the possibility of amendment. If a strong national majority were well disposed to a particular measure, it could alter the Constitution in order to give Congress the requisite power. As Madison had noted in his annual message of 1815 (in a passage that apparently failed to make the desired impression), the lack of federal authority with respect to roads and canals could be remedied in the "mode" that the Constitution itself had so "providently" supplied.[80] In vetoing the bonus bill, he again recommended that the people act in their sovereign capacity, encouraging Congress to "resort . . . to the same wisdom and virtue in the nation which established the Constitution in its actual form." This was the "safe and practicable mode" of making the improvements suggested by experience.[81]

What stands out most about these appeals is how understated and indirect they are. Though Madison repeatedly invoked the prescribed "mode" of extending the Constitution's authority, he never openly or explicitly endorsed amendment. Dwelling on the proper interpretation of the powers enumerated in Article I of the Constitution, he breathed not a word about the procedures for amendment described in Article V. His treatment of this constitutional alternative was always sotto voce, as if too emphatic a gesture toward the people might have given encouragement to those, like Jefferson, who were still eager to see them regularly consulted on matters of fundamental law. In his concern to avoid "a reckless indulgence of popular sovereignty," as Drew R. McCoy nicely puts it,[82] Madison undermined his own constitutional aims. He neglected to give the amendment process the kind of public support that might have allowed it to resolve these questions.[83]

This reluctance to press for formal constitutional change is especially regrettable in light of Madison's concern for constitutional veneration or "true opinion." Whatever dangers amendment under Article V might have entailed, it did represent respect for the Constitution and its limits. It was a principled way for the people to exercise their sovereignty and might have reinforced the distinction between constitution making and everyday politics. This was less clearly the case for precedent, which must rank as the least satisfactory aspect of Madison's views on constitutional interpretation. In its narrow Madisonian form, precedent was fairly innocuous. It certainly gave no comfort to anyone intent on further extraconstitutional acts, and it served such uncontroversial goals as stability and continuity.[84] At the same time, however, it admitted considerations into interpreting the Constitution that were at odds with the claims of originalism. For Madison, this was perhaps not so troubling. Precedent might possess an ambiguous relationship to constitutional legitimacy, but he believed that it would be invoked rarely, and he resorted to it in that spirit. Veneration for fundamental law could not be upset by a doctrine that, he hoped, might never again find expression.

Today, of course, the situation is much altered. As Henry Paul Monaghan has observed, Americans now confront a body of constitutional law composed to a large degree of such precedents—interpretations of government power and individual rights that are plainly incompatible with original understanding. Even the sternest originalists, he notes, cannot bring themselves to advocate the "massive repudiation" of the present constitutional order that strict adherence to their principles would require.[85] The reasons for this are both commonsensical and respectable, having descended from Madison's arguments for the constitutionality of the second Bank of the United States. But what is no longer so clear is that the foundation for constitutional veneration, at least as Madison understood it, remains intact. The distance between a sovereign majority and its lesser governing reflection has disappeared to a great extent, and the written Constitution seems only a distant relation of its "living" cousin.

Conclusion

The Madisonian Regime Today

Every field of study has its schemes of classification, and scholarship on the American founding is no different. As a result, Madison, like the other leading figures of his generation, is often placed into one or another scholarly box: he is said to be a liberal or a republican, a nationalist or a states'-righter, a follower of the "court" party or of its "country" rival. There is no denying the usefulness of these labels, and I have gladly availed myself of them more than once in the preceding chapters. But taxonomies seldom do justice to individuals, and this is especially true when dealing with a thinker of Madison's sophistication. Here we encounter two distinct problems, one analytical and the other practical.

In the first place, the ideological shorthand favored by students of the founding too often serves as a substitute for delving into Madison's theoretical claims; it allows a writer to dispense quickly with fundamentals and move on to the more familiar terrain of institutions and policy. Thus, before turning to a discussion of Madison's views on the separation of powers, one can create a rough-and-ready theoretical backdrop by asserting that he was a Lockean liberal or a disciple of Montesquieu. Likewise, one can claim Madison for the Scottish Enlightenment as a prelude to analyzing the extended sphere or call him a lapsed nationalist by way of introducing his differences with Hamilton over a national bank. As I hope to have demonstrated, such theoretical shortcuts are a serious mistake with respect to Madison. His political career can be understood and justified only in relation to a more comprehensive view of his first principles—principles that derive from his peculiar but in many ways compelling account of the social compact.

A second and perhaps more destructive consequence of classifying Madison according to one or another scholarly category is that it distances him from the American regime of today. After all, we do not find classical republicans or members of the country party in our own politics. To attach these labels to Madison is to suggest that he could be of interest only to an antiquarian or a reactionary. The accuracy of the "ideological" school aside, this is perhaps its most objectionable tendency. By presenting the thought of the founding era as a kind of atavism, as a backward-looking historical curiosity, writers like Gordon S. Wood and J. G. A. Pocock release us from the need to confront it in a serious, practical way. Our regime remains Madisonian in important respects, however, and we still stand to benefit from the careful consideration of Madison's principles.

This is especially true in light of various interpretations of the founding that have surfaced in recent years. At both ends of the political spectrum, and with an eye to present-day discontents, it has become fashionable to criticize the American regime for lacking any meaningful idea of citizenship or the public good. Liberalism is inevitably made the culprit—blamed for its thin, atomistic account of human nature and its emphasis on rights and interests—and Madison is often cast as its knowing accomplice. On the Right, this dissatisfaction springs from the founders' supposed indifference to public virtue. George F. Will has argued that Madison saw the "political problem . . . entirely in terms of controlling the passions that nature gives, not nurturing the kind of character that the polity might need," while Robert H. Bork believes that the founders, through their continual emphasis on personal liberty, "set in motion a tendency that . . . could and often did eventually free the individual from almost all moral and legal constraints." On the Left, the grumbling concerns the American regime's alleged failings with respect to self-government and community. For Benjamin R. Barber, liberal democracy in the United States has no use for real citizens, its democratic values having always been "prudential and thus provisional, optional, and conditional— means to exclusively individualistic and private ends." Likewise,

Richard K. Matthews blames Madison for creating an American society in which a radical devotion to property and stability has deprived the people of the right "to exercise their uniquely human . . . powers and capacities" of self-government.[1]

A good starting point for answering these charges is Madison's basic view of the Constitution, which was at once traditional and decidedly modern. On the one hand, he saw the Constitution as a regime in the classical sense, as an arrangement of offices, institutions, and powers that would give a certain character to citizens and officeholders alike. He spoke of distinctively American virtues, both public and private. On the other hand, he took this constitutional influence to be related ultimately to the claims of the social compact. His countrymen's virtues would arise from the motives of interest and pride, especially as expressed in what I have called the political right of nature, and they would be limited by the particular ends for which the regime was created—peace, prosperity, and personal security. For Madison, Americans would not be New World Spartans, but neither would they be mere self-involved bourgeoisie, entirely caught up in private affairs. Surveying the public realm, they would be vigilant, assertive, and self-reliant.

In short, Madison believed that the American regime, far from rejecting the idea of a common life, presupposes a certain consensus among citizens—a shared regard for the Constitution and a proud attachment to its authoritative ways, its rights, and its implicit duties. Though the civic virtue entailed by this common life might not be as comprehensive or robust as that described by the tradition-minded Tory or the communitarian democrat, it is real enough and has both safety and practicability to recommend it. It respects the solid human goods that are the primary ends of the American regime (thereby complementing the more commercially oriented "bourgeois" virtues). At the same time, and again by contrast to more immoderate political ideals, it allows for the pursuit of other, higher ends, both mundane and divine. Civic virtue has a central place in a liberal republic like the United States, Madison might say, but its limits must be understood and appreciated.

Insofar as current unhappiness with the American civic ethos stems from developments that long postdate the founding, Madison might be more sympathetic to present-day complaints. After all, the peculiar virtues that he associated with the American re-

gime were inseparable from its character as a limited, constitutional government. As he saw it, fidelity to the Constitution was
not just a matter of political safety, of preventing abuse by officeholders or an aroused majority; it was also a reminder to the people
of their ultimate authority over the regime and a spur to their spirited, defensive superintendence of its terms.

Such devotion to the Constitution's forms, Madison seemed to
believe, was the key to patriotism and civic satisfaction in the modern republic, where the people rule only indirectly, through their
representatives. By imposing boundaries and conditions on the
governing class, constitutional orthodoxy would compensate for
the absence of real democracy, that is, popular rule as it was practiced among the ancients. In this way, the people, though excluded
from the day-to-day politics of the nation, would nonetheless see a
constant reflection of themselves in the regime as a whole. Safe-
guarded too would be their more direct participation in the lesser
political forums provided by the states and localities.

Needless to say, this proprietary view of the Constitution no
longer prevails. As Madison saw even in his own day, the people's
pride in a government of their own making is often no match for
the urgency of their various interests and needs. Over the years,
and especially during the twentieth century, the American people
have cooperated with their elected officials in reaching beyond the
confines of the Constitution. Faced with the vicissitudes of modern
economic and social life, they have turned expectantly to their national government, asking it to take on ever greater responsibilities.
As Madison feared, utility rather than constitutionality has become the ultimate test for public policy. As a result, one seldom
hears it said anymore that the federal government simply lacks a
constitutional warrant for a given program or regulation. The argument would be seen as little more than a diversionary tactic,
prompted by the inability to block a proposal on policy grounds.
For Madison, by contrast, such limits were the deepest source of
republican dignity, the bulwarks that he expected citizens to defend in order to remind themselves of their sovereignty.

What Madison may not have fully appreciated, however carefully he couched his republican rhetoric, was that his oft-pro-
claimed principles of popular sovereignty and natural equality
posed an abiding threat to a complex arrangement like the federal

union. Alexis de Tocqueville, writing in 1835, toward the end of Madison's long life, saw this dynamic clearly.

> The idea of secondary powers, between the sovereign and his subjects, was natural to the imagination of aristocratic peoples, because such powers were proper to individuals or families distinguished by birth, education, and riches, who seemed destined to command. Opposite reasons naturally banish such an idea from the minds of men in ages of equality. ... [T]he idea of a single central power directing all citizens slips naturally into their consciousness without their, so to say, giving the matter a thought.
>
> Moreover, in politics, as in philosophy and religion, democratic peoples give a ready welcome to simple general ideas. They are put off by complicated systems and like to picture a great nation in which every citizen resembles one set type and is controlled by one single power.[2]

According to Tocqueville, Americans had resisted the inexorable pull of centralization largely because of their English pedigree. Though members of what had become the most thoroughly democratic of societies, they retained from their aristocratic forbears "the idea of individual rights and a taste for local freedom." Equality, as opposed to liberty, was "comparatively new" among them and might yet prove to be the undoing of their exceptional political institutions.[3]

In the face of so profound a democratic tendency, Madison may have been naive to hope that the Constitution's carefully delineated limits on the powers of the national government would endure and continue to shape the country's political character. Certainly the Constitution's internal architecture—the separation of powers—has fared much better over time. The conclusion seems inescapable that, compared to strict construction and federalism, the free associations celebrated by Tocqueville are a far more realistic means for preserving local liberty and its attendant political dispositions.

Still, it is easy to overlook, because of their familiarity, the elements of contemporary political life that combine the republican spirit and respect for the Constitution in a distinctively Madisonian way. One might start with the recent and much-remarked-upon effort of states and localities to take back some of the functions that the federal government has appropriated over the years. In areas like welfare, crime, and education, the initiative of late has shifted dramatically away from Washington. The reasons for this trend are complex but include, above all, growing popular doubts about the efficacy of distant, unlimited government. Once the most common rationale for expanding federal power, utility (to use Madison's term) has now become the most effective argument for confining it.

As Madison well knew, though, utility is a fickle friend of principle. If the movement now under way to restore some needed balance to the federal system is to be more than a passing fad, it cannot rest simply on the latest round of encouraging crime statistics or elementary-school test scores. Policies that bring results today may fail tomorrow. Reform must find deeper, more lasting roots.

At the institutional level, this has begun to happen in the courts, where the states are reasserting their constitutional prerogatives and making federalism a serious practical concern again. In four recent cases—*New York* v. *United States* (1992), *United States* v. *Lopez* (1995), *Seminole Tribe* v. *Florida* (1996), and *City of Boerne* v. *Flores* (1997)—the Supreme Court has rejected Congress's expansive view of its own powers and recognized the states' independent standing under the Constitution. Of particular interest for its far-reaching logic is *Lopez*, in which a slim majority of the justices affirmed that the commerce clause, the ostensible source for much of the national government's modern growth, is not infinitely elastic.[4] These rulings hardly have the makings of a return to first principles in federal-state relations, but they do point to the possibility of reinforcing and extending the boundaries that remain.

As for American political culture more generally, reverence for the Constitution does still exist in something like the form imagined by Madison. Certainly Americans of every description continue to be proud of their country's fundamental charter and to look upon it as a thing of their own making. This most often finds expression in an impassioned attachment to the Bill of Rights, a sentiment that Madison would heartily endorse, having pressed for passage of these first amendments with the very idea of cementing popular support for the new regime. Less common today is the broader Madisonian view of the Constitution as a charter of limits, but here too examples can still be found. Especially noteworthy in this regard—and paradoxically so in light of Madison's wariness of mixing politics and religion—is the Christian Right, whose members seek, among other things, to restore some vigor to local self-government and to the constitutional understandings that long sheltered it. Indignant about federal overreaching yet patriotic and (overwhelmingly) peaceable, they are a genuine modern reflection of what Madison took to be the republican spirit.

Even now, the origins of that spirit are best understood in relation to Madison's reconceived and Americanized social compact. As he knew, the social compact could no longer be treated as a thought-experiment, relevant only as a means for testing the legitimacy of existing governments. So successful were its basic principles that they had come in his day to serve as a template for practical politics, not least for the creation of new governments. Thus, if the people of the United States did not precisely understand themselves to occupy a state of nature after their break from Great Britain, they did expect to make governments much as natural men might. Because they were incapable of doing so on their own, we have Founding Fathers. Because they nonetheless retained their sovereign pride, we have American patriotism. Madison's achievement was to explain how these disparate elements could come together—and to play no small part in seeing that they did.

Notes

Abbreviations

FC   *The Founders' Constitution*, eds. Philip B. Kurland and Ralph
            Lerner, 5 vols. (Chicago: University of Chicago Press, 1987).

Federalist *The Federalist*, ed. Jacob E. Cooke (Middletown, Conn.: Wes-
            leyan University Press, 1961). Cited by essay number and page.

LJM   *Letters and Other Writings of James Madison*, 4 vols. (New York:
            R. Worthington, 1884).

MF   *The Mind of the Founder: Sources of the Political Thought of James
            Madison*, ed. Marvin Meyers (Hanover, N.H.: University Press
            of New England, 1973).

Notes   *Notes of Debates in the Federal Convention of 1787 Reported by James
            Madison*, ed. Adrienne Koch (New York: W. W. Norton & Co.,
            1966).

PAH   *The Papers of Alexander Hamilton*, eds. Harold C. Syrett and
            Jacob E. Cooke, 26 vols. (New York: Columbia University Press,
            1961–79).

PJM   *The Papers of James Madison*, eds. William T. Hutchinson,
            William M. E. Rachal, Robert A. Rutland et al., 17 vols. to date
            (Chicago and Charlottesville: University of Chicago Press and
            University Press of Virginia, 1962–).

PTJ   *The Papers of Thomas Jefferson*, eds. Julian P. Boyd et al., 27 vols.
            to date (Princeton, N.J.: Princeton University Press, 1950–).

Records   *The Records of the Federal Convention of 1787*, ed. Max Farrand, 4
            vols. (New Haven, Conn.: Yale University Press, 1937).

WJM   *The Writings of James Madison*, ed. Gaillard Hunt, 9 vols. (New
            York: G. P. Putnam's Sons, 1900–10).

Introduction: Many Madisons

1. Henry Adams's classic account of the administrations of Jefferson
and Madison is the earliest instance of such historiography. He charged that

the Republican dynasty, for all of its professions to the contrary, had finally conceded in practice "to the rule that the national government alone interpreted its own powers in the last resort." See his *History of the United States of America during the Administrations of James Madison* (New York: Library of America, 1986), pp. 1313–14. Later writers, though more sympathetic to Madison, have tended to agree, dismissing the Virginian's constitutional arguments as a stalking horse for other ends. See Irving Brant, *James Madison*, 6 vols. (Indianapolis: Bobbs-Merrill, 1941–61), 2:217; Ralph Ketcham, *James Madison: A Biography* (Charlottesville: University Press of Virginia, 1971), pp. 314–15, 605; and George W. Carey, *In Defense of the Constitution* (Indianapolis: Liberty Fund, 1995), pp. 80–94.

2. JM to C. E. Haynes, 25 February 1831, *WJM* 9:442 (emphasis added).

3. For the antitheoretical view, see Eugene F. Miller, "What Publius Says about Interest," *Political Science Reviewer* 19 (1990): 21–22; for the subtheoretical view, see Hannah Arendt, *On Revolution* (Harmondsworth, England: Penguin Books, 1965), pp. 169–78.

4. For Hobbes, see Martin Diamond, "Democracy and *The Federalist:* A Reconsideration of the Framers' Intent," *American Political Science Review* 53 (1959): 61–62; and Gary L. McDowell, "Private Conscience and Public Order: Hobbes and *The Federalist*," *Polity* 25 (1993): 421–43. For Locke, see, among many others, Louis Hartz, *The Liberal Tradition in America* (New York: Harcourt, Brace and World, 1955); Thomas L. Pangle, *The Spirit of Modern Republicanism: The Moral Vision of the American Founders and the Philosophy of Locke* (Chicago: University of Chicago Press, 1988); and Jerome Huyler, *Locke in America: The Moral Philosophy of the Founding Era* (Lawrence: University Press of Kansas, 1995).

For Hume, see Douglass Adair, "'That Politics May Be Reduced to a Science': David Hume, James Madison, and the Tenth *Federalist*," in *Fame and the Founding Fathers: Essays by Douglass Adair,* ed. Trevor Colbourn (New York: W. W. Norton & Co., 1974), pp. 93–106; and Garry Wills, *Explaining America: The Federalist* (London: Athlone Press, 1981). For Montesquieu, see Anne M. Cohler, *Montesquieu's Comparative Politics and the Spirit of American Constitutionalism* (Lawrence: University Press of Kansas, 1988).

5. Charles Beard, *An Economic Interpretation of the Constitution of the United States* (New York: Macmillan, 1913); Robert Dahl, *A Preface to Democratic Theory* (Chicago: University of Chicago Press, 1956); James MacGregor Burns, *The Deadlock of Democracy* (Englewood Cliffs, N.J.: Prentice-Hall, 1963).

6. For an attempt to summarize the debate and a complete bibliography, see Alan Gibson, "Impartial Representation and the Extended Republic: Towards a Comprehensive and Balanced Treatment of the Tenth *Federalist* Paper," *History of Political Thought* 12 (1991): 263–304.

7. Wills, *Explaining America*, pp. 180–264; Gordon S. Wood, *The Creation of the American Republic, 1776–1787* (New York: W. W. Norton & Co., 1972), pp. 606–15; J. G. A. Pocock, *The Machiavellian Moment: Florentine Political Thought and the Atlantic Republican Tradition* (Princeton, N.J.: Princeton University Press, 1975), pp. 506–52; David F. Epstein, *The Political Theory of* The Federalist (Chicago: University of Chicago Press, 1984), pp. 67–68, 109–10.

8. Richard K. Matthews, *If Men Were Angels: James Madison and the Heartless Empire of Reason* (Lawrence: University Press of Kansas, 1995). Matthews's portrait of Madison as a cold, calculating, antirepublican liberal is un-

convincing, not least for the gullibility it suggests on the part of Jefferson, Madison's longtime partner and confidant.

9. Lance Banning, *The Sacred Fire of Liberty: James Madison and the Founding of the Federal Republic* (Ithaca, N.Y.: Cornell University Press, 1995). For an earlier, abbreviated version of his argument, see Banning, "The Hamiltonian Madison," *Virginia Magazine of History and Biography* 92 (1984): 3–28.

10. See Wood, *Creation of the American Republic*; Pocock, *Machiavellian Moment*; Bernard Bailyn, *The Ideological Origins of the American Revolution* (Cambridge: Harvard University Press, 1967); Lance Banning, *The Jeffersonian Persuasion: Evolution of a Party Ideology* (Ithaca, N.Y.: Cornell University Press, 1978); and Drew R. McCoy, *The Elusive Republic: Political Economy in Jeffersonian America* (New York: W. W. Norton & Co., 1980). For a useful (if slightly outdated) overview of the literature, see Robert E. Shalhope, "Republicanism and Early American Historiography," *William and Mary Quarterly* 39 (1982): 334–56.

11. See Gary Rosen, "Madison's Madison," review of *The Sacred Fire of Liberty*, by Lance Banning, in *First Things* (April 1996): 45–47.

12. For the best examples of the older consensus among scholars of the founding, see Carl Becker, *The Declaration of Independence: A Study in the History of Political Ideas* (New York: Knopf, 1922); and Hartz, *Liberal Tradition in America*.

13. See Pangle, *Spirit of Modern Republicanism*; Paul A. Rahe, *Republics Ancient and Modern*, 3 vols. (Chapel Hill: University of North Carolina Press, 1994); Michael P. Zuckert, *Natural Rights and the New Republicanism* (Princeton, N.J.: Princeton University Press, 1994); and Huyler, *Locke in America*.

1. The Social Compact Reconsidered

1. See, for example, Gottfried Dietz, The Federalist: *A Classic on Federalism and Free Government* (Baltimore: Johns Hopkins University Press, 1960), pp. 112–13; David F. Epstein, *The Political Theory of* The Federalist (Chicago: University of Chicago Press, 1984), p. 74; Alexander Landi, "Madison's Political Theory," *Political Science Reviewer* 6 (1976): 80–81; and Thomas L. Pangle, *The Spirit of Modern Republicanism: The Moral Vision of the American Founders and the Philosophy of Locke* (Chicago: University of Chicago Press, 1988), p. 125.

2. Madison was not much for philosophical name-dropping, but Hobbes and Locke do make the occasional appearance in his writings. As a young man, Madison quoted Hobbes in his commonplace book, and at Princeton he cited both Hobbes and Locke in his notes on "logick." See Commonplace Book, 1759–72 (exact date uncertain); and Notes on a Brief System of Logick, 1766–72 (exact date uncertain), *PJM* 1:16, 35.

In his maturity, Madison included the works of both writers in the books that he recommended for purchase by Congress. Only Locke, however, is mentioned by name in Madison's own writings—on three occasions, to the best of my knowledge. See Report on Books for Congress, 23 January 1783, *PJM* 6:85; and, for references to Locke, "Spirit of Governments," 20 February 1792; "Helvidius," No. 1, 24 August 1793; and JM to Thomas Jefferson, 8 February 1825, in *MF*, pp. 183, 203, 349.

3. See Locke, *Second Treatise*, in *Two Treatises of Government*, ed. Peter Laslett, student edition (Cambridge: Cambridge University Press, 1988), secs. 97, 99 (pp. 332, 333); Hobbes, *Leviathan*, ed. C. B. Macpherson (Harmonds-

worth, England: Penguin Books, 1985), chaps. 17–18 (pp. 223–39, passim); Rousseau, *On the Social Contract,* ed. Roger D. Masters (New York: St. Martin's Press, 1978), bk. 1, chap. 6 (pp. 52–54).

4. For an exhaustive listing of Publius's use of both words, see Thomas S. Engeman et al., eds., *The Federalist Concordance* (Middletown, Conn.: Wesleyan University Press, 1980), pp. 86 ("compact"), 110 ("contracts"). These usages find confirmation in Article I, section 10 of the Constitution, which prohibits the states both from "impairing the Obligation of Contracts" and from entering into a "Compact with another State, or with a foreign Power."

5. *Federalist* 51:352.

6. Ibid., 43:297.

7. Cf. Madison's other appeals to self-preservation in *Federalist* 14:86, 38:242, and 41:270. In each case, he describes self-preservation as a compelling impulse or sentiment, overcoming ordinary political motives such as opinion, interest, and attachment to constitutional forms.

8. Jefferson's presentation of the law of nature in the Declaration of Independence is similar. While the people figure more prominently in his account, they are nonetheless "impelled" to the separation from Great Britain: "Necessity . . . constrains them to alter their former Systems of Government." Cf. Hobbes, *Leviathan,* chap. 17 (p. 223): "The finall Cause, End, or Designe of men . . . in the introduction of that constraint upon themselves, (in which wee see them live in Common-wealths) is . . . getting themselves out from [the] miserable condition of Warre." Locke, *Second Treatise,* sec. 127 (p. 352): "Thus Mankind, notwithstanding all the Priviledges of the state of Nature, being but in an ill condition, while they remain in it, are quickly driven into Society." And Rousseau, *On the Social Contract,* bk. 1, chap. 6 (p. 52): "I assume that men have reached the point where obstacles to their self-preservation in the state of nature . . . prevail over the forces each individual can use to maintain himself in that state. Then that primitive state can no longer subsist and the human race would perish if it did not change its way of life."

9. *Federalist* 40:265. Madison does nothing to indicate that he has abridged the quoted passage from the Declaration. The passage reads in full (with Madison's cut in brackets): "that whenever any Form of Government becomes destructive of these ends, it is the Right of the People to alter or to abolish it[, and to institute new Government, laying its Foundation on such Principles, and organizing its Powers in such Form,] as to them shall seem most likely to effect their Safety and Happiness." See pp. 123–24 for my discussion of this selective use of the Declaration.

10. For an illuminating discussion of the distinction—and relationship—between natural and civil rights, see Harvey C. Mansfield, Jr., *America's Constitutional Soul* (Baltimore: Johns Hopkins University Press, 1991), pp. 182–84.

11. Hobbes, *Leviathan,* chap. 14 (p. 189).

12. Ibid., chap. 14 (p. 189).

13. Ibid., chap. 6 (p. 127).

14. *Federalist* 39:250.

15. Hobbes, *Leviathan,* chaps. 6, 11 (pp. 125, 163–64).

16. *Federalist* 44:301.

17. Ibid., 51:352.

18. Epstein, *Political Theory of* The Federalist, p. 163 (emphasis in the

original), citing Locke, *Second Treatise*, secs. 95–96 (pp. 330–32). That Madison appreciated the difference between the unanimous and the majoritarian stages of the social compact is evident in his other writings. See, for example, his *Notes on Sovereignty*, 1835, *WJM* 9:570.

19. *Federalist* 43:295.

20. JM to N. P. Trist, 15 February 1830, *WJM* 9:355.

21. Locke is not alone, of course, in describing a first, unanimous stage of the social compact to be followed by a majority decision on a form of government. See Hobbes, *Leviathan*, chaps. 17–18 (pp. 227–29); and Rousseau, *On the Social Contract*, bk. 1, chap. 6 (pp. 52–54); bk. 3, chaps. 17–18 (pp. 105–7).

22. See *Federalist* 38:239. He uses similar language in *Federalist* 15:89, where he calls on the people "to deliberate and decide" on the act of the Federal Convention, and in *Federalist* 63:425, where he asserts that rash, ill-considered consent is not to be mistaken for "the cool and deliberate sense of the community."

23. Madison's "Memorial and Remonstrance" was signed by less than one-fifth of the nearly 11,000 Virginians who signed some kind of antiassessment petition. Editorial note, *PJM* 8:297–98.

24. The Supreme Court has cited the "Memorial and Remonstrance" in several important cases, primarily to shed light on the meaning of "an establishment of religion." Most members of the Court have understood the petition to enjoin an absolute separation of church and state. See *Everson* v. *Board of Education* (1947) and *McCollum* v. *Board of Education* (1948). In more recent disputes about the place of religion in American public life, the "Memorial and Remonstrance" has been used increasingly to defend claims of free exercise as well. See, for example, Michael W. McConnell, "The Origins and Historical Understanding of Free Exercise of Religion," *Harvard Law Review* 103 (1990): 1410–1517.

25. "Memorial and Remonstrance" against Religious Assessments, ca. 20 June 1785, *PJM* 8:299.

26. Ibid., p. 300.

27. Ibid., p. 299.

28. "On what principle is it that the majority binds the minority? It does not result, I conceive, from a law of nature, but from compact founded on utility. A greater proportion might be required by the fundamental Constitution of Society, if under any particular circumstances it were judged eligible." JM to Thomas Jefferson, 4 February 1790, *MF*, p. 178.

29. "Memorial and Remonstrance," *PJM* 8:299.

30. Ibid.

31. Ibid., p. 304.

32. The Virginia Declaration of Rights, taken as a whole, shows how these two sorts of rights are combined. Its opening paragraph, from which Madison borrows in the "Memorial and Remonstrance," anticipates the much more famous phrases of Jefferson's Declaration. It states that "all men are by nature equally free and independent, and have certain inherent rights, of which, when they enter into a state of society, they cannot by any compact deprive or divest their posterity; namely, the enjoyment of life and liberty, with the means of acquiring and possessing property, and pursuing and obtaining happiness and safety." The remainder of the Declaration is devoted to the particular constitutional rights that are intended to secure these "inherent" rights.

The Virginia Bill of Rights, 12 June 1776, in Henry Steele Commager, ed., *Documents of American History*, 7th ed., 2 vols. (New York: Appleton-Century-Crofts, 1963), 1:103–4.

33. "Memorial and Remonstrance," *PJM* 8:299–300.

34. Ibid., p. 304.

35. Ibid., p. 299.

36. Locke, *A Letter Concerning Toleration*, ed. James H. Tully (Indianapolis: Hackett Publishing Co., 1983), p. 42.

37. Some years earlier, as a young delegate to the state's first constitutional convention, he had succeeded in having "toleration" replaced in George Mason's original draft of the Virginia Declaration of Rights with the more uncompromising "free exercise of Religion." He had also suggested that Mason's broad qualifying statement—granting "the fullest toleration . . . unless, under colour of religion, any man disturb the peace, the happiness, or safety of society"—be replaced with the considerably more restrictive, "unless the preservation of equal liberty and the existence of the State are manifestly endangered." Declaration of Rights and Form of Government for Virginia, 16 May–29 June 1776, *PJM* 1:172–75, 177. The article on religion finally adopted by the convention contained no such qualifying statement.

38. Thomas Lindsay, "James Madison on Religion and Politics: Rhetoric and Reality," *American Political Science Review* 85 (1991): 1322.

39. "Madison's 'Detached Memoranda,'" ed. Elizabeth Fleet, *William and Mary Quarterly* 3 (1946): 559. Though it is known that these notes were made sometime after Madison's retirement in 1817, it has been impossible to date them precisely (see Fleet's introduction, pp. 534–35).

40. "Memorial and Remonstrance," *PJM* 8:299. As Madison would later write, there were those in the dispute over religious liberty in Virginia who would profane the name of Jesus Christ "by making his religion the means of abridging the natural and equal rights of all men, in defiance of his own declaration that his Kingdom was *not of this world*." "Madison's 'Detached Memoranda,'" p. 556 (emphasis added).

41. Cf. the biblical maxim adopted by Augustine in the early church's conflict with the Donatist heresy. Interpreting Luke 14.23 ("whomsoever ye shall find, compel them to come in"), Augustine wrote, "The thing to be considered when any one is coerced, is not the mere fact of the coercion, but the nature of that which is coerced, whether it be good or bad: not that any one can be good in spite of his own will, but that, through fear of suffering what he does not desire, he either renounces his hostile prejudices, or is compelled to examine truths of which he had been contentedly ignorant." *St. Augustine: The Political Writings*, ed. Henry Paolucci (Chicago: Regnery Gateway, 1962), pp. 193, 202–3. This is doubtless an instance of what the youthful Madison called the "diabolical Hell conceived principle of persecution." JM to William Bradford, 24 January 1774, *PJM* 1:106.

42. "Memorial and Remonstrance," *PJM* 8:303.

43. A full discussion of all the relevant texts is beyond our scope here, but illustrative passages include his assertion in *The Federalist* of the "dim and doubtful" character of revelation (37:237) and his observations late in life on the theological superiority of "reasoning from the effect to the cause, 'from Nature to Nature's God'" (JM to Frederick Beasley, 20 November 1825, *WJM* 9:230).

44. Lindsay, "Madison on Religion and Politics," p. 1326. For further evi-

dence from Madison's writings and a more complete discussion of his objections to revelation, see pp. 1325–29.

45. JM to Thomas Jefferson, 22 January 1786, *PJM* 8:474.

46. Hobbes, *Leviathan*, chap. 43 (pp. 611–12); Rousseau, *On the Social Contract*, bk. 4, chap. 8 (p. 131); Locke, *Letter Concerning Toleration*, p. 51.

47. *Notes on the State of Virginia*, query 18, in *The Portable Thomas Jefferson*, ed. Merrill D. Peterson, (New York: Penguin Books, 1975), p. 215.

48. Evidence for such an interpretation of Madison's views is plentiful. Before himself drafting the Bill of Rights, he feared that "infidels," among others, would be excluded from federal office if an attempt were made to give a "public definition" to the right of conscience in the Constitution (JM to Thomas Jefferson, 17 October 1788, *PJM* 11:297). As president, he used the occasion of congressionally mandated proclamations of thanksgiving to disclaim "the right to enjoin religious observances," thinking that to do otherwise would "imply and certainly nourish the erronious [*sic*] idea of a *national* religion" ("Madison's 'Detached Memoranda,'" pp. 562, 560 [emphasis in the original]). And he was no less adamant in denying government the right to appoint and salary chaplains, congressional or military, or to set aside land in unsettled districts for religious purposes (ibid., pp. 555, 558–60). Even by today's standards, Madison can only be characterized as a strict separationist.

49. "Memorial and Remonstrance," *PJM* 8:302.

50. Ibid., p. 300.

51. Background on Smith's case is drawn from Walter Berns, *The First Amendment and the Future of American Democracy* (New York: Basic Books, 1976), pp. 16–17.

52. JM from David Ramsay, 4 April 1789, *PJM* 12:44–45.

53. Speech on Citizenship, 22 May 1789, *PJM* 12:179.

54. Ibid., p. 180.

55. Cf. Locke, *Second Treatise*, sec. 211 (p. 406, emphasis in the original): "He that will with any clearness speak of the *Dissolution of Government*, ought, in the first place to distinguish between the *Dissolution of the Society*, and the *Dissolution of the Government*."

56. Speech on Citizenship, *PJM* 12:180. Madison had made a similar argument for the radical integrity of civil society in defending Virginia's exclusive right to establish the terms of the Kentucky district's separation from it. The British king had had no right to divide the American societies over which he ruled, Madison insisted, and neither did the Continental Congress: "The dissolution of the Charter [of Virginia upon the United States' declaration of independence] did not break the social compact among the people." Because "the rights of the people [of Virginia] remained entire," they could not be cut "into separate Governments without their consent." Comments on Petition of Kentuckians for Statehood, 27 August 1782, *PJM* 5:83. The editors rightly note the dubious historical basis for this claim and speculate that the writings of Locke are its true source; ibid., p. 84.

57. Like many members of the founding generation, Madison held slaves throughout a lifetime of consistent, principled opposition to the institution of slavery. The tension between his practices and his ideals is captured well by a letter that he wrote to his father about a personal slave who had accompanied him to the Continental Congress in Philadelphia: "On a view of all circumstances I have judged it most prudent not to force Billey back to Virginia even if it could be done; and have accordingly taken measures for his final separa-

tion from me. . . . I do not expect to get near the worth of him; but cannot think of punishing him by transportation merely for coveting that liberty for which we have paid the price of so much blood, and have proclaimed so often to be the right, & worthy the pursuit, of every human being." JM to James Madison, Sr., 8 September 1783, *PJM* 7:304. For an overview of Madison's relationship to the "peculiar institution," see Drew R. McCoy, *The Last of the Fathers: James Madison and the Republican Legacy* (Cambridge: Cambridge University Press, 1989), pp. 253–322.

58. Aristotle, *Politics*, trans. H. Rackham, Loeb Classical Library (Cambridge: Harvard University Press, 1932), 1280a7ff.

59. See Madison's observations on the relationship between the monarchical and the aristocratic elements in the Netherlands and in ancien régime France. JM to Edmund Randolph, 2 December 1787, *PJM* 10:289; JM to Edmund Pendleton, 20 October 1788, *PJM* 11:307.

60. Speech on Citizenship, *PJM* 12:181.

61. Cf. Aristotle, *The Politics*, trans. Carnes Lord (Chicago: University of Chicago Press, 1984), 1252b29–30: "While coming into being for the sake of living, [the city] exists for the sake of living well."

62. Ibid., 1277b10–11.

63. Epstein, *Political Theory of* The Federalist, p. 5.

64. Speech on Citizenship, *PJM* 12:180.

65. JM to George Washington, 18 October 1787, *PJM* 10:197.

66. Speech on Citizenship, *PJM* 12:180 (emphasis added).

67. Ibid., p. 181.

68. Notes on Sovereignty, 1835, *WJM* 9:570 (emphasis added).

69. Speech on Citizenship, *PJM* 12:181.

70. Notes on Sovereignty, *WJM* 9:570.

71. *Notes on the State of Virginia*, query 13, *The Portable Thomas Jefferson*, p. 170.

72. Gordon S. Wood, *The Creation of the American Republic, 1776–1787* (New York: W. W. Norton & Co., 1972), pp. 307, 310–19.

73. *Notes on the State of Virginia*, query 13, *The Portable Thomas Jefferson*, p. 170.

74. Notes for a Speech Favoring Revision of the Virginia Constitution of 1776, 14 or 21 June 1784, *PJM* 8:77–78.

75. Ibid., p. 77.

76. The people of Massachusetts speak gratefully of the "opportunity . . . of entering into an original, explicit, and solemn compact with each other, and of forming a new constitution of civil government for ourselves and our posterity." The constitution of New York declares "that no authority shall, on any pretence whatever, be exercised over the people or members of this state, but such as shall be derived from and granted by them." And Pennsylvania's constitution asserts that "whenever [the] great ends of government are not obtained, the people have a right, by common consent to change it, and take such measures as to them may appear necessary to promote their safety and happiness." See Francis Bailey, ed., *The Constitutions of the Several Independent States of America* (Philadelphia: Continental Congress, 1781), pp. 8, 63, 85.

77. The representatives of "the freemen of North Carolina" were "chosen and assembled in congress, for the express purpose of framing a constitution." Delaware's constitution was "agreed to and resolved upon" by representatives "chosen by the Freemen of the said State for that express Purpose." Likewise,

Pennsylvania's constitutional representatives met "for the express purpose of framing such a government." Ibid., pp. 150, 106, 86.

78. Notes for a Speech Favoring Revision of the Virginia Constitution, *PJM* 8:77.

79. Ibid.

80. Ibid.

81. The members of the New Hampshire congress, lamenting the "sudden and abrupt" dissolution of the colonial government, "conceive [themselves] reduced to the necessity of establishing a Form of Government, to continue during the present unhappy and unnatural contest with Great-Britain." No less desperate were representatives in New Jersey, who aver that "in the present deplorable situation of these colonies, exposed to the fury of a cruel and relentless enemy, some form of government is absolutely necessary." Bailey, ed., *Constitutions of the Several Independent States of America*, pp. 4, 78.

82. Jefferson's Draft of a Constitution for Virginia, 1783, *PTJ* 6:295.

83. Notes for a Speech Favoring Revision of the Virginia Constitution, *PJM* 8:78.

84. Ibid.

85. *Common Sense*, in *The Thomas Paine Reader*, ed. Michael Foot and Isaac Kramnick (Harmondsworth, England: Penguin Books, 1987), pp. 68–69.

86. Notes for a Speech Favoring Revision of the Virginia Constitution, *PJM* 8:78.

87. See the provisions for a constitutional convention in his bill for the Kentucky district's transition to statehood, 15 December 1786, *PJM* 9:208. The bill shows the seriousness with which Madison took the practical application of the two stages of the social compact. It required separate procedures for forming a distinct society and, subsequently, for establishing a constitution.

88. Ratification without Conditional Amendments, 24 June 1788, *PJM* 11:172. Madison did not go so far as to say that this describes how the federal Constitution came about. It is the standard that he refers to in *The Federalist*, however, when he calls the members of the Federal Convention "men of [America's] own deliberate choice." *Federalist* 38:243. I will consider later whether this is a credible claim.

89. See Madison's observations in *Federalist* 37 on the character of the relationship between representatives and their electors.

90. Ratification without Conditional Amendments, *PJM* 11:172.

91. Hobbes, *Leviathan*, chap. 21 (p. 263).

92. Samuel Stanhope Smith to JM, November 1777–August 1778, *PJM* 1:194–211 (emphasis in the original).

93. Samuel Stanhope Smith to JM, 15 September 1778, *PJM* 1:253 (emphasis in the original).

2. Pride, Property, and American Nationhood

1. *Federalist* 37:237–38 (emphasis added).

2. Ibid., 51:353.

3. Ibid., 37:237.

4. Ibid., 10:59.

5. Hobbes, *Leviathan*, ed. C. B. Macpherson (Harmondsworth, England: Penguin Books, 1985), chap. 13 (p. 186); Locke, *Second Treatise*, in *Two Treatises*

of Government, ed. Peter Laslett, student edition (Cambridge: Cambridge University Press, 1988), sec. 123 (p. 350). Hobbes was quite explicit on this point. For him, fear was the "Passion to be reckoned upon" (chap. 14, p. 200). Locke, typically, was more understated, but even for him, the property (in the widest sense) of man in the state of nature was "very unsafe, very unsecure. This makes him willing to quit this Condition, which however free, is full of fears and continual dangers" (sec. 123, p. 350). Cf. Locke's understanding of the place of "uneasiness" in human motivation: "But we being in this World beset with sundry *uneasinesses,* distracted with different *desires,* the next enquiry naturally will be, which of them has the precedency in determining the *will* to the next action? and to that the answer is, that ordinarily, which is the most pressing of those, that are judged capable of being then removed." *An Essay Concerning Human Understanding,* ed. Peter H. Nidditch (Oxford: Clarendon Press, 1975), bk. 2, chap. 21, sec. 40 (p. 257, emphasis in the original).

6. Michael J. Sandel, "The Procedural Republic and the Unencumbered Self," *Political Theory* 12 (1984): 81–96. Sandel's target, of course, is the very different sort of reductionism in the social contract of John Rawls.

7. "Preface to Debates in the Convention of 1787," *Records* 3:539. Farrand was unable to determine the exact date of the document but surmised that it was written by Madison "near the close of his life."

8. Ibid., p. 540.

9. Ibid., pp. 541, 542.

10. Ibid., p. 541.

11. JM to George Washington, 9 December 1785, *PJM* 8:438.

12. Merrill Jensen, *The Articles of Confederation: An Interpretation of the Social-Constitutional History of the American Revolution, 1774–81* (Madison: University of Wisconsin Press, 1940).

13. Jack N. Rakove, *The Beginnings of National Politics: An Interpretive History of the Continental Congress* (Baltimore: Johns Hopkins University Press, 1979), p. 190.

14. "Preface to Debates in the Convention of 1787," *Records* 3:541.

15. Ibid., pp. 542–43.

16. Ibid., p. 543. Madison crossed out the second parenthetical statement in this passage; Farrand includes it in a footnote. Cf. Rakove, *Beginnings of National Politics,* pp. 358–59, speaking of the same period: "Freed from the patriotic constraints that had always operated, although unevenly, during the war, the states were no longer obliged to defer to the wisdom of Congress and the overriding demands of the common cause. The delegates [to the Continental Congress], too, enjoyed the greater liberty and, in a sense, a greater obligation to serve as the actual representatives of their constituents. They felt less impelled to subordinate the particular desires of their states to the larger good of the union."

17. Article XIII: "And the Articles of this confederation shall be inviolably observed by every state, and the union shall be perpetual; nor shall any alteration at any time hereafter be made in any of them; unless such alteration be agreed to in a congress of the united states, and be afterwards confirmed by the legislatures of every state." The Articles of Confederation, 1 March 1781 (ratified), in Henry Steele Commager, ed., *Documents of American History,* 7th ed., 2 vols. (New York: Appleton-Century-Crofts, 1963), 1:115.

18. "A spirit of accommodation alone can render [a plan for the general liquidation and apportionment of the public debts] unanimously admissible;

a spir[it] which but too little prevails, but w[hi]ch in few instance[s] is more powerfully recommended by the occasion than the present. If our voluminous & entangled acc[oun]ts be not put into some certain course of settlement before a foreign war is off our hands it is easy to see they must prove an exuberan[t] & formidable source of intestine dissentions." JM to Edmund Pendleton, 7 February 1782, *PJM* 4:55–56.

19. *Federalist* 51:352.

20. "Preface to Debates in the Convention of 1787," *Records* 3:543.

21. Ibid., p. 539.

22. Ibid.

23. Wilson Carey McWilliams, *The Idea of Fraternity in America* (Berkeley and Los Angeles: University of California Press, 1973), p. 191; see also pp. 188–93.

24. See Ralph Ketcham, *James Madison: A Biography* (Charlottesville: University Press of Virginia, 1971), pp. 112–17.

25. Proposed Amendment of Articles of Confederation, 12 March 1781, *PJM* 3:17. Article XIII obliged every state "to abide by the determinations of the United States in Congress assembled on all questions which by this Confederation are submitted to them."

26. JM to Thomas Jefferson, 16 April 1781, *PJM* 3:72.

27. JM to Thomas Jefferson, 3 October 1785, *PJM* 8:374.

28. Irving Brant, *James Madison,* 6 vols. (Indianapolis: Bobbs-Merrill, 1941–61), 2:110.

29. Proposed Amendment of Articles of Confederation, *PJM* 3:17.

30. JM to George Washington, 16 April 1787, *PJM* 9:385.

31. See Rakove, *Beginnings of National Politics,* pp. 282–83, 313–16.

32. Report on Address to the States by Congress, 26 April 1783, *PJM* 6:489: "If the strict maxims of national credit alone were to be consulted, the revenue ought manifestly to be co-existent with the object of it; and the collection placed in every respect under that authority which is to dispense the former, and is responsible for the latter."

33. Ibid. The counterpart to the last quoted passage appears on p. 490 and reads: "Here again [in continuing to rely on state requisitions] the strict maxims of public credit gave way to the desire of Congress to conform to the sentiments of their constituents."

34. Notes on Debates, 21 February 1783, *PJM* 6:271.

35. Notes on Debates, 28 January 1783, *PJM* 6:146.

36. See *Federalist* 5–8.

37. Madison showed the true extent of his pessimism in a footnote to his record of the congressional debate on the revenue plan: "The States were jealous of each other, each supposing itself to be on the whole a creditor to the others: The Eastern States in particular thought themselves so with regard to the S[outhern] States. . . . If general funds were not introduced it was not likely the balances wd. . . . ever be discharged, even if they sd. be liquidated. The consequence wd. be a rupture of the confederacy. The E[astern] States wd. at sea be powerful & rapacious, the S[outhern,] opulent & weak. This wd. be a temptation. [T]he demands on the S[outhern] St[ate]s would be an occasion. Reprisals wd. be instituted. Foreign aid would be called in by first the weaker, then the stronger side; & finally both be made subservient to the wars & politics of Europe." Notes on Debates, 21 February 1783, *PJM* 6:272.

38. Report on Address to the States by Congress, *PJM* 6:492.

39. Ibid.

40. Ibid., p. 493.

41. The address does include a number of addenda on the discontent in the army, but these documents are more of a reassuring than of a threatening nature. As Madison says in the address itself (ibid.), the soldiers "have patiently borne, among other distresses the privation of their stipends, whilst the distresses of their Country disabled it from bestowing them; and who even now ask for no more than such a portion of their dues as will enable them to retire from the field of victory & glory into the bosom of peace & private citizenship, and for such effectual security for the residue of their claims as their Country is now unquestionably able to provide."

42. Ibid., p. 492.

43. Ibid., pp. 493–94.

44. Harvey C. Mansfield, Jr., *America's Constitutional Soul* (Baltimore: Johns Hopkins University Press, 1991), p. 131.

45. Report on Address to the States by Congress, *PJM* 6:494.

46. Gordon S. Wood, *The Creation of the American Republic, 1776–1787* (New York: W. W. Norton & Co., 1972), p. 68. Cf. Drew R. McCoy, *The Elusive Republic: Political Economy in Jeffersonian America* (New York: W. W. Norton & Co., 1980), pp. 69–70.

47. J. G. A. Pocock, *The Machiavellian Moment: Florentine Political Thought and the Atlantic Republican Tradition* (Princeton, N.J.: Princeton University Press, 1975) p. 115.

48. Ibid., p. 69.

49. See Aristotle, *Nicomachean Ethics,* trans. Hippocrates G. Apostle (Grinnell, Iowa: Peripatetic Press, 1975), 1098a8–18.

50. Ibid., 1129bff.

51. Pocock, *Machiavellian Moment,* p. 67.

52. Ibid., pp. 68, 3. Pocock's peculiar approach to republicanism is indebted to the work of Hannah Arendt, as he himself acknowledges (p. 550). Cf. Arendt, *The Human Condition* (Chicago: University of Chicago Press, 1958), p. 19: "The task and potential greatness of mortals lie in their ability to produce things—works and deeds and words—which would deserve to be and, at least to a degree, are at home in everlastingness, so that through them mortals could find their place in a cosmos where everything is immortal except themselves."

53. Report on Address to the States by Congress, *PJM* 6:494.

54. *Federalist* 56:378.

55. Michael P. Zuckert, *Natural Rights and the New Republicanism* (Princeton, N.J.: Princeton University Press, 1994), pp. 315–19.

56. Hobbes, *Leviathan,* chap. 15 (p. 216).

57. Ibid. (p. 214).

58. Ibid., chap. 26 (p. 314).

59. *The Spirit of the Laws,* trans. Thomas Nugent (New York: Hafner Publishing Co., 1966), bk. 4, chap. 5 (p. 34); chap. 7 (p. 37).

60. See Rakove, *Beginnings of National Politics,* p. 338.

61. JM to Edmund Randolph, 10 March 1784, *PJM* 8:4. Irving Brant's insistence that this passage positively explodes any effort "to interpret the doings of the thirteen states, before 1789, in terms of international action by separately independent states" is inexplicable (*James Madison* 2:312). It would seem the

opposite of Madison's intention here and of the conclusion that he would soon reach about the true nature of the Confederation.

62. "Vices of the Political System of the United States," April 1787, *PJM* 9:351.

63. *Federalist* 43:297–98: "It is an established doctrine on the subject of treaties, that all the articles are mutually conditions of each other; that a breach of any one article is a breach of the whole treaty; and that a breach committed by either of the parties absolves the others; and authorises them, if they please, to pronounce the treaty violated and void."

64. JM to George Washington, 16 April 1787, *PJM* 9:383.

65. *Federalist* 37:237–38.

66. "Vices of the Political System of the United States," *PJM* 9:353.

67. Ibid., p. 355.

68. *Federalist* 10:57.

69. "Vices of the Political System of the United States," *PJM* 9:351–52.

70. *Federalist* 10:60.

71. "Vices of the Political System of the United States," *PJM* 9:348.

72. JM to Thomas Jefferson, 16 April 1781, *PJM* 3:71.

73. *Federalist* 10:61.

74. It could be objected that those interests consistently victimized by majority faction would stand to gain under such a regime, even if it restricted their own factious opportunities. For them to prevail, however, they would have to commandeer the process of constitution making. Charles Beard made this very argument, of course. In *An Economic Interpretation of the Constitution of the United States* (New York: Macmillan, 1913), he attempted to show how an elite motivated by narrow economic interests deprived the American majority of its rightful say in the design and ratification of the Constitution. As a matter of historical record, Forrest McDonald convincingly refuted Beard's thesis in *We the People: The Economic Origins of the Constitution* (Chicago: University of Chicago Press, 1958). As a matter of constitutional theory, it is simply not how Madison, Beard's great prophet, understood these events.

75. *Federalist* 51:352.

76. Ibid., 10:59.

77. Ibid., 10:59 (emphasis added), 58.

78. Hobbes, *Leviathan*, chap. 13 (p. 186).

79. Locke, *Second Treatise*, sec. 27 (pp. 287–88).

80. Ibid., sec. 123 (p. 350).

81. *Federalist* 10:58; David F. Epstein, *The Political Theory of* The Federalist (Chicago: University of Chicago Press, 1984), pp. 73–74.

82. *Second Treatise*, sec. 98 (p. 333).

83. General Defense of the Constitution, 6 June 1788, *PJM* 11:79.

84. Ratification without Conditional Amendments, 24 June 1788, *PJM* 11:172.

85. *Federalist* 10:59.

86. Ibid., p. 56; 57:384.

87. Ibid., 51:351.

88. "Vices of the Political System of the United States," *PJM* 9:357.

89. *Federalist* 10:58.

90. Locke, *Second Treatise*, sec. 123 (p. 250).

91. Ibid., secs. 138–40 (pp. 360–62).

92. C. B. Macpherson, "The Social Bearing of Locke's Political Theory," *Western Political Quarterly* 7 (1954): 1–22.

93. Observations on Jefferson's Draft of a Constitution for Virginia, ca. 15 October 1788, *PJM* 11:287. Madison's advice took the form of comments on the appropriateness for Kentucky of Jefferson's draft constitution.

94. Ibid. (emphasis added).

95. Ibid.

96. JM to Caleb Wallace, 23 August 1785, *PJM* 8:353.

97. Observations on Jefferson's Draft of a Constitution for Virginia, *PJM* 11:288, 287.

98. *Federalist* 44:300.

99. JM to George Washington, 24 December 1786, *PJM* 9:224: "Your observations on Tob[acc]o as a commutable in [state] taxes are certainly just and unanswerable. My acquiescence in the measure was agst. every general principle which I have embraced and was extorted by a fear that some greater evil under the name of relief to the People would be substituted. . . . The original object was paper money."

100. *Federalist* 10:62, 42:283.

101. Eugene F. Miller, "What Publius Says About Interest," *Political Science Reviewer* 19 (1990): 47.

102. JM to James Monroe, 5 October 1786, *PJM* 9:141.

103. *Federalist* 57:386–87, 63:423, 51:349.

104. Ibid., 51:353.

105. Harvey C. Mansfield, Jr., "Self-Interest Rightly Understood," *Political Theory* 23 (1995): 59.

3. The Paradox of Liberal Prudence

1. Aristotle, *Nicomachean Ethics*, trans. Hippocrates G. Apostle (Grinnell, Iowa: Peripatetic Press, 1975), 1141b13.

2. Clinton Rossiter, *1787: The Grand Convention* (New York: W. W. Norton & Co., 1966), p. 54.

3. Richard Henry Lee to JM, 26 November 1784, *PJM* 8:151.

4. JM to Richard Henry Lee, 25 December 1784, *PJM* 8:201.

5. See Forrest McDonald, *E Pluribus Unum: The Formation of the American Republic, 1776–1790*, 2d ed. (Indianapolis: Liberty Fund, 1979), pp. 235–37; and Ralph Ketcham, *James Madison: A Biography* (Charlottesville: University Press of Virginia, 1971), p. 169.

6. "Preface to Debates in the Convention of 1787," *Records* 3:544–45.

7. JM to James Monroe, 30 December 1785, *PJM* 8:466, 467 n. 3. See also editorial note, p. 391.

8. JM to Thomas Jefferson, 22 January 1786, *PJM* 8:476–77 (emphasized words were written in the two men's personal code).

9. See Irving Brant, *James Madison*, 6 vols. (Indianapolis: Bobbs-Merrill, 1941–61), 2:375–87; and Ketcham, *Madison: A Biography*, pp. 169–70.

10. See Boyd, *PTJ* 9:204–8, and editorial note, *PJM* 9:115–17. The Annapolis Convention was embarrassed, in fact, by the refusal of its host state, Maryland, to send delegates out of concern for the prerogatives of the national legislature: "The measure appear'd to the Senate [of Maryland], tho' undoubtedly adopted by y[ou]r Assembly with the best intentions, to have a tendency

to weaken the authority of Congress, on which the Union, and consequently the Liberty, and Safety of all the States depend. . . . I shall only observe, that sound policy, if not the Spirit of the Confederation dictates, that all matters of a general tendency, shou'd be in the representative Body of the whole, or under its authority." Daniel Carroll to JM, 13 March 1786, *PJM* 8:496.

11. JM to George Washington, 9 December 1785, *PJM* 8:439.

12. JM to James Monroe, 19 March 1786, *PJM* 8:505.

13. JM to George Washington, 9 December 1785; JM to James Monroe, 14 March 1786; JM to Thomas Jefferson, 18 March 1786, in *PJM* 8:438, 498, 503.

14. "Preface to Debates in the Convention of 1787," *Records* 3:545. Trade wars between the states had continued to escalate; Virginia alone had complied with the most recent federal requisition; a bitter sectional dispute over navigation of the Mississippi had flared up in Congress; and, finally, the second impost proposal, the last hope for anything like federal self-sufficiency in revenue, had been killed by the New York legislature. See Brant, *James Madison* 2:382–83; and McDonald, *E Pluribus Unum*, pp. 239–44.

15. "Preface to Debates in the Convention of 1787," *Records* 3:545, 547. Madison used similar language immediately after the Federal Convention, writing of the "uneasiness" that had "prepared the public mind for a general reform." JM to Thomas Jefferson, 24 October 1787, *PJM* 10:212.

16. "Preface to Debates in the Convention of 1787," *Records* 3:545 (emphasis added). Cf. *Federalist* 40:264, where Madison used still stronger language, describing the Annapolis Convention as an instance of "a *very few* deputies, from a *very few* States," assuming the liberty of "recommending a great and critical object, wholly foreign to their commission" (emphasis in the original).

17. Bruce Ackerman, *We the People: Transformations* (Cambridge: Harvard University Press, 1998), p. 39. Ackerman gives short shrift, however, to the all-important dynamic between the participants in these conventions and the changing opinions of the people.

18. For a discussion of the possible Machiavellian inspiration for this division, see Gary Rosen, "James Madison's Princes and Peoples," in *Machiavelli's Republican Legacy*, ed. Paul A. Rahe (forthcoming).

19. JM to Thomas Jefferson, 4 December 1786, *PJM* 9:189.

20. JM to James Madison, Sr., 1 April 1787, *PJM* 9:359 (emphasis in the original).

21. JM to Edmund Randolph, 25 February 1787, *PJM* 9:299.

22. JM to George Muter, 7 January 1787, *PJM* 9:231.

23. "Preface to Debates in the Convention of 1787," *Records* 3:547.

24. Speech in the Federal Convention, 12 June 1787, *PJM* 10:49.

25. JM to Thomas Jefferson, 6 September 1787, *PJM* 10:163.

26. JM to Thomas Jefferson, 9 December 1787, *PJM* 10:313.

27. JM to Edmund Pendleton, 20 September 1787, *PJM* 10:171.

28. "Preface to Debates in the Convention of 1787," *Records* 3:547.

29. JM to Edmund Randolph, 10 January 1788, *PJM* 10:355.

30. Martin Diamond, "Democracy and *The Federalist*: A Reconsideration of the Framers' Intent," *American Political Science Review* 53 (1959): 63–64.

31. See JM to Thomas Jefferson, 19 March 1787; JM to Edmund Pendleton, 22 April 1787, in *PJM* 9:318, 395; Speech in the Federal Convention, 5 June 1787, *PJM* 10:27.

32. JM to Edmund Randolph, 10 January 1788, *PJM* 10:355.

33. Speech in the Federal Convention, 12 June 1787, *PJM* 10:49.

34. JM to Thomas Jefferson, 9 December 1787; Speech in the Federal Convention, 5 July 1787; JM to Thomas Jefferson, 19 February 1788, in *PJM* 10:313, 93, 519; Speech in the Virginia Ratifying Convention, 7 June 1788, *PJM* 11:95.

35. JM to William Short, 6 June 1787, *PJM* 10:31.

36. "Preface to Debates in the Convention of 1787," *Records* 3:546, 551.

37. Aristotle, *Nicomachean Ethics* 1144a24–1144b1.

38. JM to Edmund Randolph, 11 March 1787, *PJM* 9:307; JM to Edmund Randolph, 8 April 1787, *PJM* 9:369.

39. "Vices of the Political System of the United States," April 1787, *PJM* 9:355.

40. JM to George Washington, 7 December 1786, *PJM* 9:199.

41. JM to Edmund Pendleton, 24 February 1787, *PJM* 9:295.

42. See Douglass Adair's reflections on the importance of fame to men like Washington, Hamilton, and Jefferson. "Fame and the Founding Fathers," in *Fame and the Founding Fathers: Essays by Douglass Adair,* ed. Trevor Colbourn (New York: W. W. Norton & Co., 1974), pp. 3–26. It is worth noting that Madison did not seem to share this "ruling passion." In fact, his willingness to sacrifice the *appearance* of consistency in order to defend his fundamental principles suggests a certain indifference to matters of reputation.

43. Harry V. Jaffa, *Crisis of the House Divided: An Interpretation of the Issues in the Lincoln-Douglas Debates* (Chicago: University of Chicago Press, 1959), p. 225.

44. JM to Thomas Jefferson, 15 May 1787, *PJM* 9:415.

45. Cf. Stanley Elkins and Eric McKitrick, "The Founding Fathers: Young Men of the Revolution," *Political Science Quarterly* 76 (1961): 206–7: "Various writers [Jensen, Beard, Parrington] have said that the activities of the Federalists during this period had in them a clear element of the conspiratorial.... Though it would be wrong to think of the Constitution as something that had to be carried in the face of deep and basic popular opposition, it certainly required a series of brilliant maneuvers to escape the deadening clutch of particularism and inertia.... [The Federalists] cannot be said to have circumvented the popular will, [but they] did have to use techniques which in their sustained drive, tactical mobility, and risk-taking smacked more than a little of the revolutionary."

46. JM to James Monroe, 5 October 1786, *PJM* 9:140–41.

47. Gordon S. Wood, "Interests and Disinterestedness in the Making of the Constitution," in *Beyond Confederation: Origins of the Constitution and American National Identity,* ed. Richard Beeman, Stephen Botein, and Edward C. Carter II (Chapel Hill: University of North Carolina Press, 1987), pp. 69–109.

48. JM to George Washington, 16 April 1787, *PJM* 9:384.

49. JM to Thomas Jefferson, 24 October 1787, *PJM* 10:213.

50. Speech in the Virginia Ratifying Convention, 24 June 1788, *PJM* 11:172.

51. Aristotle, *Nicomachean Ethics* 1141b34, 30–31. For classical Greek terms from the *Nicomachean Ethics,* see rev. ed., trans. H. Rackham, Loeb Classical Library (Cambridge: Harvard University Press, 1934).

52. Ibid. (trans. Hippocrates G. Apostle), 1115a7–1117a28; 1106b36–1107a2: "[Ethical] virtue, then, is a habit, disposed toward action by deliberate choice, being at the mean relative to us, and defined by reason and as a prudent man would."

53. Ibid., 1112b33–34.

54. Ibid., 1141b25, 1142a2.

55. Ibid., 1141b27–28; Aristotle, *Art of Rhetoric*, trans. J. H. Freese, Loeb Classical Library (Cambridge: Harvard University Press, 1926), 1359b12–15. See Carnes Lord's introduction to his translation of the *Politics* (Chicago: University of Chicago Press, 1984), p. 20.

56. Aristotle, *Nicomachean Ethics* 1141b15–26.

57. Ibid., 1094a27–28.

58. Aristotle, *Politics* 1277a14–16. For classical Greek terms from the *Politics*, see the translation by H. Rackham, Loeb Classical Library (Cambridge: Harvard University Press, 1932).

59. Ibid. (trans. Carnes Lord), 1277b25–29.

60. Ibid., 1253a29–31.

61. Ibid., 1273b27–33.

62. Aristotle, *Nicomachean Ethics* 1181a2.

63. Hobbes, *Leviathan*, ed. C. B. Macpherson (Harmondsworth, England: Penguin Books, 1985), chap. 8 (p. 137).

64. Ibid., chap. 13 (p. 183).

65. Thus to "govern well a family, and a kingdome, are not different degrees of Prudence; but different sorts of businesse. . . . A plain husband-man is more Prudent in affaires of his own house, then a Privy Counseller in the affaires of another man." Ibid., chap. 8 (p. 138).

66. Ibid., chap. 13 (pp. 183–84).

67. Ibid., chap. 5 (pp. 117–18).

68. Ibid., chap. 6 (p. 127).

69. Ibid., chaps. 13–14. Cf. Hobbes, *De Cive*, chap. 1, sec. 7 (p. 115): "For every man is desirous of what is good for him, and shuns what is evil, but chiefly the chiefest of natural evils, which is death; and this he doth by a certain impulsion of nature, no less than that whereby a stone moves downward." In *Man and Citizen*, ed. Bernard Gert (Indianapolis: Hackett Publishing Co., 1991).

70. Hobbes, *Leviathan*, chap. 15 (p. 211).

71. Ibid., chap. 46 (p. 687).

72. Hobbes, *De Cive*, chap. 1, sec. 9 (p. 116).

73. Hobbes, *Leviathan*, chap. 17 (p. 227): "The only way to erect such a Common Power . . . is, *to conferre all their power and strength* upon one Man, or upon one Assembly of men, that may reduce all their Wills . . . unto one Will: which is to say, to appoint one man, or Assembly of men, to beare their Person" (emphasis added).

74. Ibid., chap. 19 (p. 241). See also, Hobbes, *De Cive*, chap. 10.

75. Hobbes, *De Cive*, preface (pp. 104–5).

76. Hobbes, *Leviathan*, chap. 17 (p. 226).

77. Locke, *Second Treatise*, in *Two Treatises of Government*, ed. Peter Laslett, student edition (Cambridge: Cambridge University Press, 1988), sec. 132 (p. 354).

78. Ibid., chap. 11.

79. Ibid., secs. 12, 124.

80. Rousseau, *Discourse on the Origin and Foundations of Inequality among Men*, in *The First and Second Discourses*, ed. Roger D. Masters (New York: St. Martin's Press, 1964), preface (p. 94).

81. Rousseau, *On the Social Contract*, ed. Roger D. Masters (New York: St. Martin's Press, 1978), bk. 2, chap. 6 (p. 67).

82. Ibid., chap. 7. See also *The Government of Poland*, trans. Willmoore Kendall (Indianapolis: Hackett Publishing Co., 1985), chap. 2.

83. Hume, "Of the Original Contract," in *Essays: Moral, Political, and Literary*, ed. Eugene F. Miller (Indianapolis: Liberty Classics, 1985), pp. 468, 474, 472, 473.

84. Rousseau, *On the Social Compact*, bk. 2, chap. 7 (p. 68). Jefferson perhaps had Rousseau in mind when he wrote to John Adams from Paris describing the Federal Convention as "an assembly of demigods." TJ to John Adams, 30 August 1787, *PTJ* 12:69.

85. Hume, "The Rise of Arts and Sciences," p. 124; "Idea of a Perfect Commonwealth," pp. 512–13, in *Essays*. Kant and Hegel took this view a step further. Radicalizing Hume's reservations about rational political activity, they attributed the perfecting of constitutions to history itself. See the eighth thesis of Kant's "Idea for a Universal History with a Cosmopolitan Intent": "One can regard the history of the human species, in the large, as the realization of a hidden plan of nature to bring about an internally . . . and also an externally perfect national constitution, as the sole state in which all of humanity's natural capacities can be developed." In Kant, *Perpetual Peace and Other Essays*, trans. Ted Humphrey (Indianapolis: Hackett Publishing Co., 1983), p. 36. Also see Hegel's observations: It "is absolutely essential that the constitution should not be regarded as something made, even though it has come into existence in time. It must be treated rather as something simply existent in and by itself, as divine therefore, and constant." At the same time, "the constitution *is*, but just as essentially it *becomes*, i.e. it advances and matures." In *The Philosophy of Right*, trans. T. M. Knox (London: Oxford University Press, 1967), sec. 273 (p. 178); addition 176 (p. 291, emphasis in the original).

86. Rousseau, *Emile*, trans. Allan Bloom (New York: Basic Books, 1979), p. 40.

87. Hume, "Of the Original Contract," in *Essays*, p. 478.

4. The Federal Convention as Founder

1. David F. Epstein, *The Political Theory of* The Federalist (Chicago: University of Chicago Press, 1984), p. 8. See his pp. 7–10 for a fuller discussion of the plan of *The Federalist*.

2. *Federalist* 37:231 (emphasis added).

3. It is a curious fact of modern scholarship on *The Federalist* that this transitional section, revealing though it is about the origins of American government, has received so little attention. Charles Beard does not mention any of the essays in this series in his *Economic Interpretation of the Constitution of the United States*, despite their obvious relevance to his thesis, nor do they receive serious consideration in *Fame and the Founding Fathers*, the collected writings of Douglass Adair. More recent commentators also give numbers 37–40 short shrift. There is no sustained discussion of them, at least as they relate to the role and significance of the Federal Convention, in George W. Carey, The Federalist: *Design for a Constitutional Republic* (Urbana: University of Illinois Press, 1989); Morton White, *Philosophy,* The Federalist, *and the Constitution* (New York: Oxford University Press, 1987); or Garry Wills, *Explaining America:* The Federalist (London: Athlone Press, 1981). Notable exceptions are Epstein, *Political*

Theory of The Federalist, and Marvin Meyers, "Founding and Revolution: A Commentary on Publius-Madison," in *The Hofstadter Aegis: A Memorial,* ed. Stanley Elkins and Eric McKitrick (New York: Knopf, 1974), pp. 3–35.

4. As Matthews puts it, noting his own debt to the work of the Frankfurt School, "If Madison worshipped a deity, it would be reason—not the substantive Reason of philosophers as diverse as Plato, Hegel, and Marcuse, but the instrumental reason of the modern age." *If Men Were Angels: James Madison and the Heartless Empire of Reason,* p. 22; see also pp. 8–9, 19.

5. Stanley Elkins and Eric McKitrick, "The Founding Fathers: Young Men of the Revolution," *Political Science Quarterly* 76 (1961): 200. For their overview of constitutional historiography up to their day, see pp. 181–200. In discussing the founding generation, Elkins and McKitrick show great respect for the nineteenth-century "legend of a transcendent effort of statesmanship" (p. 212) but insist on explaining it as a matter of sociological circumstance. Madison and his counterparts thought "in continental terms" (p. 208) not because this was the truest light in which to see American affairs, as the authors argue, but because their careers took shape within national institutions.

6. John P. Roche, "The Founding Fathers: A Reform Caucus in Action," *American Political Science Review* 55 (1961): 799–816.

7. Calvin C. Jillson, "Constitution-Making: Alignment and Realignment in the Federal Convention of 1787," *American Political Science Review* 75 (1981): 598–612.

8. Judith N. Shklar, "*The Federalist* as Myth," *Yale Law Journal* 90 (1981): 942–44.

9. JM to Thomas Jefferson, 24 October 1787, *PJM* 10:208. Even Roche, who emphasizes the mundanely political side of the Federal Convention, concedes that all of its members, "nationalists" and "states'-righters" alike, shared the same "fundamental purposes": "Basic differences of opinion emerged, of course, but these were not ideological; they were *structural.*" "The Founding Fathers: A Reform Caucus in Action," p. 803 (emphasis in the original).

10. *Federalist* 37:234–35.

11. Ibid., pp. 231–32.

12. Ibid., pp. 237–39.

13. Ibid., 18:111–13.

14. Ibid., 20:128–29 (emphasis in the original). Cf. Hamilton's similar observations in *Federalist* 15:93–94.

15. See his speeches of 30 May 1787, 29 June 1787, 30 June 1787, and 14 July 1787, in *PJM* 10:18–19, 86–87, 88–90, 100–102. This is not to say that he meant to do away with the states, only that he did not want them to have any direct role in the new government.

16. *Federalist* 37:233–34.

17. Epstein, *Political Theory of* The Federalist, pp. 111–18.

18. *Federalist* 10:61, 14:88.

19. Ibid., 37:238.

20. Ibid., pp. 233–34.

21. Ibid., pp. 234–35.

22. For the comment on Locke, see "Spirit of Governments," 20 February 1792, *MF,* p. 183. For Madison's zoological interests, see JM to Thomas Jefferson, 11 February 1784, *PJM* 7:419; Notes on Buffon's *Histoire Naturelle,* ca. May 1786; and JM to Thomas Jefferson, 19 June 1786, in *PJM* 9:29–47, 78–80. The

last item is an especially revealing instance of Madison's faith in scientific investigation. It contains a lengthy description of his dissection of a weasel and concludes with the assertion that his own findings "certainly contradict" those of Buffon.

23. *Federalist* 37:235.
24. Ibid.
25. Ibid., 43:297.
26. Ibid., 37:235–36.
27. JM to Archibald Stuart, 30 October 1787, *PJM* 10:232. *Federalist* 37 first appeared several months later, on 11 January 1788.
28. *Federalist* 9:51–52. Cf. Madison's remarks in *Federalist* 14:84–85, 88–89; 47:324; 63:427–28.
29. *Federalist* 51:349. Madison refers to prudence in its grand, political sense elsewhere in *The Federalist* as well. Thus, in concluding his account of the motives of representatives under the Constitution, he writes: "It is possible that these may all be insufficient to controul the caprice and wickedness of man. But are they not all that government will admit, and that human prudence can devise?" (57:387) At the same time, and not unexpectedly, Madison speaks of prudence in the democratized sense to which we are accustomed, particularly as it applies to business matters. Here it summarizes such bourgeois virtues as sobriety, caution, and foresight: "An individual who is observed to be inconstant to his plans, or perhaps to carry on his affairs without any plan at all, is marked at once by all prudent people as a speedy victim to his own unsteadiness and folly." "What prudent merchant will hazard his fortunes in any new branch of commerce, when he knows not but that his plans may be rendered unlawful before they can be executed?" (62:420, 421) This transformation of the meaning of prudence, well under way in Madison's time, may explain why he tends to use the word "judgment" when speaking of the intellectual virtue appropriate to politics. For an exhaustive listing of Madison's usage of "prudence," "prudent," and "prudently," see Thomas Engeman et al., eds., *The Federalist Concordance* (Middletown, Conn.: Wesleyan University Press, 1980), p. 440.
30. See Adair, "'That Politics May Be Reduced to a Science': David Hume, James Madison, and the Tenth *Federalist*," in *Fame and the Founding Fathers: Essays by Douglass Adair*, ed. Trevor Colbourn, pp. 93–106 (New York: W. W. Norton & Co., 1974); Roy Branson, "James Madison and the Scottish Enlightenment," *Journal of the History of Ideas* 40 (1979): 243–49; and Wills, *Explaining America*, pp. 179–264.
31. See his Notes for a Speech Favoring Revision of the Virginia Constitution of 1776, 14 or 21 June 1784, *PJM* 8:78; Speech on the Term of the Executive, 17 July 1787, *PJM* 10:103–4; and *Federalist* 47. For useful general discussions of Montesquieu's place in the debate over the Constitution, see James W. Muller, "The American Framers' Debt to Montesquieu," in *The Revival of Constitutionalism*, ed. James W. Muller (Lincoln: University of Nebraska Press, 1988), pp. 87–102; and Judith N. Shklar, "Publius and the Science of the Past," *Yale Law Journal* 86 (1977): 1286–96.
32. *Federalist* 20:128.
33. See, respectively, Theodore Draper, "Hume and Madison: The Secrets of Federalist Paper No. 10," *Encounter* (February 1982): 34–47; and Epstein, *Political Theory of* The Federalist, p. 101.

34. See Edmund S. Morgan, "Safety in Numbers: Madison, Hume, and the Tenth *Federalist,*" *Huntington Library Quarterly* 49 (1986): 95–112.

35. JM to N. P. Trist, February 1830, *LJM* 4:58.

36. *Federalist* 47:323–31.

37. "Helvidius," No. 1, 24 August 1793, *MF,* p. 203.

38. Wills, *Explaining America,* pp. 28–33.

39. Anne M. Cohler, *Montesquieu's Comparative Politics and the Spirit of American Constitutionalism* (Lawrence: University Press of Kansas, 1988), p. 149. For her strained defense of the dominant influence of Montesquieu, see pp. 148–69.

40. The respective demands of theory and practice seem to have directed Madison's contemporaries to very different corners of their libraries. Locke was most cited during the struggle for independence, when basic matters of political right were at issue, whereas Hume, Montesquieu, and Blackstone came to prominence at a later date, when institutions were of primary concern. See Donald S. Lutz, "The Relative Influence of European Writers on Late Eighteenth-Century American Political Thought," *American Political Science Review* 78 (1984): 189–97.

41. Thus, for example, he cited both thinkers by name in an early paper on money and its value in circulation (though dismissing their views as "manifestly erroneous"). "Money," September 1779–March 1780, *PJM* 1:302–9. Under the heading of political science I would include questions relating to "political economy"—that is, to the place of commerce in the political order of a liberal republic—in which case Adam Smith should also be added to the list of major influences on Madison. For a valuable discussion of this subject (despite a gross overstatement of the attachment of Jefferson and Madison to classical models), see Drew R. McCoy, *The Elusive Republic: Political Economy in Jeffersonian America* (New York: W. W. Norton & Co., 1980).

42. JM to N. P. Trist, February 1830, *LJM* 4:58.

43. See White, *Philosophy,* The Federalist, *and the Constitution,* pp. 3–22.

44. JM to Nicholas Biddle, 23 February 1823, *LJM* 3:302.

45. "Spirit of Governments," 20 February 1792, *MF,* p. 183.

46. JM to Thomas Jefferson, 8 February 1825, *MF,* p. 349.

47. *Federalist* 38:239.

48. Cicero, *De Re Publica,* trans. Clinton Walker Keyes, Loeb Classical Library (Cambridge: Harvard University Press, 1928), bk. 2, sec. 1 (pp. 111–13).

49. *Federalist* 38:241.

50. Madison thus offers testimony to the fact that the "self-conscious" creation of constitutions—as opposed to their growth or development—is not an eighteenth-century invention, as Charles Howard McIlwain argues in *Constitutionalism: Ancient and Modern* (Ithaca, N.Y.: Cornell University Press, 1940), pp. 14, 23.

51. Bernard Bailyn, *The Ideological Origins of the American Revolution* (Cambridge: Harvard University Press, 1967), pp. 25–26.

52. *Federalist* 38:239–41.

53. Ibid., 37:238.

54. Ibid., 38:241.

55. Ibid.

56. Remark of Pierce Butler, 5 June 1787; Speech of Gunning Bedford, 30 June 1787, in *Notes,* pp. 73, 229.

57. See "Lycurgus," in *Plutarch's Lives*, trans. John Dryden (New York: Modern Library, 1864 [date of the revised Clough edition reprinted here]), p. 53.

58. In addition to the passage cited in the preceding paragraph, see *Federalist* 2:9, 20:128. Several of these points are suggested by Charles R. Kesler, "The Founders and the Classics," in *The American Founding: Essays on the Formation of the Constitution*, ed. J. Jackson Barlow, Leonard W. Levy, and Ken Masugi (New York: Greenwood Press, 1988), p. 83.

59. Epstein, *Political Theory of* The Federalist, p. 32.

60. *Federalist* 38:240.

61. Ibid., p. 246.

62. Ibid., pp. 242–43.

63. Cf. Plato, *Gorgias*, trans. Walter Hamilton (Harmondsworth, England: Penguin Books, 1960), 464; *The Laws of Plato*, trans. Thomas L. Pangle (Chicago: University of Chicago Press, 1980), 720b–e; Aristotle, *Nicomachean Ethics*, trans. Hippocrates G. Apostle (Grinnell, Iowa: Peripatetic Press, 1975), 1141b23–24, 1104a9; and Plutarch, "Lycurgus," in *Plutarch's Lives*, p. 53.

64. See Stephen G. Salkever, "Aristotle's Social Science," *Political Theory* 9 (1981): 500–503. For a brief, helpful discussion of the differences between Plato and Aristotle in the use of this analogy (and for the source of several of my cites above), see p. 508 n. 50.

65. Gordon S. Wood, *The Creation of the American Republic, 1776–1787* (New York: W. W. Norton & Co., 1972), pp. 471–518, and "Democracy and the Constitution," in *How Democratic Is the Constitution?* ed. Robert A. Goldwin and William A. Schambra (Washington, D.C.: American Enterprise Institute, 1980), pp. 1–17; Wills, *Explaining America*, pp. 179–264.

66. *Federalist* 10:62.

67. Paul A. Rahe, *Republics Ancient and Modern*, 3 vols. (Chapel Hill: University of North Carolina Press, 1994), 3:44–45, 275 n. 60. For an overview of this question and a summary of the case against Wood and Wills, see Alan Gibson, "Impartial Representation and the Extended Republic: Towards a Comprehensive and Balanced Treatment of the Tenth *Federalist* Paper," *History of Political Thought* 12 (1991): 263–304. For the quote, see *Federalist* 10:60. Madison makes the same point more bluntly in his "Vices of the Political System of the United States," April 1787, *PJM* 9:354: "Representative appointments are sought from 3 motives. 1. ambition. 2. personal interest. 3. public good. Unhappily the two first are proved by experience to be the most prevalent."

68. *Federalist* 10:63–64.

69. Ibid., 57:384–87.

70. Martin Diamond, "Democracy and *The Federalist*: A Reconsideration of the Framers' Intent," *American Political Science Review* 53 (1959): 67.

71. *Federalist* 39:250, 251.

72. Ibid., p. 253.

73. Kesler, "The Founders and the Classics," p. 84.

74. *Federalist* 37:233.

75. Ibid., 39:250.

76. JM to James Monroe, 21 June 1786, *PJM* 9:82. Cf. *Federalist* 18:114, where Madison compares the Achaean and Amphyctionic leagues and notes "a very material difference in the genius of the two systems."

77. *Federalist* 51:351–53.

78. Ibid., 14:84.

79. JM to Edmund Pendleton, 24 February 1787, *PJM* 9:295.

80. *Federalist* 39:250.

81. Epstein, *Political Theory of* The Federalist, p. 119.

82. Thomas L. Pangle, *The Spirit of Modern Republicanism: The Moral Vision of the American Founders and the Philosophy of Locke* (Chicago: University of Chicago Press, 1988), pp. 257–61.

83. *Federalist* 57:387.

84. Ibid., 43:297.

85. Ibid., 39:251.

86. Ibid., 42:283.

87. Ibid., 51:253, 55:374, 63:425.

88. Ibid., 37:233.

89. "Republican Distribution of Citizens," 5 March 1792, *MF,* pp. 184–86.

90. Cf. Epstein, *Political Theory of* The Federalist, p. 124; and Aristotle, *Politics,* trans. H. Rackham, Loeb Classical Library (Cambridge: Harvard University Press, 1932), 1253a1–19.

91. *Federalist* 49:340–41.

92. Speech on Title for the President, 11 May 1789, *PJM* 12:155. Needless to say, Madison's quasi-classical concern for virtue can be overstated. Alexander Landi, for instance, simply cannot support the claim that Madison, "as it were, *added* Locke to Aristotle." "Madison's Political Theory," *Political Science Reviewer* 6 (1976):84 (emphasis in the original).

93. *Federalist* 40:258, 263. See also 39:253.

94. "All efforts to restore energy to the federal government have proved ineffectual, when exerted in the mode directed . . . by the confederation," announced Hugh Brackenridge in defending the Constitution. Robert Whitehall, speaking for many a fellow Anti-Federalist, thought it clear that the members of the Convention had "set aside the laws under which they were appointed." See Brackenridge, Pennsylvania House of Assembly, 28 October 1787; and Whitehall, Pennsylvania Ratifying Convention, 28 November 1787, in *FC* 1:199, 201. Only modern scholars, motivated perhaps by a desire to find an unassailable legitimacy in the founding, have maintained that there was nothing irregular in the activities of the Convention. See Forrest McDonald, *Novus Ordo Seclorum: The Intellectual Origins of the Constitution* (Lawrence: University Press of Kansas, 1985), p. 279; and Roche, "The Founding Fathers: A Reform Caucus in Action," pp. 799–800. For correctives, see Bruce Ackerman, *We the People: Transformations* (Cambridge: Harvard University Press, 1998), pp. 34–39; Elkins and McKitrick, "The Founding Fathers: Young Men of the Revolution," 209–10; Clinton Rossiter, *1787: The Grand Convention* (New York: W. W. Norton & Co., 1966), pp. 262–63; and Herbert J. Storing, *What the Anti-Federalists Were For* (Chicago: University of Chicago Press, 1981), p. 7.

95. *Federalist* 40:258–59.

96. See *Records* 3:574–75 for the commission from Delaware; ibid., pp. 559–86 for all the states. For Madison's awareness of the problem with respect to Delaware, see his Speech on Proportional Representation in the Legislature, 30 May 1787, *PJM* 10:19.

97. *Federalist* 40:259–60 (emphasis in the original).

98. As William Paterson averred in Philadelphia, "The Commissions under which we [act are] not only the measure of our power, they [denote] also the sentiments of the States on the subject of our deliberation" (speech of 9 June 1787, *Notes,* p. 95).

99. *Federalist* 40:263 (emphasis in the original).

100. See the congressional debate, *FC* 1:195–98.

101. For the commissions of Pennsylvania, New Hampshire, Delaware, Georgia, New York, South Carolina, Massachusetts, and Maryland, see *Records* 3:566, 572, 574, 577, 579–80, 581, 584, 586. See also, *Federalist* 40:258.

102. *Federalist* 40:263.

103. Richard Henry Lee, Continental Congress, 27 September 1787; Richard Henry Lee to George Mason, 1 October 1787; Luther Martin, "Genuine Information," 1788, in *FC* 1:196, 201, 203.

104. See "A Republican Federalist," No. 3, 9 January 1788, in Herbert J. Storing, ed., *The Complete Anti-Federalist*, 7 vols. (Chicago: University of Chicago Press, 1981), 4:172–73; and Martin, "Genuine Information," *FC* 1:203. For Madison's intent to make such "encroachments" on the state constitutions, see his letters to George Washington (16 April 1787) and Edmund Pendleton (22 April 1787), *PJM* 9:385, 395.

105. *Federalist* 40:263.

106. Ibid., pp. 264–66 (emphasis in the original).

107. Ibid., pp. 265–66 (emphasis in the original).

108. Ibid., p. 265.

5. Confronting Jefferson and Hamilton

1. Morton J. Frisch, *The Hamilton-Madison-Jefferson Triangle*, Ashbrook Essay no. 4 (Ashland, Ohio: John M. Ashbrook Center for Public Affairs, 1992), p. 5.

2. Richard K. Matthews, *The Radical Politics of Thomas Jefferson* (Lawrence: University Press of Kansas, 1984), p. 104 (see also pp. 98, 102, 116). For Matthews's elaboration of this view, see *If Men Were Angels: James Madison and the Heartless Empire of Reason* (Lawrence: University Press of Kansas, 1995).

3. Adrienne Koch, *Jefferson and Madison: The Great Collaboration* (New York: Knopf, 1950), p. 63.

4. See, for example, Ralph Ketcham, *James Madison: A Biography* (Charlottesville: University Press of Virginia, 1971), pp. 314–15, 605; Meyers, *MF*, pp. xlii–xliii; and George W. Carey, *In Defense of the Constitution* (Indianapolis: Liberty Fund, 1995), pp. 77–121.

5. For background on Gem and on Jefferson's activities in Paris, see Koch, *Jefferson and Madison*, pp. 75–88; and editorial note, *PTJ* 15:384–87.

6. TJ to James Madison, 6 September 1789, *PTJ* 15:392–94.

7. Editorial note, *PTJ* 15:390.

8. See Koch, *Jefferson and Madison*, pp. 82–91; and Paine, *The Rights of Man*, in *The Thomas Paine Reader*, ed. Michael Foot and Isaac Kramnick (Harmondsworth, England: Penguin Books, 1987), p. 204: "Every age and generation must be as free to act for itself, *in all cases*, as the ages and generations which preceded it. The vanity and presumption of governing beyond the grave, is the most ridiculous and insolent of all tyrannies. Man has no property in man; neither has any generation a property in the generations which are to follow" (emphasis in the original).

9. TJ to James Madison, 6 September 1789, *PTJ* 15:392–93.

10. For Madison's like usage, as well as his seeming criticisms of Locke,

see pp. 66–67. For a discussion of Jefferson's debt to Locke on property, see Koch, *Jefferson and Madison,* pp. 78–79.

11. TJ to James Madison, 6 September 1789, *PTJ* 15:395–96.

12. Charles A. Miller, *Jefferson and Nature: An Interpretation* (Baltimore: Johns Hopkins University Press, 1988), p. 163. For Jefferson's later appeals to the doctrine, also see p. 163.

13. TJ to James Madison, 6 September 1789, *PTJ* 15:396.

14. TJ to Samuel Kercheval, 12 July 1816, in *The Portable Thomas Jefferson,* ed. Merrill D. Peterson (New York: Penguin Books, 1975), p. 559.

15. Matthews, *Radical Politics of Thomas Jefferson,* p. 22.

16. JM to Thomas Jefferson, 4 February 1790, *PJM* 13:22–23. Citations of the letter are to the revised not the original text, both of which are reprinted here. The differences between the two versions are only stylistic and suggest, as the editors note, that Madison "anticipated the eventual publication of this important statement of his political philosophy" (18).

17. Matthews, *Radical Politics of Thomas Jefferson,* p. 24.

18. JM to Thomas Jefferson, 4 February 1790, *PJM* 13:22 (emphasis in the original).

19. Note during the Convention for Amending the Constitution of Virginia, December 1829, *WJM* 9:359.

20. JM to Thomas Jefferson, 4 February 1790, *PJM* 13:24 (emphasis in the original).

21. Locke, *Second Treatise,* in *Two Treatises of Government,* ed. Peter Laslett, student edition (Cambridge: Cambridge University Press, 1988), sec. 119 (pp. 347–48).

22. Hanna Pitkin, "Obligation and Consent I," *American Political Science Review* 59 (1965): 990–99; "Obligation and Consent II," *American Political Science Review* 60 (1966): 39–52. The quote is from p. 39 of the second part of the article.

23. JM to Thomas Jefferson, 4 February 1790, *PJM* 13:24.

24. Ibid.

25. Ibid.

26. *Federalist* 49:339.

27. Speech in the House of Representatives, 8 June 1789, *MF,* pp. 163–64. Consider also his description in *The Federalist* of the Constitution's "mode" for amendment: "It guards equally against that extreme facility which would render the Constitution too mutable; and that extreme difficulty which might perpetuate its discovered faults" (43:296).

28. Speech in the House of Representatives, 8 June 1789, *MF,* p. 164 (emphasis added).

29. Robert A. Goldwin, *From Parchment to Power: How James Madison Used the Bill of Rights to Save the Constitution* (Washington, D.C.: AEI Press, 1997), p. 88.

30. Bryan, "Centinel," No. 1, in Cecilia M. Kenyon, ed., *The Antifederalists* (Boston: Northeastern University Press, 1985), p. 13; Yates, "Brutus," No. 1, *FC* 1:125.

31. See TJ to James Madison, 20 December 1787; and TJ to James Madison, 15 March 1789, in *The Portable Thomas Jefferson,* pp. 428–32, 438–40.

32. *Federalist* 57:387.

33. JM to Thomas Jefferson, 4 February 1790, *PJM* 13:22.

34. *Federalist* 49:340 (emphasis in the original).

35. Koch suggests the comparison (but does not make it herself) by op-

posing the views of Jefferson (and Paine) on the question of generational obligation to those of Burke (*Jefferson and Madison*, pp. 88–91). For more explicit presentations of Madison as a conservative, see Garry Wills, *Explaining America: The Federalist* (London: Athlone Press, 1981), pp. 24–33; Drew R. McCoy, *The Last of the Fathers: James Madison and the Republican Legacy* (Cambridge: Cambridge University Press, 1989), pp. 39–64; and Miller, *Jefferson and Nature*, p. 162.

36. Quoted by Wills, *Explaining America*, p. 30.

37. Quoted by McCoy, *Last of the Fathers*, p. 59.

38. Thomas L. Pangle, *The Spirit of Modern Republicanism: The Moral Vision of the American Founders and the Philosophy of Locke* (Chicago: University of Chicago Press, 1988), p. 298 n. 5. Harry V. Jaffa rightly asks whether such "secular" veneration is an adequate source of stability and moral restraint, though in his admiration for Lincoln's remedy, "a political religion," he fails to develop Madison's alternative as fully as he might. See *Crisis of the House Divided: An Interpretation of the Issues in the Lincoln-Douglas Debates* (Chicago: University of Chicago Press, 1959), pp. 230–32, 236–42.

39. Montesquieu, *The Spirit of the Laws*, trans. Thomas Nugent (New York: Hafner Publishing Co., 1966), author's explanatory notes, p. lxxi.

40. Montesquieu's account of the "great operative principles of government" could be credited with but a "portion of truth," according to Madison ("Spirit of Governments," 20 February 1792, *MF*, p. 183).

41. See Montesquieu, *Spirit of the Laws*, bk. 3, chaps. 3–5 (pp. 20–24); bk. 8, chap. 16 (pp. 120–21). Cf. *Federalist* 9:50: "It is impossible to read the history of the petty Republics of Greece and Italy, without feeling sensations of horror and disgust at the distractions with which they were continually agitated, and at the rapid succession of revolutions, by which they were kept in a state of perpetual vibration, between the extremes of tyranny and anarchy."

42. Aristotle, *Politics*, trans. H. Rackham, Loeb Classical Library (Cambridge: Harvard University Press, 1932), 1277b25–32.

43. Wills, *Explaining America*, p. 26.

44. See James Morton Smith, "Virginia and Kentucky Resolutions," in *James Madison and the American Nation, 1751–1836: An Encyclopedia*, ed. Robert A. Rutland (New York: Simon and Schuster, 1994), p. 422.

45. Kentucky Resolutions, 16 November 1798; and Kentucky Resolutions, 22 February 1799, in Henry Steele Commager, ed., *Documents of American History*, 7th ed., 2 vols. (New York: Appleton-Century-Crofts, 1963), 1:179, 181, 184.

46. Virginia Resolutions, 24 December 1798, in Commager, ed., *Documents of American History* 1:182. Madison had foreseen the possibility of such intervention even as he worked to establish a far more powerful national government: "If it be asked, what is to be the consequence, in case Congress shall misconstrue this part of the Constitution [the 'necessary and proper' clause], and exercise powers not warranted by its true meaning? . . . [I]n the last resort, a remedy must be obtained from the people, who can by the election of more faithful representatives, annul the acts of the usurpers. The truth is, that this ultimate redress may be more confided in against unconstitutional acts of foederal than of the State Legislatures, for this plain reason, that as every such act of the former, will be an invasion of the rights of the latter, these will be ever ready to mark the innovation, to sound the alarm to the people and to

exert their local influence in effecting a change of foederal representatives." *Federalist* 44:305.

47. Report on the Virginia Resolutions, 1799–1800, *MF,* p. 270 (emphasis added).

48. I am persuaded by Madison's defense of the Virginia Resolutions in his Notes on Nullification, 1835–36 (*MF,* pp. 418–42), and see no reason to agree with Frisch, who equates "interposition" with "nullification" and asserts that both, in their "essence," are "suspensive or preventative and not merely declaratory of opinion" (*The Hamilton-Madison-Jefferson Triangle,* pp. 24–25).

49. Notes on Nullification, 1835–36, *MF,* pp. 418, 429 (note).

50. AH to Edward Carrington, 26 May 1792, *PAH* 11:427 (emphasis in the original).

51. Ibid., p. 438.

52. Ibid., pp. 437, 440, 442.

53. At one extreme is McDonald, who charges Madison with self-promotion and simple political expediency. See *Alexander Hamilton: A Biography* (New York: W. W. Norton & Co., 1979), pp. 175, 177–86, 199–201. At the other, Brant and Ketcham attempt to place Madison's actions in a more sympathetic light while still acknowledging his inconsistency. See, respectively, *James Madison,* 6 vols. (Indianapolis: Bobbs-Merrill, 1941–61), 3:331–33; and *Madison: A Biography,* pp. 314–15.

54. Gaillard Hunt, *The Life of James Madison* (New York: Doubleday, Page & Co., 1902), p. 211; Brant, *James Madison* 3:332.

55. Carey, *In Defense of the Constitution,* pp. 107–16.

56. JM to C. E. Haynes, 25 February 1831, *WJM* 9:442.

57. Speeches of 26 June 1787 and 18 June 1787, in *Notes,* pp. 195–96, 134–35.

58. Speech of 18 June 1787, *Notes,* pp. 138–39, 136.

59. For a useful discussion of Hamilton's plan of government and its reception at the Federal Convention, see John C. Miller, *Alexander Hamilton: Portrait in Paradox* (New York: Harper & Row, 1959), pp. 163–73.

60. See Speech on Assumption of the State Debts, 2 March 1790; JM to Edmund Pendleton, 4 March 1790; and JM to Henry Lee, 13 April 1790, in *PJM* 13:80, 85, 147.

61. In his desire to save some part of Madison's legacy for broad construction of the Constitution, Irving Brant reverses these priorities, arguing that disagreement with Hamilton "on social and economic matters . . . grew until it produced a change in Madison's political and constitutional views" (*James Madison* 2:217). Drew R. McCoy also reduces the Madison-Hamilton dispute to questions of political economy, though with the rather different intent of claiming Madison for the eighteenth-century English "country" party (*Elusive Republic,* pp. 136–65).

62. Jack N. Rakove, *James Madison and the Creation of the American Republic* (Glenview, Ill.: Scott, Foresman, 1990), p. 91.

63. Interview with N. P. Trist, 27 September 1834, *Records* 3:534.

64. Hamilton declared such a purpose in a personal memorandum written as the Federal Convention drew to a close: "If the government is adopted, it is probable general Washington will be the President of the United States. This will insure a wise choice of men to administer the government and a good administration. A good administration will conciliate the confidence and

affection of the people and perhaps enable the government to acquire more consistency than the proposed constitution seems to promise for so great a Country. It may then triumph altogether over the state governments and reduce them to an intire subordination, dividing the larger states into smaller districts." Conjectures about the New Constitution, 17–30 September 1787, *PAH* 4:276.

65. "An Opinion on the Constitutionality of an Act to Establish a Bank," 23 February 1791, *PAH* 8:100, 102–3, 106, 105 (emphasis in the original).

66. Ibid., pp. 105, 103, 98 (emphasis in the original). Cf. *Federalist* 78:524, where Hamilton spoke of a "limited constitution" as one that contained "certain specified exceptions to the legislative authority." On this view, acts were unconstitutional not when they extended beyond enumerated powers but when they were contrary to the "tenor"—that is, the *general* meaning and intent—of the Constitution.

67. "Report on Manufactures," 5 December 1791, *PAH* 10:302–3 (emphasis in the original).

68. "The Farmer Refuted," 23 February 1775, *PAH* 1:88 (emphasis added).

69. See Gerald Stourzh, *Alexander Hamilton and the Idea of Republican Government* (Stanford, Calif.: Stanford University Press, 1970), pp. 24–26; and Mackubin Thomas Owens, Jr., "Alexander Hamilton on Natural Rights and Prudence," *Interpretation* 14 (1986): 331–51.

70. "The Farmer Refuted," 23 February 1775, *PAH* 1:87.

71. Ibid., p. 86.

72. Locke, *Second Treatise,* sec. 139 (pp. 361–62). Locke's reasoning is similar in defending executive prerogative (though in this instance it is a question of legal rather than of constitutional right). Ibid., chap. 14 (pp. 374–80).

73. Ibid., chap. 11 (pp. 355–63); sec. 107 (p. 338); sec. 143 (p. 364).

74. See Harvey Flaumenhaft, *The Effective Republic: Administration and Constitution in the Thought of Alexander Hamilton* (Durham, N.C.: Duke University Press, 1992), pp. 61–65; and Stourzh, *Hamilton and the Idea of Republican Government*, pp. 40–44, 56–63.

75. Speech on the Bank Bill, 2 February 1791, *PJM* 13:373–78 (emphasis in the original); at the Federal Convention of 18 August 1787 and 14 September 1787, in *Notes*, pp. 477–78, 638.

76. Speech on the Bank Bill, 2 February 1791, *PJM* 13:379–80.

77. Speech on the Bank Bill, 8 February 1791, *PJM* 13:384.

78. *Federalist* 39:256.

79. As Madison summarized the matter when forced to revisit it during his retirement, the powers of the state governments "are understood to extend to all the Acts whether as means or ends required for the welfare of the Community, and falling within the range of just Government. To withhold from such a Government any particular power necessary or useful in itself, would be to deprive the people of the good dependent on its exercise." JM to Spencer Roane, 2 September 1819, *MF,* p. 362. Cf. his Report on the Virginia Resolutions, 1799–1800, *MF,* p. 255, where he wrote that the "peculiar character of the [national] government" is to be "possessed of particular and definite powers only, not of the general and indefinite powers vested in ordinary governments."

80. Speech on the Bank Bill, 2 February 1791, *PJM* 13:380–81.

81. Speech on the Bank Bill, 8 February 1791, *PJM* 13:386–87.

82. JM to Henry Lee, 1 January 1792, *PJM* 14:180 (emphasis in the original).

83. JM to Henry Lee, 21 January 1792, *PJM* 14:193.

84. See Colleen A. Sheehan, "Madison's Party Press Essays," *Interpretation* 17 (1990): 360–63.

85. "A Candid State of Parties," 26 September 1792, *MF,* pp. 189–90.

86. Michael P. Zuckert, *Natural Rights and the New Republicanism* (Princeton, N.J.: Princeton University Press, 1994), pp. 312–13. As Zuckert shows, Wood and Pocock (as well as others following their lead) overlook this instrumental relationship in their zeal to discover a more classical and moralistic strain of American republicanism.

87. "Spirit of Governments," 20 February 1792, *MF,* pp. 183–84.

88. "Consolidation," 5 December 1791, *MF,* pp. 181–82 (emphasis in the original).

89. "Government of the United States," 4 February 1792, *PJM* 14:218.

90. "Charters," 18 January 1792, *PJM* 14:192 (emphasis in the original).

91. "Who Are the Best Keepers of the People's Liberties?" 20 December 1792, *PJM* 14:426.

92. "Universal Peace," 2 February 1792, *MF,* pp. 192–93.

6. The Legitimate Meaning of the Constitution

1. *Federalist* 44:304.

2. Ibid., 37:236.

3. JM to Henry Lee, 25 June 1824, *LJM* 3:442.

4. Irving Brant, *James Madison,* 6 vols. (Indianapolis: Bobbs-Merrill, 1941–61), 3:332–33.

5. Paul C. Peterson, "The Problem of Consistency in the Statesmanship of James Madison," in *The American Founding: Politics, Statesmanship, and the Constitution,* ed. Ralph Rossum and Gary L. McDowell (Port Washington, N.Y.: Kennikat Press, 1981), p. 125.

6. George W. Carey, *In Defense of the Constitution* (Indianapolis: Liberty Fund, 1995), p. 80. See also John Zvesper, "The Madisonian Systems," *Western Political Quarterly* 37 (1984): 236–56.

7. See Lance Banning, *The Sacred Fire of Liberty: James Madison and the Founding of the Federal Republic* (Ithaca, N.Y.: Cornell University Press, 1995), pp. 244–47, 332–33, 347.

8. See JM to Edmund Pendleton, 8 January 1782, *PJM* 4:22–23 (national bank); Proposed Amendment of Articles of Confederation, 12 March 1781, *PJM* 3:17 (coercion); Protest of Virginia Delegates, 10 October 1781, *PJM* 3:285 (territorial disputes); JM to Edmund Pendleton, 25 June 1782, *PJM* 4:369 (trade); JM to Edmund Randolph, 16 June 1783, *PJM* 7:159 (peacetime army); JM to Edmund Pendleton, 28 July 1783, *PJM* 7:257 (jurisdiction over permanent seat); and JM to James Monroe, 27 November 1784, *PJM* 8:156 (Indian affairs).

9. Proposed Amendment of Articles of Confederation, 12 March 1781, *PJM* 3:17; JM to Edmund Pendleton, 8 January 1782, *PJM* 4:23.

10. This held as well for the Federal Convention. As Banning has shown, even while advocating such measures as a national veto over local legislation, Madison assumed that the new government would be one of enumerated powers and that the states would retain much of their authority: "Madison was a

determined 'nationalist' only in his view of how the new regime should work, not in his opinion of the work it ought to do" (see *Sacred Fire of Liberty*, pp. 158–64).

11. JM to Edmund Randolph, 4 June 1782, *PJM* 4:314.

12. Speech on Removal Power of the President, 16 June 1789, *PJM* 12: 225–29.

13. See David F. Epstein, *The Political Theory of* The Federalist (Chicago: University of Chicago Press, 1984), p. 44: "Borrowing the terms from Hamilton quoted earlier, *Federalist* 44's language implies that government may use all means which are 'usefu[l]' if they are proper, and all means which are 'essential' even if they are improper." For a similarly unconvincing attempt to derive broad construction from *Federalist* 44, see Garry Wills, *Explaining America:* The Federalist (London: Athlone Press, 1981), pp. 49–50.

14. *Federalist* 44:304.

15. Remark on Amendments to the Constitution, 18 August 1789, *PJM* 12:346.

16. See Peterson, "The Problem of Consistency in the Statesmanship of James Madison," p. 127.

17. See *Federalist* 44:303: If the Federal Convention had followed the Articles of Confederation in prohibiting the exercise of any power not expressly delegated, "it is evident that the new Congress would be continually exposed as their predecessors have been, to the alternative of construing the term 'expressly' with so much rigour as to disarm the government of all real authority whatever, *or with so much latitude as to destroy altogether the force of the restriction*" (emphasis added).

18. JM to James Monroe, 27 November 1784, *PJM* 8:156; *Federalist* 40:259, 44:304–5. H. Jefferson Powell has attempted to describe these common-law assumptions in some detail. He argues that the founders, following the traditions of the metropole, emphasized "intent" in legal construction but that they understood it as a product of the "interpretive process" rather than as "some fixed meaning that the author locks into the document's text at the outset." Raoul Berger has provided an important corrective to this view, especially where Madison is concerned. See H. Jefferson Powell, "The Original Understanding of Original Intent," *Harvard Law Review* 98 (1985): 885–948; and Raoul Berger, "'Original Intention' in Historical Perspective," *George Washington Law Review* 54 (1986): 296–337.

19. Paul Finkelman, "The Constitution and the Intentions of the Framers: The Limits of Historical Analysis," *University of Pittsburgh Law Review* 50 (1989): 360, 363–64. Madison, then a member of the House, was joined in opposition by two other representatives who had been present in Philadelphia. It should be noted as well that Madison did, on occasion, resort to the intentions of the framers in later years, but only in private correspondence and only when their views did not conflict with those of the ratifiers.

20. Speech in the House of Representatives, 6 April 1796, *Records* 3:374.

21. JM to Thomas Ritchie, 15 September 1821, *LJM* 3:228.

22. Donald O. Dewey, "James Madison Helps Clio Interpret the Constitution," *American Journal of Legal History* 15 (1971): 45–47.

23. JM to John J. Jackson, 27 December 1821, *WJM* 9:74–75 ("forming" is not emphasized in the original).

24. See the speech of Attorney General Edwin Meese before the American Bar Association, 9 July 1985: "Those who framed the Constitution chose

their words carefully; they debated at great length the most minute points. The language they chose meant something. It is incumbent upon the Court to determine what that meaning was." Federalist Society, *The Great Debate: Interpreting Our Written Constitution* (Washington, D.C.: Federalist Society, 1986), pp. 9–10. Though critics have properly stressed Meese's frequent appeals to the specific intent of the members of the Federal Convention, it should be noted that he often spoke more broadly of original intent: "The approach this administration advocates is rooted in the text of the Constitution as illuminated by those who drafted, proposed, and ratified it. . . . Our approach understands the significance of a written document and seeks to discern the particular and general principles it expresses." Speech before the Washington, D.C., chapter of the Federalist Society, 15 December 1985, ibid., pp. 35–36.

25. Former Justice Department spokesman Terry Eastland, as quoted in Jack N. Rakove, "Mr. Meese, Meet Mr. Madison," *Atlantic Monthly,* December 1986, p. 79. Rakove objects to the appropriation of Madison by conservatives like Eastland and asserts, astonishingly, that Madison would have preferred to leave the question of minority and individual rights "to the arbitrary will of federal judges" rather than "the judgment of democratic majorities within the states" (p. 82). Needless to say, Madison did not wish to see any officer under the Constitution exercise an "arbitrary will," nor was his sole concern the protection of minority and individual rights. To the extent that he favored national intervention to protect these rights, it was to be *legislative,* in the form of a veto, thus securing a proper degree of both impartiality and responsibility. He was unsuccessful, of course, in having such a provision included in the Constitution and thereafter defended the instrument as it was ratified rather than as it might be. In appealing to Madison's early support for a national veto, Rakove, like those whom he criticizes, relies on Madison's specific and subjective intent at the moment of framing.

26. Quoted in Gary L. McDowell, "The Politics of Original Intention," in *The Constitution, the Courts, and the Quest for Justice,* ed. Robert A. Goldwin and William A. Schambra (Washington, D.C.: American Enterprise Institute, 1989), p. 15.

27. As Alexis de Tocqueville observed in discussing the "great parties" of this era, the Federalists, with their aristocratic principles, arose in large part from the peculiar circumstances of the day (the "ruin of the first Confederation made the people afraid of falling into anarchy," etc.). With time and a more settled state of affairs, it became apparent that the Federalists' principles "were inapplicable in their entirety to the society they wished to control." See *Democracy in America,* trans. George Lawrence (New York: Harper & Row, 1966), vol. 1, part 2, chap. 2 (pp. 174–78).

28. JM to Joseph C. Cabell, 18 September 1828, *LJM* 3:639–40.

29. See Dewey, "Madison Helps Clio Interpret the Constitution," 39–42.

30. JM to Spencer Roane, 6 May 1821, *MF,* p. 366. See also his speech in the House of Representatives, 6 April 1796, *Records* 3:372–75.

31. JM to Spencer Roane, 2 September 1819, *MF,* p. 361.

32. See the speech of Associate Justice William Brennan at Georgetown University, 12 October 1985: "In its most doctrinaire incarnation, this view demands that Justices discern *exactly what the Framers thought* about the question under consideration and simply follow that intention in resolving the cases before them. It is a view that feigns self-effacing deference to the *specific judgments* of those who forged our original social compact. But in truth it is little

more than arrogance cloaked as humility. It is arrogant to pretend that from our vantage we can gauge accurately the intent of the Framers on the application of principle to specific, contemporary questions" (*Great Debate*, p. 14, emphasis added). See also Stephen Macedo, *The New Right v. The Constitution* (Washington, D.C.: Cato Institute, 1987), pp. 7–23; and Jack N. Rakove, *Original Meanings: Politics and Ideas in the Making of the Constitution* (New York: Knopf, 1996), pp. 3–22.

33. JM to Spencer Roane, 6 May 1821, *MF*, p. 365; JM to M. L. Hurlbert, May 1830, *WJM* 9:372.

34. JM to Henry Lee, 21 January 1792; JM to Edmund Pendleton, 21 January 1792, in *PJM* 14:193–94, 195. JM to Thomas Ritchie, 15 September 1821; JM to Thomas Jefferson, 27 June 1823; JM to Henry Lee, 25 June 1824; JM to Andrew Stevenson, 25 March 1826, in *LJM* 3:228, 325, 442, 522.

35. *Federalist* 37:236.

36. JM to Henry Lee, 25 June 1824, *LJM* 3:442.

37. JM to Converse Sherman, 10 March 1826, *LJM* 3:519.

38. See Dewey, "Madison Helps Clio Interpret the Constitution," p. 51 n. 41.

39. Justice Brennan at Georgetown University, 12 October 1985, in *Great Debate*, p. 17.

40. JM to Spencer Roane, 2 September 1819, *MF*, p. 361. See also Speech on the Bank Bill, 2 February 1791, *PJM* 13:380–81; JM to Edward Livingston, 17 April 1824, *WJM* 9:188; and JM to Andrew Stevenson, 17 November 1830, *Records* 3:489.

41. JM to Spencer Roane, 2 September 1819, *MF*, pp. 361–62.

42. Speech on the Bank Bill, 2 February 1791, *PJM* 13:375.

43. Report on the Virginia Resolutions, 1799–1800, *MF*, p. 253. For Madison's wider discussion of the incompatibility of the common law with the American regime, see pp. 247–53.

44. Robert H. Bork, *The Tempting of America: The Political Seduction of the Law* (New York: Free Press, 1990), p. 144. For another contemporary defense of originalism that is indebted to Madison, see McDowell, "Politics of Original Intention," pp. 2–5.

45. Bork, *Tempting of America*, p. 218.

46. Ibid., p. 141.

47. Ibid., p. 145.

48. Ibid., pp. 27–28. As Bork writes of Chief Justice John Marshall, who wrote the opinion, "The Federalists stood for a much stronger national government than did the Jeffersonians. Today, it seems difficult to see the point in the struggle to draft and ratify the Constitution if Jefferson and his followers were correct" (p. 21). For obvious reasons, Bork does not number Madison among these "followers." Meese seems to share this reasoning: "Marshall was keeping faith with the original intention that Congress be free to elaborate and apply constitutional powers and principles" (speech before the Washington, D.C., chapter of the Federalist Society, 15 November 1985, in *Great Debate*, p. 35).

49. Macedo, *New Right v. The Constitution*, p. 25 (emphasis added).

50. Bork, *Tempting of America*, p. 139.

51. Indeed, *mutatis mutandis*, Bork's view of the Constitution often echoes Hamilton's: "The orthodoxy of our civil religion, which the Constitution has aptly been called, holds that we govern ourselves democratically, except

on those occasions, few in number though critically important, when the Constitution places a topic beyond the reach of majorities" (*Tempting of America*, p. 153).

52. Report on the Virginia Resolutions, 1799–1800, *MF*, p. 238.

53. JM to Spencer Roane, 6 May 1821, *MF*, p. 366.

54. JM to N. P. Trist, December 1831, *WJM* 9:476.

55. *Federalist* 10:60: "If a faction consists of less than a majority, relief is supplied by the republican principle, which enables the majority to defeat its sinister views by regular vote: It may clog the administration, it may convulse the society; but it will be unable to execute and mask its violence under the forms of the Constitution."

56. See Drew R. McCoy, *The Last of the Fathers: James Madison and the Republican Legacy* (Cambridge: Cambridge University Press, 1989), pp. 91–92.

57. JM to Thomas Ritchie, 18 December 1825, *WJM* 9:231–32.

58. See Paul Finkelman, "Bank of the United States," in Robert Rutland, ed., *James Madison and the American Nation, 1751–1836: An Encyclopedia* (New York: Simon and Schuster, 1994), p. 28.

59. JM to Charles Jared Ingersoll, 25 June 1831, *MF*, p. 393; JM to C. E. Haynes, 25 February 1831; JM to N. P. Trist, December 1831, in *WJM* 9:442, 476.

60. JM to Spencer Roane, 6 May 1821, *MF*, p. 366.

61. JM to Charles Jared Ingersoll, 25 June 1831, *MF*, p. 393.

62. JM to Spencer Roane, 2 September 1819, *MF*, pp. 359–61.

63. JM to Charles Jared Ingersoll, 25 June 1831, *MF*, p. 392.

64. JM to N. P. Trist, December 1831, *WJM* 9:477.

65. JM to Charles Jared Ingersoll, 25 June 1831, *MF*, p. 392–93.

66. See Finkelman, "The Constitution and the Intentions of the Framers," pp. 366–68, who fails to grasp the conservative aim behind Madison's understanding of precedent and blithely suggests that "'the father of the Constitution' intended the nation's frame of government to be a 'living Constitution.'"

67. Bruce Ackerman, *We the People: Foundations* (Cambridge: Harvard University Press, 1991). Setting aside their very different attitudes toward such extraconstitutional activity, Ackerman's requirements are akin to Madison's in important respects.

68. Though Madison would doubtless agree with Akhil Reed Amar that the people possess ultimate authority over the Constitution, he recognized—as Amar does not—that exercising such sovereignty outside the terms of the Constitution would effectively dissolve the regime (see Amar, "Philadelphia Revisited: Amending the Constitution Outside Article V," *University of Chicago Law Review* 55 [1988]: 1043–1104).

69. JM to Spencer Roane, 2 September 1819, *MF*, p. 360.

70. See McCoy, *Last of the Fathers*, pp. 99–103.

71. See "Vices of the Political System of the United States," April 1787, *PJM* 9:350; and Madison's remarks in the Federal Convention, 14 September 1787, *Notes*, p. 638. Such a power would have taken the form of granting corporate charters and was rejected at the Federal Convention.

72. See Stuart Leibiger, "Cumberland Road," in Rutland, ed., *Madison and the American Nation*, pp. 105–6.

73. Annual Message to Congress, 5 December 1815, *MF*, p. 304.

74. See Drew R. McCoy, *The Elusive Republic: Political Economy in Jeffersonian America* (New York: W. W. Norton & Co., 1980), pp. 121–22.

75. Veto Message, 3 March 1817, *MF*, pp. 308–9.

76. JM to James Monroe, 27 December 1817, *LJM* 3:55–56 (emphasis in the original).

77. Ibid., p. 56.

78. JM to Thomas Jefferson, 17 February 1825, *LJM* 3:483. See also JM to Henry St. George Tucker, 23 December 1817, *LJM* 3:54 (notable as well for its rare display of Madisonian sarcasm): "I am not unaware that my belief, not to say knowledge, of the views of those who proposed the Constitution, and, what is of more importance, my deep impression as to the views of those who bestowed on it the stamp of authority, may influence my interpretation of the Instrument. On the other hand, it is not impossible that those who consult the instrument without a danger of that bias, may be exposed to an equal one in their anxiety to find in its text an authority for a particular measure of great apparent utility."

79. JM to Spencer Roane, 6 May 1821, *MF*, p. 364.

80. Annual Message to Congress, 5 December 1815, *MF*, p. 305.

81. Veto Message, 3 March 1817, *MF*, p. 309. Cf. JM to Spencer Roane, 2 September 1819, *MF*, p. 361.

82. McCoy, *Last of the Fathers*, p. 72; see also his discussion of this question, pp. 71–73.

83. See JM to Thomas Ritchie, 18 December 1825, *WJM* 9:233.

84. For a similar defense of *stare decisis* in constitutional adjudication, see Bork, *Tempting of America*, pp. 155–59.

85. Henry Paul Monaghan, "Stare Decisis and Constitutional Adjudication," *Columbia Law Review* 88 (1988): 723–73.

Conclusion: The Madisonian Regime Today

1. George F. Will, *Statecraft as Soulcraft: What Government Does* (New York: Simon and Schuster, 1983), p. 39; Robert H. Bork, *Slouching Towards Gomorrah: Modern Liberalism and American Decline* (New York: ReganBooks, 1996), p. 58; Benjamin R. Barber, *Strong Democracy: Participatory Politics for a New Age* (Berkeley and Los Angeles: University of California Press, 1984), p. 4; Richard K. Matthews, *If Men Were Angels: James Madison and the Heartless Empire of Reason* (Lawrence: University Press of Kansas, 1995), p. xvi.

2. Tocqueville, *Democracy in America*, trans. George Lawrence (New York: Harper & Row, 1966), vol. 2, part 4, chap. 2 (p. 668).

3. Ibid., chap. 4 (pp. 675–76).

4. Supporters of the law in question, which prescribed federal criminal penalties for possession of a firearm in a school zone, asserted that it involved commerce in various (admittedly indirect) ways. In language reminiscent of Madison's case against Hamilton and the Marshall Court, Chief Justice William Rehnquist rejected such latitude. "If we are to accept the Government's arguments," he wrote, "we are hard-pressed to posit any activity by an individual that Congress is without power to regulate" (*The New York Times*, 27 April 1995, p. D24).

In dissenting, Justice Stephen Breyer defended the Court's "rational basis" test for such regulation and described the many ways, however indirect, in which guns in schools can be said to affect commerce. As he wrote, "Courts must give Congress a degree of leeway in determining the existence of a significant factual connection between the regulated activity and interstate commerce both because the Constitution delegates the commerce power directly to Congress and because the determination requires an empirical judgment of a kind that a legislature is more likely than a court to make with accuracy." Cf. Madison's strictures on *McCulloch* v. *Maryland* (JM to Spencer Roane, 2 September 1819, *MF,* pp. 359–60):

> What is of most importance [in the decision] is the high sanction given to a latitude in expounding the Constitution which seems to break down the landmarks intended by a specification of the Powers of Congress, and to substitute for a definite connection between means and ends, a Legislative discretion as to the former to which no practical limit can be assigned. . . . Does not the Court . . . relinquish by their doctrine, all controul on the Legislative exercise of unconstitutional powers? According to that doctrine, the expediency & constitutionality of means for carrying into effect a specified Power are convertible terms; and Congress are admitted to be Judges of the expediency.

Bibliography

Ackerman, Bruce. *We the People: Foundations.* Cambridge: Harvard University Press, 1991.

———. *We the People: Transformations.* Cambridge: Harvard University Press, 1998.

Adair, Douglass. *Fame and the Founding Fathers: Essays by Douglass Adair.* Edited by Trevor Colbourn. New York: W. W. Norton & Co., 1974.

Adams, Henry. *History of the United States of America during the Administrations of James Madison.* New York: Library of America, 1986.

Amar, Akhil Reed. "Philadelphia Revisited: Amending the Constitution Outside Article V." *University of Chicago Law Review* 55 (1988): 1043–1104.

Arendt, Hannah. *The Human Condition.* Chicago: University of Chicago Press, 1958.

———. *On Revolution.* Harmondsworth, England: Penguin Books, 1965.

Aristotle. *Nicomachean Ethics.* Translated by H. Rackham. Rev. ed. Loeb Classical Library. Cambridge, Mass.: Harvard University Press, 1934.

———. *Nicomachean Ethics.* Translated by Hippocrates G. Apostle. Grinnell, Iowa: Peripatetic Press, 1975.

———. *Politics.* Translated by H. Rackham. Loeb Classical Library. Cambridge: Harvard University Press, 1932.

———. *The Politics.* Translated by Carnes Lord. Chicago: University of Chicago Press, 1984.

———. *Art of Rhetoric.* Translated by J. H. Freese. Loeb Classical Library. Cambridge: Harvard University Press, 1926.

Augustine. *St. Augustine: The Political Writings.* Edited by Henry Paolucci. Chicago: Regnery Gateway, 1962.

Bailey, Francis, ed. *The Constitutions of the Several Independent States of America.* Philadelphia: Continental Congress, 1781.

Bailyn, Bernard. *The Ideological Origins of the American Revolution.* Cambridge: Harvard University Press, 1967.

Banning, Lance. *The Jeffersonian Persuasion: Evolution of a Party Ideology.* Ithaca, N.Y.: Cornell University Press, 1978.

———. "The Hamiltonian Madison." *Virginia Magazine of History and Biography* 92 (1984): 3–28.

———. "Jeffersonian Ideology Revisited: Liberal and Classical Ideas in the New American Republic." *William and Mary Quarterly* 43 (1986): 3–19.

——. "Some Second Thoughts on Virtue and the Course of Revolutionary Thinking." In *Conceptual Change and the Constitution,* edited by Terence Ball and J. G. A. Pocock, pp. 194–212. Lawrence: University Press of Kansas, 1988.

——. *The Sacred Fire of Liberty: James Madison and the Founding of the Federal Republic.* Ithaca, N.Y.: Cornell University Press, 1995.

Barber, Benjamin R. *Strong Democracy: Participatory Politics for a New Age.* Berkeley and Los Angeles: University of California Press, 1984.

Beard, Charles. *An Economic Interpretation of the Constitution of the United States.* New York: Macmillan, 1913.

Becker, Carl. *The Declaration of Independence: A Study in the History of Political Ideas.* New York: Knopf, 1922.

Berger, Raoul. "'Original Intention' in Historical Perspective." *George Washington Law Review* 54 (1986): 296–337.

Berns, Walter. *The First Amendment and the Future of American Democracy.* New York: Basic Books, 1976.

Bork, Robert H. *The Tempting of America: The Political Seduction of the Law.* New York: Free Press, 1990.

——. *Slouching Towards Gomorrah: Modern Liberalism and American Decline.* New York: ReganBooks, 1996.

Brann, Eva T. H. "Madison's 'Memorial and Remonstrance': A Model of American Eloquence." *St. John's Review* (Summer 1981): 55–73.

Branson, Roy. "James Madison and the Scottish Enlightenment." *Journal of the History of Ideas* 40 (1979): 235–50.

Brant, Irving. *James Madison.* 6 vols. Indianapolis: Bobbs-Merrill, 1941–61.

Burns, James MacGregor. *The Deadlock of Democracy.* Englewood Cliffs, N.J.: Prentice-Hall, 1963.

Carey, George W. The Federalist: *Design for a Constitutional Republic.* Urbana: University of Illinois Press, 1989.

——. *In Defense of the Constitution.* Indianapolis: Liberty Fund, 1995.

Cicero. *De Re Publica.* Translated by Clinton Walker Keyes. Loeb Classical Library. Cambridge: Harvard University Press, 1928.

Cohler, Anne M. *Montesquieu's Comparative Politics and the Spirit of American Constitutionalism.* Lawrence: University Press of Kansas, 1988.

Commager, Henry Steele, ed. *Documents of American History.* 7th ed. 2 vols. New York: Appleton-Century-Crofts, 1963.

Cropsey, Joseph. *Political Philosophy and the Issues of Politics.* Chicago: University of Chicago Press, 1977.

Dahl, Robert. *A Preface to Democratic Theory.* Chicago: University of Chicago Press, 1956.

Dewey, Donald O. "James Madison Helps Clio Interpret the Constitution." *American Journal of Legal History* 15 (1971): 38–55.

Diamond, Martin. "Democracy and *The Federalist:* A Reconsideration of the Framers' Intent." *American Political Science Review* 53 (1959): 52–68.

——. "The Federalist, 1787–1788." In *History of Political Philosophy,* 3d ed., edited by Leo Strauss and Joseph Cropsey, pp. 659–79. Chicago: University of Chicago Press, 1987.

Dietz, Gottfried. The Federalist: *A Classic on Federalism and Free Government.* Baltimore: Johns Hopkins University Press, 1960.

Draper, Theodore. "Hume and Madison: The Secrets of Federalist Paper No. 10." *Encounter* (February 1982): 34–47.

Elkins, Stanley, and Eric McKitrick. "The Founding Fathers: Young Men of the Revolution." *Political Science Quarterly* 76 (1961): 181–216.

Engeman, Thomas S., et al., eds. *The Federalist Concordance.* Middletown, Conn.: Wesleyan University Press, 1980.

Epstein, David F. *The Political Theory of* The Federalist. Chicago: University of Chicago Press, 1984.

Farrand, Max, ed. *The Records of the Federal Convention of 1787.* 4 vols. New Haven, Conn.: Yale University Press, 1937.

Federalist Society. *The Great Debate: Interpreting Our Written Constitution.* Washington, D.C.: Federalist Society, 1986.

Finkelman, Paul. "The Constitution and the Intentions of the Framers: The Limits of Historical Analysis." *University of Pittsburgh Law Review* 50 (1989): 349–98.

Flaumenhaft, Harvey. *The Effective Republic: Administration and Constitution in the Thought of Alexander Hamilton.* Durham, N.C.: Duke University Press, 1992.

Frisch, Morton J. *The Hamilton-Madison-Jefferson Triangle.* Ashbrook Essay no. 4. Ashland, Ohio: John M. Ashbrook Center for Public Affairs, 1992.

Gibson, Alan. "Impartial Representation and the Extended Republic: Towards a Comprehensive and Balanced Treatment of the Tenth *Federalist* Paper." *History of Political Thought* 12 (1991): 263–304.

Goldwin, Robert A. *From Parchment to Power: How James Madison Used the Bill of Rights to Save the Constitution.* Washington, D.C.: AEI Press, 1997.

Hamilton, Alexander. *The Papers of Alexander Hamilton.* Edited by Harold C. Syrett and Jacob E. Cooke. 26 vols. New York: Columbia University Press, 1961–79.

Hartz, Louis. *The Liberal Tradition in America.* New York: Harcourt, Brace and World, 1955.

Hegel, G. W. F. *The Philosophy of Right.* Translated by T. M. Knox. London: Oxford University Press, 1967.

Hobbes, Thomas. *Leviathan.* Edited by C. B. Macpherson. Harmondsworth, England: Penguin Books, 1985.

———. *Man and Citizen* (De Homine and De Cive). Edited by Bernard Gert. Indianapolis: Hackett Publishing Co., 1991.

Hume, David. *Essays: Moral, Political, and Literary.* Edited by Eugene F. Miller. Indianapolis: Liberty Classics, 1985.

Hunt, Gaillard. *The Life of James Madison.* New York: Doubleday, Page, & Co., 1902.

Huyler, Jerome. *Locke in America: The Moral Philosophy of the Founding Era.* Lawrence: University Press of Kansas, 1995.

Jaffa, Harry V. *Crisis of the House Divided: An Interpretation of the Issues in the Lincoln-Douglas Debates.* Chicago: University of Chicago Press, 1959.

Jefferson, Thomas. *The Papers of Thomas Jefferson.* Edited by Julian P. Boyd et al. 27 vols. to date. Princeton, N.J.: Princeton University Press, 1950–.

———. *The Portable Thomas Jefferson.* Edited by Merrill D. Peterson. New York: Penguin Books, 1975.

Jensen, Merrill. *The Articles of Confederation: An Interpretation of the Social-Constitutional History of the American Revolution, 1774–81.* Madison: University of Wisconsin Press, 1940.

Jillson, Calvin C. "Constitution-Making: Alignment and Realignment in the Federal Convention of 1787." *American Political Science Review* 75 (1981): 598–612.

Kant, Immanuel. *Perpetual Peace and Other Essays*. Translated by Ted Humphrey. Indianapolis: Hackett Publishing Co., 1983.

Kenyon, Cecilia, ed. *The Antifederalists*. Boston: Northeastern University Press, 1985.

Kesler, Charles R. "The Founders and the Classics." In *The American Founding: Essays on the Formation of the Constitution*, edited by J. Jackson Barlow, Leonard W. Levy, and Ken Masugi, pp. 57–90. New York: Greenwood Press, 1988.

Ketcham, Ralph. *James Madison: A Biography*. Charlottesville: University Press of Virginia, 1971.

Koch, Adrienne. *Jefferson and Madison: The Great Collaboration*. New York: Knopf, 1950.

Kurland, Philip B., and Ralph Lerner, eds. *The Founders' Constitution*. 5 vols. Chicago: University of Chicago Press, 1987.

Landi, Alexander. "Madison's Political Theory." *Political Science Reviewer* 6 (1976): 73–111.

Levinson, Sanford. "'Veneration' and Constitutional Change: James Madison Confronts the Possibility of Constitutional Amendment." *Texas Tech Law Review* 21 (1990): 2443–60.

Lindsay, Thomas. "James Madison on Religion and Politics: Rhetoric and Reality." *American Political Science Review* 85 (1991): 1321–37.

Locke, John. *An Essay Concerning Human Understanding*. Edited by Peter H. Nidditch. Oxford: Clarendon Press, 1975.

——. *A Letter Concerning Toleration*. Edited by James H. Tully. Indianapolis: Hackett Publishing Co., 1983.

——. *Two Treatises of Government*. Edited by Peter Laslett. Student edition. Cambridge: Cambridge University Press, 1988.

Lutz, Donald S. "The Relative Influence of European Writers on Late Eighteenth-Century American Political Thought." *American Political Science Review* 78 (1984): 189–97.

McConnell, Michael W. "The Origins and Historical Understanding of Free Exercise of Religion." *Harvard Law Review* 103 (1990): 1410–1517.

McCoy, Drew R. *The Elusive Republic: Political Economy in Jeffersonian America*. New York: W. W. Norton & Co., 1980.

——. *The Last of the Fathers: James Madison and the Republican Legacy*. Cambridge: Cambridge University Press, 1989.

McDonald, Forrest. *We the People: The Economic Origins of the Constitution*. Chicago: University of Chicago Press, 1958.

——. *Alexander Hamilton: A Biography*. New York: W. W. Norton & Co., 1979.

——. *E Pluribus Unum: The Formation of the American Republic, 1776–1790*. 2d ed. Indianapolis: Liberty Fund, 1979.

——. *Novus Ordo Seclorum: The Intellectual Origins of the Constitution*. Lawrence: University Press of Kansas, 1985.

McDowell, Gary L. "The Politics of Original Intention." In *The Constitution, the Courts, and the Quest for Justice*, edited by Robert A. Goldwin and William A. Schambra, pp. 1–24. Washington, D.C.: American Enterprise Institute, 1989.

——. "Private Conscience and Public Order: Hobbes and *The Federalist*." *Polity* 25 (1993): 421–43.

Macedo, Stephen. *The New Right v. The Constitution*. Washington, D.C.: Cato Institute, 1987.

McIlwain, Charles Howard. *Constitutionalism: Ancient and Modern.* Ithaca, N.Y.: Cornell University Press, 1940.

McWilliams, Wilson Carey. *The Idea of Fraternity in America.* Berkeley and Los Angeles: University of California Press, 1973.

Macpherson, C. B. "The Social Bearing of Locke's Political Theory." *Western Political Quarterly* 7 (1954): 1–22.

Madison, James. *Letters and Other Writings of James Madison.* 4 vols. New York: R. Worthington, 1884.

———. *The Writings of James Madison.* Edited by Gaillard Hunt. 9 vols. New York: G. P. Putnam's Sons, 1900–10.

———. "Madison's 'Detached Memoranda.'" Edited by Elizabeth Fleet. *William and Mary Quarterly* 3 (1946): 534–68.

———. *The Papers of James Madison.* Edited by William T. Hutchinson, William M. E. Rachal, Robert A. Rutland, et al. 17 vols. to date. Chicago and Charlottesville: University of Chicago Press and University Press of Virginia, 1962–.

———. *Notes of Debates in the Federal Convention of 1787 Reported by James Madison.* Edited by Adrienne Koch. New York: W. W. Norton & Co., 1966.

———. *The Mind of the Founder: Sources of the Political Thought of James Madison.* Edited by Marvin Meyers. Hanover, N.H.: University Press of New England, 1973.

Madison, James, Alexander Hamilton, and John Jay. *The Federalist.* Edited by Jacob E. Cooke. Middletown, Conn.: Wesleyan University Press, 1961.

Mansfield, Harvey C., Jr. *America's Constitutional Soul.* Baltimore: Johns Hopkins University Press, 1991.

———. "Self-Interest Rightly Understood." *Political Theory* 23 (1995): 48–66.

Matthews, Richard K. *The Radical Politics of Thomas Jefferson.* Lawrence: University Press of Kansas, 1984.

———. *If Men Were Angels: James Madison and the Heartless Empire of Reason.* Lawrence: University Press of Kansas, 1995.

Meyers, Marvin. "Founding and Revolution: A Commentary on Publius-Madison." In *The Hofstadter Aegis: A Memorial,* edited by Stanley Elkins and Eric McKitrick. New York: Knopf, 1974.

Miller, Charles A. *Jefferson and Nature: An Interpretation.* Baltimore: Johns Hopkins University Press, 1988.

Miller, Eugene F. "What Publius Says about Interest." *Political Science Reviewer* 19 (1990): 11–48.

Miller, John C. *Alexander Hamilton: Portrait in Paradox.* New York: Harper & Row, 1959.

Monaghan, Henry Paul. "Stare Decisis and Constitutional Adjudication." *Columbia Law Review* 88 (1988): 723–73.

Montesquieu. *The Spirit of the Laws.* Translated by Thomas Nugent. New York: Hafner Publishing Co., 1966.

———. *De L'Esprit des Lois.* 2 vols. Paris: Garnier-Flammarion, 1979.

Morgan, Edmund S. "Safety in Numbers: Madison, Hume, and the Tenth *Federalist.*" *Huntington Library Quarterly* 49 (1986): 95–112.

Muller, James W. "The American Framers' Debt to Montesquieu." In *The Revival of Constitutionalism,* edited by James W. Muller, pp. 87–102. Lincoln: University of Nebraska Press, 1988.

Owens, Mackubin Thomas, Jr. "Alexander Hamilton on Natural Rights and Prudence." *Interpretation* 14 (1986): 331–51.

Paine, Thomas. *The Thomas Paine Reader.* Edited by Michael Foot and Isaac Kramnick. Harmondsworth, England: Penguin Books, 1987.

Pangle, Thomas L. *The Spirit of Modern Republicanism: The Moral Vision of the American Founders and the Philosophy of Locke.* Chicago: University of Chicago Press, 1988.

Peterson, Paul C. "The Problem of Consistency in the Statesmanship of James Madison." In *The American Founding: Politics, Statesmanship, and the Constitution,* edited by Ralph Rossum and Gary L. McDowell, pp. 122–34. Port Washington, N.Y.: Kennikat Press, 1981.

Pitkin, Hanna. "Obligation and Consent I." *American Political Science Review* 59 (1965): 990–99.

———. "Obligation and Consent II." *American Political Science Review* 60 (1966): 39–52.

Plato. *Gorgias.* Translated by Walter Hamilton. Harmondsworth, England: Penguin Books, 1960.

———. *The Laws of Plato.* Translated by Thomas L. Pangle. Chicago: University of Chicago Press, 1980.

Plutarch. *Plutarch's Lives.* Translated by John Dryden. New York: Modern Library, 1864 (date of the revised Clough edition reprinted here).

Pocock, J. G. A. *The Machiavellian Moment: Florentine Political Thought and the Atlantic Republican Tradition.* Princeton, N.J.: Princeton University Press, 1975.

Powell, H. Jefferson. "The Original Understanding of Original Intent." *Harvard Law Review* 98 (1985): 885–948.

Rahe, Paul A. *Republics Ancient and Modern.* 3 vols. Chapel Hill: University of North Carolina Press, 1994.

Rakove, Jack N. *The Beginnings of National Politics: An Interpretive History of the Continental Congress.* Baltimore: Johns Hopkins University Press, 1979.

———. "Mr. Meese, Meet Mr. Madison." *Atlantic Monthly,* December 1986, pp. 77–86.

———. *James Madison and the Creation of the American Republic.* Glenview, Ill.: Scott, Foresman, 1990.

———. *Original Meanings: Politics and Ideas in the Making of the Constitution.* New York: Knopf, 1996.

Roche, John P. "The Founding Fathers: A Reform Caucus in Action." *American Political Science Review* 55 (1961): 799–816.

Rosen, Gary. "Madison's Madison." Review of *The Sacred Fire of Liberty,* by Lance Banning. *First Things* (April 1996): 45–47.

———. "James Madison and the Problem of Founding." *Review of Politics* 58 (1996): 561–95.

———. "James Madison's Princes and Peoples." In *Machiavelli's Republican Legacy,* edited by Paul A. Rahe. Forthcoming.

Rossiter, Clinton. *1787: The Grand Convention.* New York: W. W. Norton & Co., 1966.

Rousseau, Jean-Jacques. *The First and Second Discourses.* Edited by Roger D. Masters. New York: St. Martin's Press, 1964.

———. *On the Social Contract.* Edited by Roger D. Masters. New York: St. Martin's Press, 1978.

———. *Emile.* Translated by Allan Bloom. New York: Basic Books, 1979.

———. *The Government of Poland.* Translated by Willmoore Kendall. Indianapolis: Hackett Publishing Co., 1985.

Rutland, Robert, ed. *James Madison and the American Nation, 1751–1836: An Encyclopedia*. New York: Simon and Schuster, 1994.

Salkever, Stephen G. "Aristotle's Social Science." *Political Theory* 9 (1981): 479–508.

Sandel, Michael J. "The Procedural Republic and the Unencumbered Self." *Political Theory* 12 (1984): 81–96.

Shalhope, Robert E. "Republicanism and Early American Historiography." *William and Mary Quarterly* 39 (1982): 334–56.

Sheehan, Colleen A. "Madison's Party Press Essays." *Interpretation* 17 (1990): 355–77.

Shklar, Judith N. "Publius and the Science of the Past." *Yale Law Journal* 86 (1977): 1286–96.

———. "*The Federalist* as Myth." *Yale Law Journal* 90 (1981): 942–53.

Storing, Herbert J. *What the Anti-Federalists Were For*. Chicago: University of Chicago Press, 1981.

———, ed. *The Complete Anti-Federalist*. 7 vols. Chicago: University of Chicago Press, 1981.

Stourzh, Gerald. *Alexander Hamilton and the Idea of Republican Government*. Stanford, Calif.: Stanford University Press, 1970.

Tocqueville, Alexis de. *Democracy in America*. Translated by George Lawrence. New York: Harper & Row, 1966.

White, Morton. *Philosophy*, The Federalist, *and the Constitution*. New York: Oxford University Press, 1987.

Will, George F. *Statecraft as Soulcraft: What Government Does*. New York: Simon and Schuster, 1983.

Wills, Garry. *Explaining America:* The Federalist. London: Athlone Press, 1981.

Wood, Gordon S. *The Creation of the American Republic, 1776–1787*. New York: W. W. Norton & Co., 1972.

———. "Democracy and the Constitution." In *How Democratic Is the Constitution?* edited by Robert A. Goldwin and William A. Schambra, pp. 1–17. Washington, D.C.: American Enterprise Institute, 1980.

———. "Interests and Disinterestedness in the Making of the Constitution." In *Beyond Confederation: Origins of the Constitution and American National Identity*, edited by Richard Beeman, Stephen Botein, and Edward C. Carter II, pp. 69–109. Chapel Hill: University of North Carolina Press, 1987.

Zuckert, Michael P. "Federalism and the Founding: Toward a Reinterpretation of the Constitutional Convention." *Review of Politics* 48 (1986): 166–210.

———. *Natural Rights and the New Republicanism*. Princeton, N.J.: Princeton University Press, 1994.

Zvesper, John. "The Madisonian Systems." *Western Political Quarterly* 37 (1984): 236–56.

Index